RALPH ELLISON AND KENNETH BURKE

Ralph Ellison and Kenneth Burke

At the Roots of the Racial Divide

BRYAN CRABLE

University of Virginia Press

CHARLOTTESVILLE AND LONDON

University of Virginia Press

© 2012 by the Rector and Visitors of the University of Virginia
Printed in the United States of America on acid-free paper

First published 2012

9 8 7 6 5 4 3 2 1

LIBRARY OF CONGRESS CATALOGING-IN-PUBLICATION DATA

Crable, Bryan, 1970–
 Ralph Ellison and Kenneth Burke : at the roots of the racial divide / Bryan Crable.
  p. cm.
 Includes bibliographical references and index.
 ISBN 978-0-8139-3215-6 (cloth : alk. paper)
 ISBN 978-0-8139-3216-3 (pbk. : alk. paper)
 ISBN 978-0-8139-3217-0 (e-book)
  1. Ellison, Ralph—Criticism and interpretation.   2. Burke, Kenneth, 1887–1993—
Criticism and interpretation.   3. Race awareness—United States—History.   4. United
States—Race relations—History—20th century.   I. Title.
PS3555.L625Z634   2011
818'.5409—dc23

                                                                    2011023085

A book in the American Literatures Initiative (ALI), a collaborative
publishing project of NYU Press, Fordham University Press, Rutgers
University Press, Temple University Press, and the University of Virginia
Press. The Initiative is supported by The Andrew W. Mellon Foundation.
For more information, please visit www.americanliteratures.org.

Yo, Joy. To you.

CONTENTS

ACKNOWLEDGMENTS

Many events, large and small, conspired to help me write this book. (Unfortunately for me, I have surely forgotten many of them.) My parents were among the strongest influences on my choice of vocation, both as a teacher and as a scholar. Both are writers, and both spent decades teaching, at the college (dad) and secondary (mom) level. They also first connected me to Kenneth Burke. Burke was central to my father's dissertation, and so, as the story goes, when I was a toddler the family camped in Florida so that my father could interview Burke. At one point during this trip, Malcolm Cowley's wife, Muriel, taught me the word "moon" (she did a good job; I haven't forgotten it). This early association prepared me to study Burke's work in earnest.

I have my parents to thank for another vital contribution to this book. Though I grew up in the Midwest—and in locales that were more homogeneous in population than not—my early experiences were reflective of our American diversity. Since my earliest playmates and friends formed a veritable Rainbow Coalition, I had a different experience of race than many white peers—something I found out in seventh grade when our social studies teacher gave a portion of one class to the telling of anti-black jokes. This is not to say that I grew up innocent of race or racism. But I did grow up differently than many of my peers, and I do have my parents to thank for that.

This particular project, however, has its specific genesis in more recent history. During my second year at Villanova, my department chair (and friend) Terry Nance encouraged me to participate in an interdisciplinary, team-taught institute in our honors program. We even hit upon a title: "Race, Rhetoric, and the Reality of Racism." After receiving the blessing of the director of the program, Edwin Goff, I collaborated with four colleagues on the design of and readings for the nine-credit course. I can honestly say that without this intensive semester alongside them, I would not be the thinker, or the person, I am today. This book and I owe an immense debt to them: Maghan Keita, Kevin Miles, Crystal Lucky, and Carol Anthony.

Further, during that semester, Crystal assigned Ralph Ellison's "Change the Joke and Slip the Yoke" in preparation for a lecture by Kimberly Benston. Reading these pages, I was hooked—and struck by the Burkean flavor of the essay. When I mentioned this to Crystal and Benston, I first learned of the personal and intellectual connection between Burke and Ellison.

This news arrived at a critical time. My junior sabbatical was to follow on the heels of that semester, and I was searching for a project. Joy Cypher (about whom more later) made a suggestion—Why don't you make this the subject of your sabbatical?—that was truly the genesis for this book. In addition to this valuable sabbatical time, along the way I have also benefited immensely from two Strategic Communication Research Grants from the Graduate Programs of Villanova's Department of Communication. Ten years later, I feel that I have finally been able to do this relationship, and these two men, justice.

I also, of course, have other debts to acknowledge. I still reap the benefits of the education I received at Purdue University, especially under the tutelage of Calvin Schrag, Martin Matustik, and Lewis R. Gordon. Without the education that they provided me in existential phenomenology and its roots, I would not read Burke the way that I do. William K. Rawlins also was generous in agreeing to provide an independent study on Burke when I was turned away by others. Robert Wade Kenny, although not at Purdue, not only agreed to be on my doctoral committee, but was also my most challenging reader. My interpretation of Burke is heavily indebted to him.

Calvin Schrag insists that we, as professors, learn more from our students than we ever acknowledge. Thus, I would like to thank the students with whom these ideas (in one form or another) were discussed. That includes the fifteen students of the Race Institute, and especially Dr. Jasmine Cobb, who has been a source of conversation upon matters of race since 2001. (I still reflect upon her insightful senior thesis, a Goffmanean view of racial "passing.") I am also thankful to the students in my 2004 honors seminar on Burke and Ellison, where I worked out early versions of these ideas—and especially Erin Arizzi, who used the course to work out a few ideas of her own regarding the "bureaucratization of the imaginative." Finally, the Spring 2010 students of "Rhetoric, Identity, and Conflict" were quite tolerant when I wove drafts of my chapters into course topics.

I have also been given several opportunities, over the years, to present material on the Burke-Ellison relationship. Many of these have transpired thanks to Jack Selzer, whom I met during my first visit to the Kenneth Burke Papers at Penn State. Jack has been a wonderful mentor and source of friendship. He assisted me in the archives and asked me to give a featured address at the 2005 Kenneth Burke Society Triennial Conference, an experience that led to my essay's inclusion in his edited volume, *Kenneth Burke and His Circles*. Since I also draw heavily upon his two books on Burke, I owe him a great deal. I have others to thank at Penn State, of course; Keith Gilyard and Robin Schulze were generous with an invitation to a daylong symposium on Ellison and his work. They, and the other participants, were very helpful in pushing me to incorporate more Ellisonian elements into my habitually Burkean perspective.

I have to also thank those whose labor helped make this book possible. Nathan Taylor was an able research assistant, and his slogging made my own more bearable. Leah Jehan of the Beinecke Rare Book and Manuscript Library at Yale University was quick to respond to a long-distance request for a letter housed in the Richard Wright Papers. Dr. Alice Birney and the Library of Congress staff were immensely helpful during my visits to D.C. Jeannette Sabre and Sandra Stelts from the Penn State Special Collections staff are angels. I am also thankful to Phoebe Pettingell for her interest in my work, and her willingness to let me quote from the Stanley Edgar Hyman Papers. John F. Callahan, similarly, in his role as literary executor for Ralph Ellison, has been more than generous. He gave me access to the Ellison Papers at a time when few were granted such access. I will never forget his encouragement and his willingness to take a chance on a young scholar. I am likewise immensely grateful to the Ralph and Fanny Ellison Foundation for its support and permission to quote from the Ellison Papers.

I also could not have completed this project without the assistance of the Kenneth Burke Literary Trust, and especially Anthony and Michael Burke. This is not a hagiographic project regarding "K.B.," though I believe that it *is* very Burkean. Their support of this project, despite the portions that might be a little uncomfortable, is a testament to them.

Excerpts from the Kenneth Burke archives are published with the permission of the Kenneth Burke Literary Trust.

Much of this book is new, and has been glimpsed only in fragments in my conference presentations. However, portions of chapter 2 were previously published as "Race and *A Rhetoric of Motives*: Kenneth Burke's Dialogue with Ralph Ellison," *Rhetoric Society Quarterly* 33, no. 3 (2003): 5–25. Used by permission. Portions of chapter 3 were previously published as "From Acceptance to Rejection: Kenneth Burke, Ralph Ellison, and *Invisible Man*," in *Kenneth Burke and His Circles*, edited by Jack Selzer and Robert Wess (West Lafayette, Ind.: Parlor Press, 2008), 3–26. Used by permission. I am grateful to Taylor & Francis, and to David Blakesley and Parlor Press for their permission to use these materials.

These remarks would certainly be incomplete without acknowledgment of the labors that began when mine ended. I want to express my gratitude to the staff at the University of Virginia Press, who have been wonderful throughout the publication process. Though I've worked with many great folks at UVa, I want especially to thank my editor, Cathie Brettschneider. She saw promise in my initial prospectus, provided invaluable editorial advice on the manuscript, and displayed immense patience (and faith) as I missed multiple deadlines. I am also immensely grateful to Susan Murray for her professional and thorough copyediting of the finished manuscript. Moreover, I am fortunate and honored to have this book included in the American Literatures Initiative, and to have had the support and assistance of managing editor Tim Roberts and his team at the ALI. All of these folks have made the transition from manuscript to published book more humane and transparent for a first-time author.

Finally, my friends and colleagues have played an important role in this process, though I can name only a few. Loretta Chiaverini and Maria DiStefano are the best administrative staff and people that I could ever imagine working with—and they saved me on more than one occasion during the writing of this book. Crystal Lucky gave great feedback on early chapters, as did John C. Carr. My father, Richard Crable, read four chapters and gave invaluable editorial advice. Their work helped me avoid many errors, though they are not responsible for those remaining. Corey Anton has been a vital interlocutor; he and I "grew up" together during our doctoral studies, and I owe much to our fifteen-plus years of conversations. During the 2010 Eastern Communication Association convention, David Levasseur started a conversation over dinner that shaped chapter 5. My yogis helped balance me during the writing of this book, but I especially want to thank Asha for her memorable phrase—uttered to help us through "half pigeon" pose—which I appropriated for chapter 5: from the turmoil to the peace.

Without Joy Marie Cypher, though, none of this would matter. She is my spouse, and also my friend, companion, and intellectual "sparring partner." She not only helped me through the points of despair, frustration, and/or anger, but also tolerated my solitary hours locked away on our third floor. She was graciously willing to read every word of this book; given its length, that is no small gift. Joy plays more of a role in my thinking then she likely even knows. For all this and more, it is to her that this book is dedicated.

A Note about Archival Materials

In addition to the published works written by both Kenneth Burke and Ralph Ellison, in the chapters that follow I draw extensively upon unpublished archival materials by and concerning these men. I have had the privilege and good fortune to spend a great deal of time investigating the Kenneth Burke Papers, housed in the Rare Books and Manuscripts Collection, Pattee Library, Pennsylvania State University. I draw on materials from the "Burke 1" and "Burke 2" collections within the archive, primarily the folders containing correspondence with Ellison and Hyman (though, in chapter 1, I also draw on some of Burke's early correspondence with Malcolm Cowley, and in chapter 5, I draw on some of the "Burke 3" material on "Myth"). Letters and materials cited from this collection are abbreviated in the notes as "Kenneth Burke Papers."

I have also spent a great deal of time in the Manuscript Reading Room in the James Madison Memorial Building of the Library of Congress in Washington, D.C., poring over the Ralph Ellison Papers, the Stanley Edgar Hyman Papers, and the Shirley Jackson Papers. Letters and materials from these collections are identified in the notes by the collection name. My examination of the Jackson Papers was limited to the folders in box 7 labeled "Burke, Mr. and Mrs. Kenneth, 1954–1962" and "Ellison, Fanny (Mrs. Ralph Ellison), 1953–1962," as well as the folder in box 43 labeled "Burke, Libby [*sic*], 1945–1950, undated." My investigation of the Hyman Papers was more extensive, though my citations reference the folders of correspondence in box 4 entitled "Burke, Kenneth, 1940–1951," the folders of correspondence in box 5 labeled "Burke, Kenneth, 1952–1970, undated," and the folders of correspondence in box 6 labeled "Ellison, Ralph and Fanny, 1942–1970." However, following the LOC Finding Aid for the Ralph Ellison Papers, materials from this (newly opened) collection are specifically cited in the endnotes by box and folder number, for ease of reference for scholars interested in consulting them.

Finally, those interested in a firsthand glimpse of the marginalia and notations in Ellison's copies of Burke's books should plan to visit Ellison's personal library, which is permanently housed in the Rare Books and Special Collections Reading Room in the Thomas Jefferson Building of the Library of Congress in Washington, D.C. All references to Ellison's copies of books are drawn from my examination of this collection.

RALPH ELLISON AND KENNETH BURKE

Introduction

In the preface to *Counter-Statement*, Kenneth Burke reflected upon the relationship between a writer and her social context, distinguishing between two types of writing: pamphleteering and inquiry. Pamphleteering, he suggested, represents a reaction, corrective or supportive, to the writer's environment: "In so far as an age is bent, a writer establishes equilibrium by leaning (leaning either as his age leans, or in the direction opposite to his age)."[1] Yet, he noted, the writer need not simply lean: "A writer will also desire to develop an equilibrium of his own, regardless of external resistances—and this we might call inquiry." Since these modes of linguistic action rarely appear in pure form, a writer will typically display evidence of both impulses, and likely "will not be sure just when he is inquiring and when pamphleteering."[2]

These oft-quoted sentences are more than observations on the writer's craft; they represent an apt description of Burke's own career. Though *Counter-Statement* represented his first sustained strivings toward equilibrium, for forty years Burke published books that fleshed out his perspective on the nature of self, symbols, and society. These works won him accolades, and a kind of cult status, among some readers: "With a kind of limitless fertility Burke has done everything in criticism's bag of tricks, including several things he put there."[3] Later, this body of work was hailed as a foundation of New Criticism, contemporary philosophies of language, and the modern study of rhetoric.[4] Burke's writings cemented his reputation as an eclectic, innovative thinker, yet he never received the public accolades given to many of his peers.[5] To the general public, Burke displayed less pamphleteering than inquiry, with the independence of his thought underscored by "difficult," "obscure" prose. As one profile of Burke noted, "most commentators found him too unconventional, too idiosyncratic. He has been dismissed as a 'Yankee crank,' a 'crackpot with a panacea,' and a 'circus rider.'"[6]

The complex nature of Burke's writings aside, emphasis upon his uniqueness, or idiosyncrasy, overlooks the many points where Burke's texts respond to the events and trends surrounding their creation. Burke's concepts, in short, were not forged in isolation from the social context that produced the man and his writings. As Selzer argues, "Burke's independence has been overstated, and it has been too easy to excuse him from membership in formative cultural groups that gave Burke his intellectual lifeblood—and that drew lifeblood from him."[7]

Since Burke's life spanned nearly all of the twentieth century, his writings reflect many of that century's key debates: over modernism, capitalism, communism, Marxism, war, ecology, and the rise of science and technology.[8] However, for one notable reader, they offered insight into another divisive twentieth-century issue, one rarely associated with Burke: the nature and meaning of *race*. Emerging into a world where his identity as a black man was *the* difference that made a difference—an America deeply "bent" by racial discrimination and violence—Ralph Ellison found in Kenneth Burke's work the resources needed to establish his own equilibrium.

Although Ellison produced brilliant essays on American literature and the American "racial divide" (preserved in *Shadow and Act, Going to the Territory,* and the *Collected Essays of Ralph Ellison*), he is remembered for his fiction. *Invisible Man,* the only novel he published during his lifetime, catapulted Ellison from relative obscurity to national prominence—earning Ellison a National Book Award, membership in the American Academy of Arts and Letters, and a permanent place in the list of canonical American writers of his, or any, century. Despite Ellison's inability to publish a sequel, *Invisible Man* remains "one of the jewels of twentieth-century American fiction."[9]

Scholarship on Ellison's use of Burkean concepts is now common—especially, as described in chapter 3, regarding *Invisible Man*—but such accounts rarely capture the importance of Burke's writings for Ellison. Ellison studied Burke's writings intently, and, as he later wrote Burke, these writings supplied the *foundation* for his own perspective: "That is why I feel really indebted to you. Essentially the Negro situation is irrational to an extent which surpasses that of the rest of the world—though God knows that sounds impossible. Your method gave me the first instrument with which I could orientate myself." Without the assistance of Burke's "counter-statement," Ellison continued, "coming from where I do in American society, I would not be at home in this rather cockeyed world."[10]

These passages suggest the full impact of Burke's work on Ellison. Using the resources he found in Burke's writings, Ellison crafted his perspective on race and identity in America. For Ellison, this perspective represented, quite literally, a counter-statement—an opportunity to lean against the prevailing American discourse surrounding race, and thereby gain equilibrium in a "rather cockeyed world."

Yet, Ellison's Burkean perspective met resistance from Burke himself—a point lost in most accounts linking the two men. Indeed, Burke's reply to the above-quoted letter expressed misgivings regarding Ellison's ideas: "Thanks much for your kindly references to my work. But as regards the high percentage of indignation with which you apparently propose to write on the conditions of the Negro, I find it extremely awkward to reply." He admitted that his hesitation was likely due to their differing locations in "the white-black opposition," adding: "Whenever I am with a Negro, I think of myself as white; so I do not see how I could reasonably expect that a Negro should similarly consider our culture in any but racial terms."[11]

These passages express discomfort, not with Ellison's praise—after all, Burke's files are stuffed with "fan mail" from readers of his work—but with something more fundamental. Ellison's letter celebrated their overlapping points of view, but Burke's reply interposed a distance between them. Where Ellison saw an extension of Burke's work to the matter of race, Burke saw a significant difference in emphasis; further, Burke's letter attributed this *perspectival* difference to a more fundamental *racial* difference.

More significantly, this exchange, far from an isolated incident, exemplifies the distance that interrupted the Burke-Ellison friendship at key points, producing significant moments of silence, conflict, and misunderstanding between the two men. This awkwardness is treated within chapters 2, 3, and 4 of the present book; we might be tempted to dismiss moments such as these, or attribute them to a clash of personalities, but both Burke and Ellison call attention to the importance of awkwardness in social interaction. Burke's *A Rhetoric of Motives* emphasizes the significance of interactional hesitation and embarrassment since "any variants, however twisted or attenuated, of embarrassment in social intercourse [are] a sign of a corresponding mystery of communication," the mystery arising when "'different kinds of beings' communicate with each other."[12] Following Burke's own cues, then, might we not see in Burke's sense of embarrassment—and, indeed, in awkward moments in their relationship as a whole—a sign of something more than a clash of personalities, but of what Ellison termed the "psychological distance created by race manners"?[13]

By demanding a rigid physical separation between white and black Americans, Ellison famously observed, American racial discourse simultaneously opened a ritual distance between them—a distance "not so much spatial as psychological; while [white and black Americans] might dress and often look alike, seldom on deeper levels do they think alike."[14] In Burke's reply to Ellison, we see a familiar reinscription of the divide between white and black Americans, and—in the "awkward" nature of his reply—the distance that Burke felt between Ellison's social location and his own. Burke's letter thus foreshadows the argument that will be unfolded over the course of this book: the Burke-Ellison relationship was, through and through, *American*.

In one sense, this is a rather simple observation. Burke and Ellison are two men who embraced the (quintessentially American) opportunity to remake themselves—two men whose desire to know and to create led them out of the classroom and into the intellectual circles of New York City. Further, unlike so many of their friends, both men resisted the urge to seek exile in Europe when the American political climate shifted in the 1940s and 1950s.[15] One could even make the argument that few other twentieth-century intellectuals were as committed, on both philosophical and moral grounds, to American democracy.

By describing their friendship as thoroughly American, I mean that these men, and their relationship, signify something important about our culture. As chapter 1 illustrates, these two men reflect differences of origin—geographical, generational, and racial—which, in other national contexts, would have prohibited the formation of any intellectual or personal relationship. By grasping the intellectual and existential possibilities open to them, these men were able to craft, from their different origins, a deep intellectual and personal bond. They shared geographical proximity,[16] a dear friend (Stanley Edgar Hyman), and a common perspective on the relationship between art, symbols, and society. However, just as it was the American context that fostered their relationship, it also made their relationship an uneasy one.

It is thus my contention that the Burke-Ellison relationship reflects an even more vital, complex feature of American life: the uneasy, unstable relationship between white and black Americans generated (and reinforced) by the American "racial divide."[17] I read the Burke-Ellison relationship as this divide writ small; their friendship embodies the "antagonistic cooperation"—or unsteady mixture of trust and mistrust, connection and separation—that has long characterized the relationship between blacks and whites. The two were deeply connected, intellectually and personally; however, engrained social divisions produced hesitation, embarrassment, mystery, and estrangement where Burke and Ellison might have found unity.

In order to lay the foundation for this argument, chapter 1 focuses upon the early years of both men. Rather than strictly focusing upon biography, the chapter embeds their lives within a broader discussion of American racial discourse in the early twentieth century. Chapters 2 and 3 build upon this narrative, examining the intellectual exchanges between the men during the 1940s and 1950s, beginning with Ellison's "Richard Wright's Blues" and ending with *Invisible Man*. Drawing upon published works and unpublished correspondence, I trace the awkward moments that arose during these years, moments that centered on matters of race—and were serious enough to threaten their relationship, especially in the wake of *Invisible Man*. Moving, in a sense, from literary biography to theory, chapter 4 clarifies the nature of these relational disruptions, connecting them to the broader assumptions lying within American racial discourse. This chapter argues that, although Ellison drew heavily upon Burke's writings in order to establish a sense of equilibrium, Burke was unable to fully break away from the confines of the American racial divide. By delineating the differences between Burke's positive, dialectical, and ultimate terms—and applying them to matters of race—this chapter demonstrates that Burke himself suggests the insufficiency of his habitually binaristic vocabulary of race.

Even from this basic outline, it is evident that my overall intent is not to idealize this fascinating friendship. Neither, though, is it to dismiss the importance of the relationship—or demonize either man. The exchanges between Burke and Ellison produced disagreement and misunderstanding, but they also provoked both toward new insights; the sociohistorical conditions that made this fifty-year friendship fractious thus charged it with intellectual significance. We could, I would claim, no more have *Invisible Man* without Burke than we could have *A Rhetoric of Motives* without Ellison. As a consequence, this relationship serves not only as a telling illustration of racial conflict, but as an Ellisonian reminder of the connection that lies beneath our racial divisions.

This connection between Burke and Ellison is, then, as much the focus of this book as the distance that interrupted their friendship. Scholars have long recognized that Ellison employed Burkean concepts in his writings on race; less common, though, is the recognition of the unanalyzed remainder, the resources in Burke's work that can release new insights within Ellison's. Over the course of several decades, Ellison developed an integrative theoretical framework, one that challenged the divide between black and white Americans, but he failed to achieve the ultimate vocabulary that Burke's *Rhetoric* advocates. In this way, I believe that Burke's ultimate order enables the completion of the project begun by Ellison—the creation of a properly complex approach to the study of race.

As chapter 5 argues, this combination of insights from Burke and Ellison has much to offer our own twenty-first-century struggles over the nature and meaning of race in America. Though the election of Barack Obama was supposed to spell the end of our "racial divide," subsequent events have demonstrated otherwise. As a result, the conceptual framework outlined in this chapter represents an alternative to the racial binarism that remains as dominant today as it was in 1942, when the friendship between Burke and Ellison began. By transcending the dialectical division between black and white, a Burkean-Ellisonian vocabulary of race represents the ultimate vocabulary advocated by Burke. It also, though, represents the vocabulary required if we are to successfully challenge our long-standing American investment in the discourse of racial binarism.

Indeed, their relationship itself demonstrates that our customary discourse about race is not inevitable, nor is it sufficiently complex. As chapter 1 suggests, Burke's early years were spent immersed in assumptions about race that, though problematic, were pluralistic, not polar. The shift, from this racial discourse to one premised on binarism, demonstrates that we can adopt a different way of speaking about race—because we have done so in the past. By attending to the hesitation and awkwardness marking their relationship, as in chapters 2, 3, and 4, we can also point toward the deformations and limitations produced by a binaristic approach to race.

However, most powerfully, the Burke-Ellison relationship provides important *intellectual* resources for the critique of this racial binary. The interaction and disagreements between these two critics point toward the possibility of something indicated by Burke, and begun by Ellison: a different way of speaking (and thinking) about race and identity. By uniting these two figures, as chapter 5 argues, we suggest a new possibility: an ultimate vocabulary of race. Transformative moments alone, as in the case of Obama, are not sufficient to produce lasting change; change, as Burke and Ellison both realized, requires a transformative discourse. By uniting Burke and Ellison, I hope to help speak a new conception of race into existence—so that new deeds might follow these new words.

1 /   Birth of an Ancestor

But perhaps you will understand when I say . . . that while one can do nothing about choosing one's relatives, one can, as artist, choose one's "ancestors."

—RALPH ELLISON, COLLECTED ESSAYS

In one famous episode in the history of American letters, during the summer of 1945 an aspiring writer with an unlikely name holed up in a barn in Vermont—to escape New York, improve his health, and gain inspiration. Though Ralph Waldo Ellison had planned to continue writing about a fictional Tuskegee airman-turned-POW, he found himself unable to ignore a nagging inner voice. This strange voice interrupted his novel-in-progress, diverting Ellison's attention with the provocative assertion, "I am an invisible man."[1] Six decades later, the line has become inseparable from Ellison's achievement as a novelist, and his incisive commentary on the American "racial divide."

Thanks to the success of *Invisible Man*, many readers are familiar with its origins and plotline, and with the arc of Ellison's entire career as a novelist: Ellison's wrestling with the manuscript over the course of several years, until its publication in 1952; the book's immediate critical and popular success, including its selection for a National Book Award; and Ellison's unsuccessful struggle to produce a sequel.[2] At the same time, the attention given this landmark novel has eclipsed another aspect of Ellison's career: his essays on race in/and America.[3] By ignoring the impulse to reduce Ellison to *Invisible Man*—and examining his entire body of work, both fiction and nonfiction—we can begin to recognize the power of this work for the theorizing of race and identity in contemporary America. However, any study of Ellison's critical perspective remains incomplete without the inclusion of another oft-overlooked dimension of Ellison's life: his intellectual and personal relationship with fellow American author Kenneth Burke.

Burke is an unlikely figure to link with Ellison—and not simply because his origins (geographic, generational, and racial) contrasted sharply with Ellison's own. Biography aside, Burke is simply not known for his writings on issues of race.[4] Despite this seeming divergence of interests, Ellison found much in Burke's work that spoke to the significance of race in American culture; thus, although Ellison did not place the label on Burke, it is clear that the latter served as one of Ellison's most important "ancestors."[5] This term, borrowed from Ellison's essay "The World and the Jug," indicates a specific type of relationship for a young artist. Unlike "relatives," who populate an artist's environment or whose connection is cemented by the fact of birth, "ancestors" are persons an artist seeks out— those whose achievements represent a standard the artist strives to reach.[6] It is clear from Ellison's writings that Burke played a key ancestral role for Ellison; their relationship arose not from a common background, but from an overlap of sensibilities, a shared perspective on the nature of language, identity, and social reality. As I argue over the next three chapters, it is this perspective, originally derived from Burke's work, that Ellison playfully altered and embodied in the now-famous voice of *Invisible Man*'s narrator.

In November 1945, three months after this voice announced itself to Ellison, he sat with pen and paper, filling eleven legal-sized pages with a letter to Burke—even sketching a rough caricature of Burke in the left margin. Ellison's intention had been to craft a letter of thanks; his summer retreat had been made possible by a grant from the Julius Rosenwald Fund, which Ellison had received at Burke's recommendation.[7] However, the letter grew beyond its intended task, toward a broader consideration of Ellison's relationship to Burke: "I started once before right after I received the Rosenwald Fellowship with the intention of thanking you for having recommended me. But when I had begun it occurred to me that the whole business was a little bit ridiculous; I was about to thank you for a minor favor while leaving the major debt unmentioned. For I realized then that my real debt to you lies in the many things I've learned (and continue to learn) from your work." This debt, Ellison continued, could never be fully repaid, but charged his writing with a special responsibility: to match, in quality, the work that inspired it. Perhaps, Ellison mused, the nascent *Invisible Man* would express the gratitude his letter could not: "I am writing a novel now and perhaps if it is worthwhile it will be my most effective means of saying thanks. Anything else seems to me inadequate and unimaginative."[8]

Indicating Ellison's regard for Burke's opinion, the letter also sought Burke's advice. Ellison outlined, in broad strokes, the nature and tone of the novel-in-progress: "I've deliberately written in the first person, couched much of it in highly intellectualized concepts, and proceeded across a tight rope stretched between the comic and the tragic; but withal I don't know where I'm going." The central obstacle to the book's success, Ellison wrote, lay well beyond its pages: "In our culture the blacks have learned to laugh at what brings tears to white eyes and vice versa, and that makes it hard as hell for a Negro writer to call his shots." Since Burke represented a source of artistic inspiration—and had written extensively on problems of meaning and perspective—Ellison hoped Burke would have an answer to a vital question: "How will a Negro writer who writes out of his full awareness of the complexity of western personality, and who presents the violence of American culture in psychological terms rather than physical ones—how will such a writer be able to break through the stereotype-armored minds of white Americans so that they can receive his message?"[9]

With this question, Ellison invited Burke to join him in a dialogue on issues of race in America—to focus their shared perspective upon the American racial hierarchy. Instead, Ellison's question hung in the air between them; although Burke would later reply to some of the points raised by Ellison, the opportunity represented by this letter was, tragically, missed.

Yet, it is my contention that this episode marks not the end of the story, but its beginning. If we interrogate this strained exchange more closely, we discover a vital link between the Burke-Ellison friendship and the changing conception of race in American culture. The relationship between these two men sheds new light not only upon these central figures' lives and thought, but also—more crucially—upon the American racial drama that contextualized and shaped their lives and thought.

Race matters have always played a decisive role in American society; as Matthew Jacobson persuasively argues, "Race and races are American history."[10] Yet, Ellison's question to Burke was posed at an important moment in the history of the American conception of race. The early to mid-1940s represent not only the pre–civil rights era, but the solidification of the binaristic view of race: race as a question of black and white.[11] In their struggles to connect, Burke and Ellison reflect the consequences of this Manichean division between black and white Americans. Though their friendship was marked by the mystery of race, there remain unexplored possibilities in their relationship—resources that could have allowed them to jointly grapple with this division. By attending to the Burke-Ellison friendship, we can thus reflect upon the construction of the American "racial divide"—and help combat its malign magic. Read in this way, the story of the Burke-Ellison friendship is as relevant now as when Ellison crafted his letter to Burke.

To do justice to the complex story of this relationship, however, we cannot begin in 1945, with Ellison's missive to Burke. Instead, we must trace the trajectories that brought both men to this point, reembedding their biographies, their perspectives, and their relationship within the curve (or boomerang) of American history—and, most especially, American attitudes toward and discourse surrounding race.

Burke's Pittsburghian Origins

On 5 May, 1897, the "smoky inferno" of Pittsburgh, Pennsylvania, welcomed the arrival of Kenneth Duva Burke, the son of James Burke and Lillyan May Duva Burke.[12] The "steel city" of Kenneth's birth was hailed as the nation's foremost producer of steel and iron, though this achievement was not without detrimental effect. The steel industry spurred automation and corporate expansion, but undermined other types of economic activity; it produced many new jobs for unskilled workers, but devalued the abilities of skilled craftsmen.[13] These economic developments further exacerbated the tensions rising in the city (and the nation) around issues of race.

However, these tensions, like their causes, were complex. In the America of Burke's birth, anxieties over race were not solely centered upon black Americans. In the waning years of the nineteenth century, for example, not only had Congress acted to curtail the rights of Native Americans, it had also created a law banning Chinese immigration into the country.[14] Yet, indicating widespread antiblack sentiment, the end of the nineteenth century marked a significant shift in the social and legal status of black Americans.

In 1896, less than a year before Burke was born, the Supreme Court in *Plessy v. Ferguson* had affirmed the constitutionality of race-based segregation. By establishing the "separate but equal" standard for public accommodation—arguing that animosity toward black Americans was natural, and immune to legislative action—the decision sanctioned the "Jim Crow" laws adopted by legislatures across the South.[15] Although these states had passed segregationist laws prior to the decision, afterward they institutionalized *Plessy v. Ferguson* with a decided thoroughness.

Jim Crow laws decreed that black Americans had to attend separate schools, ride in separate railway cars, eat in separate sections of restaurants, swear on separate Bibles, convalesce in separate hospitals, and rest in separate cemeteries. There was, in essence, no part of public life left untouched by these laws.[16]

In response to Jim Crow and the bleak economic and agricultural conditions in the South, the dawn of the twentieth century found an increasing number of black Americans seeking better lives in the North. The "Great Migration" resulted in the relocation of 5 million black Americans from the South—with the heaviest migration occurring just after World War I.[17] Because of the rapid expansion of Pittsburgh's heavy industry, however, steady migration to the city began at an earlier date.[18] "Between 1870 and 1900 the rate of population growth for black Pittsburgh was greater than during any other period . . . making the Pittsburgh black community the sixth largest in the nation"[19]—with its population doubling between 1890 and 1900.[20]

However, reflecting the complexities of race during this period, tensions in Pittsburgh were not simply a result of black Americans' quest to seek new opportunities in the North. Between the last decades of the nineteenth century and World War I, millions of immigrants, largely from eastern and southern Europe, swelled the population of the United States but—unlike previous immigrants from England, Germany, and Ireland—settled in the urban, industrialized areas of the Northeast.[21] The "steel city" proved as attractive to these immigrants as to black Americans fleeing the South: by 1900, Pittsburgh contained the sixth-largest Polish and Italian communities in the nation.[22]

Upon their arrival, Poles, Italians, and black migrants all sought jobs calling for unskilled or semiskilled labor—yet, given the antiblack sentiment common in Pittsburgh's steel industry and building trades, they rarely vied for the same jobs. As open positions were overwhelmingly awarded to immigrants, black Americans were forced to work as laborers, or in service and transportation.[23] Though southern and eastern Europeans thus benefited from antiblack racism, in Pittsburgh relations between black Americans and immigrants bore little resemblance to the segregated ideal of Jim Crow.

Complete segregation was made impossible in 1875, when Pittsburgh closed its black schools—making it "one of the few large cities with a desegregated [educational] system."[24] Further, the black community was not ghettoized, as elsewhere in the North, so areas of the city with a substantial number of black residents often included a sizable immigrant population.[25] This meant that black, Polish, and Italian communities occupied the same neighborhoods—even, at times, sharing space within the same rooming houses and apartment buildings.

This residential and educational integration does not mean that Pittsburgh was free of prejudice. On the contrary, the city's housing patterns were a product of discriminatory practices—but practices aimed *equally* at black Americans and Polish and Italian immigrants. As "the poorest and least desired immigrants," members of these communities "received the least desirable land—that with the highest density, that with the oldest and most deteriorated housing, or that located on the most formidable terrain."[26]

This shared stigma—the undesirability that united these disparate communities—also frustrates any attempt to impose a binaristic racial frame upon Burke's early years. Though, in the twenty-first century, the temptation is to read Pittsburgh's social scene as oppositional, to "Anglo-Saxon" Americans, blacks, Poles, and Italians were *all* members of inferior racial groups. At the dawn of the twentieth century, "the Negro," "the Hunkie," and "the Wop" alike were described as grave threats—threats of "racial degeneration"—to America's Anglo-Saxons.[27] This was neither a simple rhetorical flourish nor a conflation of race and ethnicity. Members of the "Negro," "Slav," and "Italian" races were perceived as having physiological and psychological characteristics marking them as distinct from, and inferior to, America's dominant Anglo-Saxons.[28] To be Italian or Polish at this time meant that you were not white—or, at least, not *unambiguously* white, not white *enough*.[29]

For those, like Burke, growing up in Pittsburgh in the early 1900s, these attitudes were as pervasive as smoke from the city's factories. As he later reflected, "I grew up in an uncouth age and neighborhood in which it was taken for granted that minorities 'normally' referred to one another as Dagoes, Hunkies, Niggers, Micks, Kikes, and such, along with our sound suspicion that we were all minorities of one sort or another."[30] This apologia—offered for the "bumpy passages" in Burke's early fiction—could also apply to portions of his correspondence that appear, to contemporary eyes, racist or anti-Semitic.[31] Burke's use of these epithets certainly illustrates that Pittsburgh's integrated neighborhoods were not free of racial stigma. As a third-generation American, Burke grew up with family stories that would have reflected the prejudice accompanying the immigrant experience—and perhaps prompted Burke's "suspicion" that he, too, was a minority, even if he could not claim membership within the groups "recognized" as such by the epithets of his youth.

Whether or not Burke's minority status was granted by his peers, he internalized the markers of, and proprieties surrounding, Pittsburgh's racial identities; when asked by an interviewer about his "background," Burke's catechistic answer emphasized citizenship, religion, and what would now be termed "ethnicity": "Both my parents were raised in Pittsburgh. They were both Protestant. Their parents were immigrants. My mother's side was French and German. My father's side was Irish and German."[32] A similar precision characterized a 1933 portrait of Burke: "The name sounds Irish and Roman Catholic; but the author is mostly German, and more French than Irish, and his family's religion he has described as 'Protestantism merging into nothing.'"[33] A 1915 letter from Malcolm Cowley only differed from these accounts by suggesting there was more Irish in Burke's heritage than he would want to admit. Cowley's letter even divined the tenor of an upcoming reunion from their racial backgrounds: "You—who are gifted and cursed with the intensity of an Irish nature, will have either a pleasing surprise or bitter disappointment, depending on which convolution you are in at the time. And I, the German-English-Irish-Scotch moderate, will find the visit about as I expected."[34]

These passages suggest the importance that Burke and his contemporaries placed upon proper identification: Burke was not a recent immigrant, but a third-generation American; not Catholic, but Protestant; not Irish (at least in his eyes), but German or French. These distinctions, like the slurs Burke recalled from his youth, matched Pittsburgh's (and America's) racial hierarchies at the dawn of the twentieth century: Protestants over Catholics and Jews, Anglo-Saxons over blacks, Celts, Poles, and Italians. As a result, though he might have suspected otherwise, even in the early 1900s Burke occupied a quite favorable position within the American racial drama.

Burke's socialization into these hierarchies was as much a reflection of location as generation. Since his father, James, was "a minor clerk in a detail and supply department" for General Electric's Westinghouse Plant, Burke spent his early years living near the factory, in Pittsburgh's East Liberty section.[35] Although this neighborhood had traditionally been populated by Germans and Irish,[36] by the time Burke was in high school, surveys of East Liberty's residents included growing numbers of black and Italian families.[37] Such an alteration in the complexion—in every sense of the word—of East Liberty likely lent increased salience to the hierarchies and epithets learned (and hurled) by the neighborhood's children.

However, race was not the only distinction to make a difference to Burke and his contemporaries; the young residents of East Liberty also learned important lessons about class. According to Burke, this hierarchy supplemented racial measures of status, helping to place, quite literally, even those, like Burke, identified as Anglo-Saxon and Protestant. Given the link between class and residence, a map of Pittsburgh revealed to the initiated reader the economic topography of the city. Those, like Burke, who did not occupy the city's finest suburbs keenly felt the resulting diminution of status: "(Imagine the stigma, for instance, of living in Brushton rather than Homewood, or Homewood rather than Squirrel Hill, and so on.)."[38]

Perhaps because Burke occupied a privileged position within Pittsburgh's racial hierarchy, he was more attuned to the power of its economic analogue to create "stigma." Compared to Squirrel Hill, East Liberty conferred an ambiguous status upon its residents. Although the neighborhood was filled with working-class families—often Westinghouse employees—its transportation options and housing also made it an attractive location for Pittsburgh's rising middle class.[39] In addition, East Liberty's mixed population distinguished it from affluent suburbs that had few, if any, black residents.[40] Economically, at least, this neighborhood thus represented a fitting location for Burke's childhood; like East Liberty, the Burke family was located somewhere on the border between working class and middle class.

Since he was a clerk at Westinghouse, James's income exceeded that of his laboring neighbors. The Burkes were not far removed from the working class, however; their hold on a middle-class existence was a tenuous one, at best. As Burke later recalled, "The way things were in those days, you were always broke," since James "had one of those jobs where you were laid off periodically."[41] The layoffs were a regular occurrence for the family because "any time [Westinghouse] had financial troubles, he got thrown out of work."[42] The family maintained their home in East Liberty throughout Burke's early years, but after he turned four, the family moved farther from the city center—facing Burke with the "stigma" of a Brushton address.[43]

Perhaps reflecting these economic struggles, James tried to instill pragmatic values in Kenneth—emphasizing the importance of earning a good wage. James's desire for a secure, middle-class life created tension in their relationship; as Burke later explained: "He was worried about me because I wasn't enough interested in making money. That was his thing; he spent his whole life under a cloud of a million dollars."[44] Fixated on Kenneth's lack of ambition, James disapproved of his son's literary aspirations.[45] Yet, James and Lillyan also nurtured an appreciation for the creative and the aesthetic in their young son. Burke's son Anthony summarized the family's contradictory nature as "working class, but with an academic flair."[46]

Thanks to Lillyan, the Burke household was filled with music, instilling in Kenneth an early appreciation for tonality and rhythm. Despite his contempt for the artistic life, there was more to James than the quest for monetary success; Kenneth later characterized his father as someone who "would have been wonderful if he'd had a good education. He had a great deal of ability, he was a wonderful raconteur, and he had a beautiful tenor voice."[47] James was a frustrated inventor (whose inventions, unwanted by American industry, littered the family home),[48] but he "spent his whole life unsuccessfully submitting short stories to the *Saturday Evening Post*."[49]

This eclectic, even paradoxical, familial context conspired with accidental events to set the foundation for Kenneth's later career. Burke had a near-death experience at age two, breaking his neck in a fall. Although he miraculously healed, the injuries left an indelible mark on him.[50] Physically, he was never the same; he began to suffer from "sinking" fits or spells, "where he felt as if the earth would swallow him up. During these spells, Burke would cry until his father returned from work, often in the middle of the day, to calm him."[51]

However, the accident was to play a second, even more important, role in charting Burke's future. In Lillyan's opinion, the "sinking" spells testified to Kenneth's sensitive nature. To avoid triggering them, she treated him as fragile, even barring him from attending school for two years. When he asked permission to join his friends at school, she pacified him with a dictionary, which he dutifully dragged around the family's home. Whether or not this was the intended effect, Kenneth also set about trying to master the text. In a late interview, he explained that "she gave me the 'Good Book,' but with no instructions on how to figure out what was inside it"—yet, at a certain point, "the damn thing began to make sense. And before long I had it pretty well figured out."[52]

After mastering the dictionary, he was more than prepared for the moment when his mother relented, and he attended school for the first time.[53] Burke's desire to build upon this lexicographical foundation, combined with his newfound love of books, led him to enroll in a "better" school, by "registering under [his] grandmother's name."[54] Using her address, Burke attended school in East Liberty, beginning with the Margaretta Grammar School. This led to a momentous event: during his eighth-grade year at the Liberty School, he reconnected with someone who would become his lifelong friend: Malcolm Cowley.[55]

Burke and Cowley first met as children—Cowley's father was the Burke family's physician—but lost contact when Burke's family moved to Brushton.[56] When they met again at Liberty and enrolled together at Peabody High School, their friendship was renewed and reinvigorated. Their bond was cemented by shared loneliness, love of the library, and taste in literature. Soon, the two became inseparable—key figures in the "literary crowd" at Peabody High, which Cowley described as "composed of boys who made good marks in English Composition, read books that weren't assigned for reading, were shy, noisy, ill dressed, and helped to edit the school magazine."[57] Burke and Cowley were part of the first class of students to attend Peabody—a new school created by the expansion and conversion of Burke's old grammar school, Margaretta.[58] Cowley recalled Peabody as "well equipped," and that "the atmosphere of the school was prosperous and middle class."[59]

Perhaps reflecting the newness of the school and its "prosperous" student body, Peabody boasted a well-credentialed faculty. Burke studied Greek for two years at Peabody under "a Harvard man" who "taught in the high school because the pay was better."[60] As a result, Burke was afforded an astonishingly robust education; he was introduced to H. L. Mencken's literary and cultural magazine, *Smart Set*, which was devoted to "ridiculing genteel American culture"—including James Burke's beloved *Saturday Evening Post*.[61] Burke and Cowley went on to devour the work of James, Emerson, and Twain, as well as "Ibsen, Strindberg, Pinero, Shaw, Schnitzler, Sudermann, Hauptmann. Then came the Russians, 'with attachment particularly to Chekhov's plays and the self-interfering characters of Dostoevsky.'"[62]

Burke's graduation in the spring of 1915 signaled the beginning of his critical career. Yet, though he left it behind, the city of his birth provided him more than a lifelong friend in Cowley—and more than an education in the hierarchies of race and class. His instructors at Peabody instilled in him a deep appreciation for the European authors responsible for the modernist strains in American literature.[63] Just as important, the environment of his early years generated an appreciation for "art that ran counter to the general nature of things, as a kind of counterprinciple."[64] Burke's first "counterprinciple" was a pure aestheticism, opposed to his father's financial ambitions and the choking pollution of the city: "That's where I got my whole horror of technology. God, Pittsburgh . . . terrifying place in that time."[65] Over the next twenty years, Burke's work developed in complexity, but his appreciation for "counterprinciples" remained constant. The embodiment of this attitude in Burke's critical perspective proved significant in another way: two decades later, it triggered a watershed moment in the development of an aspiring writer named Ralph Ellison.

A Product of the Territory

At a 1979 festival held in his honor, Ellison reflected upon the role played by chance, and "unknown history," in the determination of human character. "Geography," he concluded, "is fate."[66] Just as Burke's perspective was shaped by Pittsburgh's smokestacks and invectives, Oklahoma provided the raw materials for Ellison's. Suggesting the complexities hidden in Ellison's phrase, these disparate beginnings (geographical and otherwise) led to a striking accord of sensibilities—though that would have seemed unlikely on 1 March 1913, when Ellison was born in an Oklahoma City rooming house.[67]

Like many black Americans during the 1900s, Ralph's parents, Lewis and Ida Ellison, had sought an escape from the choking restrictions of Jim Crow's South. Rejecting a northern migration, Lewis and Ida had seen promise in Oklahoma's combination of freedom and frontier. Slavery had existed in the Indian Territory prior to Emancipation—imported with the Native American tribes forced to walk the "Trail of Tears."[68] However, matters had changed greatly by 1889, when the area was opened to broader settlement—and after control over its affairs was wrested from the "Five Civilized Tribes." Since the federal government had barred discrimination in the newly opened land, black Americans from elsewhere in the country joined the mad scramble for homesteads. Ellison's birthplace, Oklahoma City, literally rose overnight, as twelve thousand settlers gobbled up the ground around the Oklahoma Station railway stop.[69]

For Lewis and Ida, Oklahoma represented "a territory of hope, and a place where they could create their own opportunities"; they could stake out their own land and, even more importantly, they were able to vote.[70] Oklahoma's black community was thus afforded a quality of life superior to that of any southern state. As a result, Ellison wryly recalled, Oklahoma's black residents "were often charged by exasperated white Texans with 'not knowing their place.'"[71] During this time, advocates like Edward P. McCabe even founded black-only towns—envisioning a state reserved exclusively for black Americans—and advertised the virtues of the Territory throughout the South.[72]

Formal statehood for Oklahoma in 1907 ended the dreams of those like McCabe. Within its constitution, the state's racial complexity was reduced to a simple binary: "Though Oklahoma had a large number of blacks, whites, and American Indians, as well as Mexicans, everyone was considered a member of the white race except those with 'African' blood."[73] The new legislature also passed a series of statutes mandating segregation in railway transportation, marriage, and education. In 1910, this segregationist attitude was again written into the state constitution, when an amendment linking voting to literacy—with a "grandfather clause" exempting white voters—effectively disenfranchised Oklahoma's black residents.[74]

Despite this encroachment of the Deep South into Oklahoma, Ida and Lewis remained hopeful—especially when the United States Supreme Court declared the "grandfather clause" unconstitutional in June 1915. Their hopes were extinguished when the Oklahoma legislature immediately circumvented the ruling. The state's new election law adhered to the *letter* of the ruling, but ensured that the decision would have little impact. Under this law, the majority of black Oklahomans were again prevented from participating in the electoral process.[75]

Like all black Oklahomans, Ida and Lewis mourned the end of freedom in the state. Lewis had to take work where he could find it, traveling to Texas when nothing satisfactory was available in Oklahoma City.[76] Yet, over the course of Ralph's childhood, the Ellison family battled to overcome these obstacles and improve their station; after Lewis parlayed his earnings into ownership of an ice and coal business, the family moved to a larger home at a more prosperous address.[77] This upward trajectory was forever altered on 19 June 1916, when Lewis slipped down a flight of stairs while delivering ice. He sustained a serious wound from the ice and was immediately hospitalized; the injury was compounded by a preexisting stomach condition, and rapidly produced an uncontrollable infection. One month later, Lewis died following an experimental surgery. For the three-year-old Ralph, who had accompanied his father on the fateful delivery, the "terrible fact" of Lewis's death was the end of the world.[78]

Since Ida had given birth to another son, Herbert, in June, Lewis's death left her with medical bills, no source of income, and two small boys to raise.[79] The accident "devastated the family emotionally and financially," and "marked the beginning of years of no-frills living."[80] This dramatic change in the family's economic status forced the Ellisons to move from their new home and find lodging elsewhere—an experience that would become characteristic of Ralph's childhood. Though she had not worked prior to Lewis's death, afterward Ida was forced to take a series of low-paying service jobs, with most of her paycheck devoted to rent. Under these conditions, if a job disappeared or an employer became unbearable, the family also lost its home. On several occasions, Ida moved her sons out of Oklahoma City, even out of Oklahoma, in search of better wages; however, it was never long before, exhausted and dispirited, Ida would bring the boys back to the familiar streets of Oklahoma City.[81]

Ralph hated the family's nomadic existence, especially after he realized the significance of the moves—their reflection of the Ellisons' place in Oklahoma's economic hierarchy. He became increasingly aware of the differences between his family and the wealthier black families who took pity on them: "The ragtag pilgrimage of the Ellison family from house to house across Oklahoma City became the nine-year-old boy's unspoken shame."[82] Like Burke, Ralph learned to connect geography and class—and to track changes in the family's economic standing through visible indicators like house size, presence of others in the home, neighborhood type, and proximity of white families. Though Ida worked to instill a sense of pride in Ralph that countered these signs of class, she could not control the reaction of others in the community: "As Ralph grew into adolescence and young manhood, he watched his mother slip down the social ladder until, in the end, she had lost whatever cachet she had brought with her to Oklahoma as a pretty young bride." Ralph was forced to recognize that the wealthy families who helped Ida "were *not* his family, that he was a recipient of their charity, that his mother was a servant, and that he would largely be on his own in the world."[83]

This economic stigma was compounded by his humiliating encounters with Oklahoma's white population. In an increasingly segregated Oklahoma City, Ralph learned the significance of the "brief impersonal encounters, stares, vocal inflections, hostile laughter, or public reversals of private expectations" that marked his interaction with whites;[84] he learned that to be black was to be deemed inferior and denied opportunities. According to Ralph, one of his earliest experiences of discrimination occurred in 1919, when he began first grade. Though he lived one block away from a new, well-equipped school, Ida informed Ralph that he would instead have to walk eight blocks, to the school reserved for black students: Frederick Douglass Elementary School. Not only was Douglass much older than the school nearby, but his path to Douglass involved a walk through the red-light district and a dangerous crossing of busy railroad tracks.[85]

This early lesson in Oklahoma's racial hierarchy was reinforced by the state's Jim Crow–style laws. These laws confronted Ralph in a myriad of everyday situations, such as the streetcar—when he was forced to sit in the back, separated from the "whites-only" seats by a divider.[86] More troubling to a child Ralph's age, Oklahoma City passed an ordinance barring unaccompanied blacks from visiting the zoo. Although Ida decided to challenge the law directly—by taking her sons to see the animals—the resulting confrontation with an angry white man made a deep impression on Ralph. He characterized it as "another lesson in the sudden ways good times could be turned into bad when white people looked at your color instead of *you*."[87]

Ralph soon learned that his skin color could result in more than a few angry words—that violence was often the result when "good times . . . turned into bad." These lessons were partly provided by the Ku Klux Klan, whose rebirth coincided with the first ten years of Ralph's life; although originally associated with the days of Reconstruction, the Klan reappeared across the country following the success of the 1915 film *The Birth of a Nation*. By 1920, the KKK had appeared in Oklahoma City, and by 1923 it claimed to have more than one hundred thousand members across the state—including prominent state and local officials.[88]

Yet, the KKK was only one source of the violence aimed at the black communities during Ralph's youth. Lynching had been a horrific facet of American life since the second half of the nineteenth century.[89] In the early decades of the twentieth century, Congress repeatedly demonstrated its unwillingness to pass a law banning lynching, despite the efforts of such groups as the National Association of Colored Women and the National Association for the Advancement of Colored People.[90] As a result, whether instigated by the Klan or by an angry mob, during Ralph's childhood, "the number of lynchings nationwide, which had been declining for some years, rose sharply. In 1917, thirty-six blacks were lynched; in 1919, the number was approximately seventy-six, including ten black soldiers still wearing their uniforms."[91] Some of these incidents were sparked by white outrage at the sight of uniformed black Americans—suggesting one of the many ways in which World War I contributed to this racial violence.[92]

After the war's end, demobilized black soldiers decried the contradiction between their "fight for democracy" abroad and their treatment at home.[93] Many even resolved to challenge threats to black individuals or their freedoms. These men embodied the determination of black communities across the country to resist antiblack racism at any cost—to meet violence with violence. Oklahoma, as Ellison recalled, was one of the states thereby converted into a battleground: "I know that a great number of the people I grew up with were armed, and during the 1920s when there was a lot of trouble, I've seen them produce those arms and stand waiting."[94] Such confrontations were common when a member of the black community was lynched—or threatened with lynching. Ellison witnessed at least one such event in his hometown: "A man was lynched in Chickasha, and his body was brought over to Oklahoma City for burial. The members of the white mob telephoned to Oklahoma City that they were coming over to drag this body back. And the Negroes sent word: 'Come on. We'll be waiting.' And they were waiting. Jack Walton was mayor at the time. I was out there when he came out and took a stand with the Negroes to keep this thing from exploding."[95]

In one respect, Ellison's experience was unusual; authorities did not often "stand with the Negroes" during this period. Even if they did, given the combustible conditions of the time, these confrontations rarely ended without an explosion—often quite literally. In Chicago, for example, "between 1917 and 1921 fifty-eight homemade bombs were thrown into communities composed of newly arrived Negroes."[96] Far from isolated incidents, these bombings were indications of the hostility aimed at black communities; from 1917 to 1921, an epidemic of violent race riots swept across the country, when racially charged confrontations degenerated into open warfare. During the "Red Summer" of 1919, between twenty-five and fifty-six race riots occurred, where mobs engaged in systematic acts of destruction aimed indiscriminately at black individuals and communities; the riots killed scores, wounded thousands, and damaged millions of dollars of black-owned property.[97]

Ralph personally witnessed the devastation created by "the worst [race riot] in the twentieth century and possibly in American history," which took place in Tulsa, Oklahoma, on 30 June 1921.[98] The Ellison family—on their way to Gary, Indiana, in search of opportunity—had stopped in Tulsa in early 1921. While there, Ralph had seen firsthand the fine black-owned homes and thriving businesses in the neighborhood of Greenwood. A few months later, when the family was forced to retrace their steps to Oklahoma City, he was stunned to see "that Greenwood had been devastated and all but destroyed by bomb and fire."[99]

The turbulence and violence of these postwar years deepened Ralph's grim education in the significance of his racial identity. Less evident, given the strict segregation championed in his home state, was the battle raging at this time over the nature of whiteness. Like most Oklahomans, Ellison had become accustomed to thinking of race in oppositional terms—a pattern of thought reinforced by the antiblack violence of the 1920s. Since Oklahoma's segregationist constitution excluded only those "of African descent" from the white race, the state had both defined race as a battle between two opponents ("Africans" vs. "whites") and papered over other racial divisions through a blanket attribution of whiteness.[100] Elsewhere in the country, however, and especially in the industrial Northeast, race was hardly a tidy division between black and white.[101]

Engineering America's Racial Composition

Oklahoma's definition of race reflected that state's traditions, but did not address the nation's preoccupation with the immigrant, which had not diminished in the years since Burke's childhood; if anything, concern over immigration had intensified in the Northeast, thanks to a shift in American foreign policy. Concerned about the economic implications of industrialism, policymakers had used diplomatic and militaristic means to extend American influence to far-flung areas of the globe. Though imperial adventures had expanded the reach of U.S. exports, these efforts threatened to produce a flood of racially "inferior" immigrants—from such places as Samoa, Hawaii, Guam, the Philippines, Cuba, Puerto Rico, and Panama.[102] At the turn of the century, nativist passions had been aroused by the arrivals from southern and eastern Europe; prominent Anglo-Saxon or "Old Stock" Americans saw the surge in non-European immigration as a further dilution of the nation's vitality through "massive influxes of inferior 'stock.'"[103]

The only solution, according to the nativists, was to halt the influx of these problematic arrivals—to retake control of the nation's population and to intelligently engineer its racial composition. This solution received official sanction when Senator William Paul Dillingham became chairman of the United States Immigration Commission. Under his leadership, the commission worked to ensure that "those new arrivals who were still allowed entry . . . once again 'looked exactly like Americans.'"[104] As this quote from Dillingham suggests, the commission's efforts were grounded in the assumption that the questions of immigration and race were one and the same.

Not surprisingly, then, in 1911 Dillingham's commission sponsored the publication of A Dictionary of Races or Peoples. This widely cited text recognized the five major "varieties" of humankind identified by Johann Blumenbach in 1775, but further divided American immigrants into forty-five distinct races, thirty-six of which were European.[105] In other words, like the residents of Burke's East Liberty neighborhood (and unlike the framers of Oklahoma's constitution), the *Dictionary* refused to fold all Europeans into a unified white race. Dillingham's typology was soon replaced in the popular imagination, however, by one that consolidated the thirty-six European races into three: Nordics, Alpines, and Mediterraneans.

This tripartite scheme, popularized by Madison Grant's *The Passing of the Great Race*, also organized these races into a hierarchy. Grant placed the "Nordic" race, the race truly able to claim whiteness, at the top, the Alpine between, and the Mediterranean at the bottom.[106] The success of this typology was due to its rhetorical appeal—since "Nordic" was more inclusive than "Anglo-Saxon"—and its ability to unite the political and the racial. Although Grant's book was first published in 1916, it attained its greatest popularity during the postwar "Red Scare," given the heightened salience of his descriptions of physiologically and psychologically inferior races. Reinforcing the belief that radicalism (like inferiority) was physiologically evident, that it could be seen, Grant "scientifically" traced the spread of bolshevism to arriving hordes of Alpines and Mediterraneans.[107]

Grant's work also won him a leading place on the Eugenics Committee of the United States Committee on Selective Immigration. This committee's research led directly to the Johnson-Reed Act of 1924, a decisive victory for those (like Grant) desperate to halt the immigration of "inferior" races into America.[108] Moreover, this "triumph of eugenic logic was not a political anomaly, the fleeting victory of so many cranks and crackpots."[109] On the contrary, between 1910 and 1930, a majority of the American public saw little difference between advocating the restriction of immigration and the scientific control of the nation's racial "stock"—since both aimed to ensure the continued dominance of the superior "Nordic" race.

The popularity of the eugenics movement derived partly from widespread faith in the progressive march of science, and partly from acceptance of the racial differences catalogued by Grant and his allies. Public support was also cultivated and reinforced by the promotion of eugenicist studies—studies that isolated the racial "causes" of social ills. In this effort, the eugenics movement was able to count on a more tangible type of support: generous financial awards from the United States government and from prestigious private foundations.

Just as Congress funded committees to promote and apply the science of eugenics, wealthy philanthropists like the Carnegies and Rockefellers donated substantial sums to establish centers of eugenics research. These organizations worked to sway public perception and national policy regarding the link between race and deviance.[110] From criminal behavior to prostitution to birth control to drug abuse, there was little in social life that was not investigated for its racial significance—with the results trumpeted to a receptive public. Illustrating the mainstream nature of the eugenics movement, the Bureau of Social Hygiene—a Rockefeller-funded organization founded upon a racialist view of crime—even hired a prominent young critic named Kenneth Burke to ghostwrite a book on "dangerous drugs."[111]

A Young Aesthete, or Among the Villagers

Burke's work for the Bureau of Social Hygiene played a significant role in such works as *Permanence and Change* (1935) and *The Philosophy of Literary Form* (1941), but he initially saw it as glorified moonlighting—a way to support his family, and tolerable only insofar as it did not interfere with his literary career.[112] By the time that Burke accepted a position with the bureau (in the late 1920s), he had begun to realize the promise that he had shown as a member of Peabody's "literary crowd." Indeed, according to one memoir of the period, even by "1922 and '23 Burke was one of [America's] most promising literary figures."[113]

Burke's personal choices had facilitated the rapid rise of his career; after graduation, he had moved with his family from Pittsburgh to Weehawken, New Jersey, and immersed himself in the artistic environment of Greenwich Village.[114] At first, to support his intellectual pursuits, and likely to appease his father, Burke worked for a bank; his tenure in the workaday world lasted only until the spring of 1916, however, when he enrolled in Ohio State University. After one semester, Burke remained enthusiastic about art, but not about Ohio State, so he dropped out and returned to New Jersey.[115] He spent 1917 commuting from Weehawken to classes at Columbia University, but then made a decision that would define his future: at Columbia, "there were a lot of courses I wanted to take, and I had to take so many prerequisite courses before I could get to them that I said to my father, hell, Pap, I'll save you some money—and persuaded him to let me go down to the Village and rent a room and read all the books by myself."[116] As Burke explained in a 6 January 1918 letter to Cowley, he had resolved to make himself into an artist, with

Greenwich Village his classroom: "I shall get a room in New York and begin my existence as a Flaubert. . . . I don't want to be a virtuoso; I want to be a—a—oh hell, why not? I want to be a—yes—a genius."[117]

With his father's "tuition" money in his pocket, Burke spent 1918–22 in rooming houses in the Village, where he "lived on iron rations of oatmeal and milk twice a day and worked at stories and essays which he was very eager to publish before his funds gave out."[118] Suspicious of the jingoism surrounding the war effort, rejected from military service, and in need of additional income, Burke spent the war years working first in a shipyard and then, as he later recalled, "for an anarchist in a little 42nd Street office making gauges to check gauges that were used to regulate the mass production of munitions."[119] When not working, or debating his peers, Burke wrote and revised poetry and short pieces of fiction—a few of which were published in small, experimental periodicals.[120]

Consequently, as the war ended and peacetime activities resumed, Burke found himself at the forefront of what his friend Cowley famously named the "Youngest Generation": the artists and intellectuals fomenting a modernist revolution in American arts and letters.[121] The central figures in this movement, including Burke, were synonymous with the suddenly chic confines of Greenwich Village.[122] Beyond their common location, they were united by their disillusion with postwar American culture, and by their commitment to an experimental, avant-garde aesthetic. Some, like Cowley, felt Europe was a better environment for their artistic development, while others sought refuge in pastoral settings, in an attempt "to correct the alienating aspects of urban life and to sustain creative vigor."[123]

For Burke, not long removed from Westinghouse's smokestacks, rural settings held a strong appeal. Before and after his marriage to Lily Batterham in 1919, Burke spent his summers away from the noise and expense of the Village—using stays in New York State (1919), North Carolina (1920), and Maine (1921) to reconnect with the immediacy of subsistence living.[124] In 1922, Burke seized an opportunity to make this "agro-bohemian" (and anti-Pittsburgh) lifestyle permanent; borrowing three hundred dollars from his father, Burke and Lily purchased an old house, together with seventy acres, in Andover, New Jersey.[125] Since the house combined proximity to the city with near-primitive living conditions, Burke and Lily overlooked the building's state of disrepair and decay.[126]

By the time they moved into the house in April 1922, Burke had begun to earn positive reviews from editors for his stories, essays, and reviews. Some of his fiction and criticism had even been accepted for publication

in the prestigious modernist periodical the *Dial*—regarded as "the greatest American magazine of arts and letters of our [twentieth] century."[127]
Although Burke was eventually described as "the great discovery of the
Dial, next to [E. E.] Cummings,"[128] of more immediate importance—as
Burke pondered his finances in May 1922—was the unexpected invitation to serve as the *Dial's* temporary assistant editor, an offer he later
called one of the "two moments that most changed me."[129] His editorial work won him the praise of the staff, and by January 1923, he was
named the *Dial's* acting managing editor. This second interim position
cemented his relationship with the magazine and enhanced his literary
reputation; it also helped win Burke's loyalty. Burke remained connected
to the *Dial* until the periodical's demise in 1929—winning the prestigious Dial Award for 1928, the last one in its history.[130]

When his last full-time position at the *Dial* ended in 1926, Burke's
sister-in-law and future wife, Elizabeth (Libbie) Batterham, helped him
secure a salaried post as a research assistant for Colonel Arthur Woods.[131]
Though less providential than the invitation to join the *Dial*, his job as
a ghostwriter "made a terrific difference," Burke later recalled, in his life
and literary development.[132] Burke remained in Woods's employment
from the summer of 1926 to the summer of 1927, and from October 1928
to mid-1931, eventually resigning because these studies of narcotics and
drug trafficking were hindering his creative efforts. Even so, Burke found
the position difficult to relinquish since it was quite lucrative, bankrolled
by the Laura Spelman Rockefeller Memorial Trust and the (Rockefeller-
funded) Bureau of Social Hygiene.[133]

The steady income from these positions enabled Burke to spend the
decade contributing to a variety of experimental periodicals and projects, completing freelance translations, and producing the essays and
fiction that comprised the foundation of *The White Oxen* (1924), *Counter-Statement* (1931), and *Towards a Better Life* (1932). Although Burke
would soon question his commitment to "a rather pure aestheticism,"
in these early works Burke focused upon questions eternal and formal,
not temporal and social.[134] This was no accident; as Burke explained to
Cowley in 1923, he intentionally avoided pressing issues of the day: "I am
not interested primarily in American business, nor the Japanese problem on the coast, nor the one big union, nor the *New York Journal*. I
am interested primarily in the possibility of turning out solid boulders
of art." To do otherwise, Burke continued, was to embrace a different
conception of art: "You propose to write the work of art for a continent.
I propose to write the work of art for about twelve people. This involves a

great difference. It means, simply, that I look upon writing as I look upon smoking, as a personal enjoyment."[135]

Even when Burke commented on current events, he did not abandon this aestheticist concern for the eternal; the resulting political viewpoint was an odd amalgam of East Liberty and Greenwich Village. A 1923 letter to Cowley, for example, cited Pittsburgh's racial hierarchies in its support for immigration restriction, redefining the issue as an artistic one of "fit" between sensibility and environment: "Not merely Southern Italians and Slavs are undesirable immigrants, but everyone is an undesirable immigrant, since the state of ebullition is preserved by any new influx. Ebullition prevents the erection of satisfactory forms about life; ebullition is wholesome only when it is a direct transition from one form to another." Though Burke's diagnosis of the situation differed from that of Grant and the eugenicists, his proposed solution was identical: "With immigration stopped, America's economic disturbances would clarify within twenty years; . . . it would involve no noticeable changes in the present landscape. With unlimited immigration (rank prophecy) we shall eventually have a bloody revolution, blind and ugly, or rather a prolonged succession of uprisings, local civil wars, which produce absolutely nothing."[136] This passage may explain why Burke had few qualms about working (via Woods) for the Bureau of Social Hygiene.[137]

Regardless, Burke soon tempered his youthful equation of writing and smoking, and began to address the social implications of art. By the end of the decade, Burke's interest in the artist's social context led him to analyze the shift from an agrarian to an industrial economy, the growth of technologies, and the clashes between "bohemian" and "bourgeois" values[138]—but did not also lead him to reflect upon the race-based conflicts roiling the nation or to reconsider his views on immigration. Years later, Cowley suggested a possible explanation for these (characteristically modernist) gaps in Burke's conscience: "It has to be said that the men of the Lost Generation were white, middle-class, mostly Protestant by upbringing, and mostly English and Scottish by descent. . . . In other words, these writers had what would come to be regarded as a privileged background, though the notion would have seemed preposterous to them when they were twenty."[139]

Just as the young Burke suspected that he, too, was a minority, the Villagers failed to recognize their enviable position in the American racial hierarchy—even though, as Cowley points out, they were not simply of European descent, but fully "Nordic."[140] Little wonder, then, that they did not see the need to incorporate racial equality into their "system of

ideas," as they did, for example, with "female equality."[141] This unacknowledged privilege also explains why, during this decade, Burke did
not give serious attention in his essays or correspondence to lynching,
race riots, immigration reform, the Klan, or Marcus Garvey—the latter
of whose efforts to turn Harlem into the epicenter of a black separatist
movement unfolded a short distance from Burke's Village haunts.[142]

Gazing at the landscape of 1920s America, Burke, like his fellow Villagers, recognized the significance of industrialization, but not the nation's struggles over race and immigration. Though the postwar era, as
we have seen, opened with a spasm of race-based violence, Burke (like
his fellow Villagers) seems almost completely insulated from these
events. Those black Americans living through the "Red Summer," for
example, would not have recognized the description of 1919 America
offered by Burke's colleague Gorman Munson: "The wonderful times
of peace were at hand, and the young generation in America looked to
the future with a confidence that would be impossible to the generations that followed."[143]

The Villagers' unacknowledged racial privilege was evident in their
deliberate self-segregation; though they lived a short distance from the
black writers creating a "Harlem Renaissance," as Selzer notes, "the
Greenwich Villagers at this time do seem to have quarantined themselves pretty completely from the artists of Black Manhattan."[144] As
Cowley later admitted, for the members of his "Youngest Generation,"
if Harlem was considered at all, it was as a means to achieve "the *escape
toward the primitive*."[145] Yet, even as Burke and the other Villagers were
choosing to ignore the concerns—and even the existence—of the black
community, in Oklahoma City Ellison was immersing himself in the
modernist aesthetic that these racially privileged artists were perfecting
and promoting.

From the Territory to Tuskegee

Ironically, Ellison's exposure to Burke and the Greenwich Villagers
was facilitated by Jim Crow. During Ellison's childhood, a black minister
challenged the segregation of Oklahoma City's library—since there was
no separate facility for black residents, and no law banning them from
the "whites-only" facility. City authorities, unwilling to desegregate the
library, hastily created the Dunbar Branch of the Oklahoma City Library
in late 1921. However, their hurried efforts prevented them from separating books according to readers' age; for Ellison, this meant that he was

free to engage adult texts, both classic and contemporary—and not just those written by black authors. Thus, antiblack racism gave Ellison the opportunity to read fiction from Dreiser, Lewis, Twain, and Cooper—as well as nonfiction like Freud's *The Interpretation of Dreams*.[146]

The library's eclectic (but impressive) holdings also deepened his understanding of contemporary developments in American literature and art—developments that he had first been exposed to thanks to his mother. Interested in encouraging her son's intellectual pursuits, Ida regularly brought him castoff reading material from her white employers. Because this meant that Ellison had been raised on a steady diet of *Vanity Fair* and *Literary Digest*, unlike his peers and neighbors he "had the luxury of becoming familiar with famous names and the high culture associated with them."[147] Even before graduating from high school, Ellison had thus read articles by and about modernists like T. S. Eliot, Igor Stravinsky, Marcel Proust, Edna St. Vincent Millay—and Kenneth Burke.[148]

Books and magazines were not the only means by which Greenwich Village was imported into segregated Oklahoma City. Since Ida also brought home opera recordings, music played a central role in Ellison's childhood—often the same music that Burke and his circles were enjoying. At the same time, these scavenged recordings had to compete for Ellison's attention with Oklahoma City's flourishing community of jazz musicians, some of whom achieved national fame.[149]

Awakened to the possibilities opened to those with musical training, Ellison took up the trumpet and, in 1926, joined the Douglass High School Band, directed by the classically inclined Zelia Breaux. Under her tutelage, Ellison was steeped in musical theory, harmony, melody, and the classical tradition. Although he keenly felt the tension between Breaux's emphasis and the jazz that filled Oklahoma City's nightclubs, he had tremendous respect for her opinion.[150] Determined to improve himself as a musician, Ellison also took a series of lessons in trumpet and symphonic composition from Ludwig Herbestreit, a talented, white, classically trained musician—who avoided the censure of his neighbors by having Ellison cut his grass.[151]

Encouraged by Breaux and Herbestreit, Ellison decided that his best chance for success was not in performing, but in symphonic composition. After graduating from high school in the spring of 1932, he therefore determined to begin his classical career.[152] At first, he was not even inclined to apply to college since he had little money of his own and his mother was unable to afford the tuition. With the support of friends and teachers, however, Ellison slowly began to explore options for advanced education. The resulting uncertainty over his future finally dissipated when Ellison received a response from the new school for music at Tuskegee Institute. Entranced by the radio broadcast of the Tuskegee Choir's performance at the opening of Radio City Music Hall, he had applied to the school in the hope of working with their conductor, William Levi Dawson.[153]

Thanks to a fortuitous series of events, Ellison was accepted for the fall 1933 term, granted a scholarship, and promised a position in the band. According to the offer of admission, to secure his scholarship Ellison simply had to find his way to Tuskegee—almost immediately. With little money and no transportation, Ellison despaired of claiming his place at the school. At the last moment, a family friend, Charlie Miller, provided a solution: they would hop freight trains all the way from Oklahoma City to Alabama.[154] Ellison was apprehensive about this plan, but not as much as Ida was; hoboing was dangerous. If mother and son had forgotten this, they would have been reminded by the court-mandated retrial of the "Scottsboro Boys," which was then under way. This case involved nine black men charged—and speedily convicted, on the basis of scant evidence—with raping two white women while hoboing through Alabama. The case had gained national visibility, thanks to a campaign by the NAACP and the Communist Party; ultimately, the Supreme Court had overturned the convictions and ordered a new, and fair, trial.[155]

Despite this grim reminder of what could happen to young black men caught riding the rails, Ellison and Charlie left Oklahoma City on 20 June 1933, bound for Tuskegee. The four-day trip involved a roundabout route (initially heading north, to avoid Arkansas), the separation of the two men, and a terrifying encounter with railroad detectives in Decatur, Alabama, but the plan worked: Ellison arrived in time to claim his scholarship.[156] This is not to say he arrived unscathed: his Tuskegee "entrance picture shows him with the left side of his forehead heavily bandaged, and an open gash alongside his right eye, just below the temple."[157] After having his wounds dressed by the school's physician, Ellison was assigned a bed, a meal ticket, a job, and a place in the band; with his immediate future secure, he settled into his new surroundings.[158]

In some respects, it was an easy adjustment. Tuskegee represented a fresh start for Ellison; he put Oklahoma City behind him, throwing himself into the military-style regimen of rehearsal, work (in the bakery), and class.[159] Though the toil involved was not always welcome, the results were: Ellison's skill on the trumpet earned him the nickname

"Sousa," and, by the end of 1933, recognition as "a rising star in music at Tuskegee."[160] He also took advantage of the school's extracurricular opportunities, such as stage plays, film screenings, and the KiYi Club, which "served the more cultivated student intellectuals and artists at Tuskegee."[161]

In other respects, reminders of his Oklahoma City childhood were difficult to ignore. Alabama's version of Jim Crow was painfully familiar—and more frustrating, since white Alabamans expected (and demanded) his silent acquiescence.[162] Just as troubling for Ellison were the reminders of his family's class status. Not only was he too poor to join the students headed home during breaks, but his status at Tuskegee was perpetually threatened by a lack of funds. When Ida was unable to send money to cover expenses, Ellison was forced to rely on the generosity of wealthier teachers, administrators, and friends in order to ensure his continued enrollment. Further, since Ellison's friends tended to be from the upper echelons of Tuskegee students, and since his work in the band entailed public performances, his lack of funds was highly visible—his haircut, shoes, and clothes making his poverty harder to ignore, and more embarrassing, than it had been in Oklahoma.[163]

Persevering despite these financial challenges, Ellison maintained his precarious hold on college life, and seemed poised to realize his aspirations. His grades were strong and his musical performances won him praise—of all save Professor Dawson, whom Ellison ultimately despaired of impressing. Yet, Ellison's time at Tuskegee took him in unexpected directions; in 1932, he viewed the school as his path to the symphony, but by mid-1934, he began to gravitate instead toward literature.[164]

This shift in interest was partly a response to Dawson's emotional distance; it was also encouraged by Ellison's second job at Tuskegee, working in the Frissell Library. Ellison had been a voracious reader during his days in the Dunbar Branch, and Frissell reawakened his appetite—while giving him access to a richer store of books and periodicals. Given his undemanding job, Ellison was able to spend hours perusing Frissell's holdings; these habits distinguished him from his peers and drew the attention of the library's head, Walter Williams.[165]

Impressed by Ellison's eclectic but extensive literary background, Williams befriended the younger man and began to serve as Ellison's mentor. Ellison even began to try his hand at verse—but it was not until the 1935–36 academic year that Ellison began to study literature.[166] Although he had pondered a career in writing during the preceding summer—when a barbershop copy of *Esquire* had introduced him to

Hemingway[167]—Ellison's change of direction was largely motivated by his coursework with Morteza Sprague.[168] The young, demanding aesthete Sprague replaced Williams as Ellison's mentor, and, through his classes on the British novel, expanded Ellison's knowledge of the literary canon. Further, it was Sprague who guided Ellison through the modernist work that cemented his change of vocation: T. S. Eliot's *The Waste Land*.[169]

Ellison's encounter with this text was a decisive moment; as he would later describe it, "*The Waste Land* seized my mind."[170] In part, this was because the poem presented an imposing challenge for Ellison—a heady collage of allusions, motifs, and references that demanded more from him than any text ever had. More importantly, however, it also represented the transformative possibilities of modernist literature. To the astonishment of the young Ellison, *The Waste Land* referenced black culture as well as white, folklore as well as literature. Eliot's poem incorporated features of the classical tradition, but simultaneously featured "a style of improvisation—that quality of improvising which is very close to jazz."[171] As he laboriously tracked down Eliot's citations and the wealth of commentaries on Eliot, Ellison found himself increasingly interested in the mechanics of the poem—and, more broadly, in the writing process itself.[172]

Although these efforts made Ellison more at home in the literary world, they made him less comfortable in his immediate surroundings. In his early days at Tuskegee, Ellison had sought the company of fellow students, especially those participating in the intellectual conversations of the KiYi Club; but, as Ellison followed the clues in Eliot's text, he "quickly outshot the depth of his class" and had little time for his less diligent peers.[173] He became increasingly dissatisfied with Tuskegee's conservative racial and economic politics—and their embodiment in the school's genteel standards (emphasizing propriety, humility, and deference), teachings on the sociology of race, and commitment to vocational training.[174] Eliot provided Ellison the first stirrings of a counterattitude, involving both an integrative view of art and something more personal: "I began to see my own possibilities with more objective and in some ways more hopeful eyes."[175]

Perhaps prompted by a spring semester meeting with one of the foremost figures in the Harlem Renaissance, Alain Locke; by his Eliot-induced explorations of Burke's Greenwich Village; by a teacher's suggestion that he study sculpture in Harlem; by the rumors that Tuskegee's music school was to be eliminated; or by his mother's relocation to Ohio—or, more likely, a combination of these—Ellison decided to spend the summer of 1936 in New York. He initially described the trip as a way to earn money for his final year of tuition; yet New York represented something more important: the opportunity to grow as an artist.[176] Reflecting upon this decision in later years, he wrote, "I was both young and bookish enough to think of Manhattan as my substitute for Paris, and of Harlem as a place of Left Bank excitement."[177] Entranced by his image of this intellectual and artistic mecca, Ellison packed his belongings and boarded a bus to New York. This journey ultimately led to much more than a summer job; when Ellison returned to Tuskegee, it was as a literary celebrity—not as a student.[178]

New York in White, Black, and Red

Ellison's road was one that had been traveled by millions of other black Americans during the Great Migration; "like many young Negroes of the time," he recalled, "I thought of [New York] as the freest of American cities, and considered Harlem as the site and symbol of Afro-American progress and hope."[179] Though the Great Migration swelled the black populations of most urban centers in the industrial Northeast, the city's long-standing equation with freedom made it an especially appealing destination; between 1910 and 1920 alone, there was an 80 percent jump in the number of New York's black residents.[180] The city's black population expanded again after passage of the National Origins Act, since immigration restriction also eliminated cheap immigrant labor. Because American industry still required a pool of unskilled (and poorly paid) workers, corporations chose "to bring black folks northward, and then to segregate them into isolated neighborhoods and into the most menial, backbreaking, and pretechnological tasks in the industrial sector."[181] The increase of these so-called "Negro jobs" contributed to the exponential growth of Harlem's black community during the late 1920s.[182]

By the time Ellison arrived in July 1936, this industry-facilitated demographic shift had begun to produce a decisive shift in New York's (and America's) discourse about race.[183] Although Nordicism had fired the imagination of racially privileged New Yorkers in the 1920s, with the cessation of immigration from southern and eastern Europe, the racial classifications championed by Dillingham and Grant lost their currency. In the mid-1930s, the gulf separating Alpines, Mediterraneans, and Nordics seemed narrow—in comparison to that separating all of them from their new black neighbors. Simultaneously, as Jacobson notes, "the overall center of gravity of [existing] immigrant populations shifted toward an American-born generation for whom the racial oppressions of the Old World . . . were far less significant than American white privilege where immediate racial experience was concerned."[184] When, added to these changes in the status and attitude of immigrants, "northeastern Americans had to grapple with 'the Negro' at close range, in face-to-face situations, and in unprecedented numbers," the stage was set for a consolidation of "white" identities, and a new, binaristic account of race.[185]

Over the course of the 1930s, northern whites' importation of southern "negrophobia," discomfort over the rising black population, and response to scarcity of goods, homes, and jobs led to their designation of "the Negro" as America's primary "race problem" and, correspondingly, segregation as *the* racial issue of American political discourse."[186] Racial differences between Europeans diminished (to later reemerge as "ethnicities"), and American discourse on race focused on the opposition between "whites" or "Caucasians" and "the Negro."[187] After the 1930s, to think about race, or in racial terms, was to assume a fundamental distinction between the *essentially white* and *essentially black*. "Racial binarism" was a relatively new discourse when Ellison disembarked in New York, but it was a powerful one—since it "would come to dominate American political culture for the balance of the twentieth century."[188]

Though its foundations were laid by immigration reform, the Great Depression played a decisive role in reinforcing this new conception of race. To be sure, the market crash of 1929 affected all Americans; how could it not, since "in a few short weeks it had blown into thin air *thirty billion dollars*—a sum almost as great as the entire cost to the United States of its participation in the World War, and nearly twice as great as the entire national debt."[189] At the same time, the Depression did not affect Americans equally; it "dealt a staggering blow to blacks. It magnified all their traditional economic liabilities. It created newer and harsher ones."[190] Nor did the New Deal's programs help Americans equally. Since Roosevelt's fragile political coalition included racist southern Democrats, "the great majority of New Dealers accepted discrimination against blacks as an inevitable cost of economic recovery and relief."[191]

The government's inattention to the economic struggles of black Americans was especially devastating in New York. According to one estimate, "the unemployment rate for Harlem blacks hovered between one-and-a-half and three times that of the whites in New York City, and the social dislocations imposed by joblessness were proportionately more severe."[192] Even in 1935—six years after the crash—the jobless rate among black New Yorkers topped 50 percent.[193] Unemployment remained rampant in the black community largely because the unskilled, low-wage jobs they had traditionally held ("Negro jobs") were either eliminated or given to whites.[194]

Another effect of the Depression was a sharpening of the distinction between black and white Americans. With employers hiring whites (Nordic, Alpine, or Mediterranean) before blacks, federal recovery programs disproportionately benefiting the same groups, and the government tacitly (or explicitly) accepting discriminatory practices in housing and in the workplace, many black Americans saw little to distinguish one group of whites from another. Many whites, in turn, resented the competition posed by black Americans for jobs, homes, and federal dollars. Under such conditions, racial binarism flourished.

During this same period, however, the Communist Party attempted to work across the divide—though its 1928 adoption of the slogan, "Black and white, unite and fight," reflected, rather than challenged, racial binarism.[195] Throughout the 1920s, the party protested the violence faced by black Americans, hoping to create a crossracial movement uniting all members of the working class.[196] Although originally a national effort, by the early 1930s, "Harlem was chosen by the Party as the 'concentration point' of its strategy to win influence in Black America"—because it was "convinced that the Party's progress in that community would be crucial to its overall success."[197]

The Communist Party's early appeals to Harlemites failed, but, as the Depression deepened, it scored victories with specific campaigns in the community targeting lynching, unemployment, discrimination, and police brutality. A few prominent successes in the early 1930s also elevated the party's status in Harlem. The first was the recruitment of the well-known and well-respected author Langston Hughes—followed by public protests, led by the party, on behalf of the Scottsboro Boys. The latter were especially significant, since "the huge turnout of left-wing whites for Harlem Scottsboro protests showed Harlemites that they had new allies in their struggle against racial injustice and helped convince them that they could fight effectively for their interests in the streets as well as in the courts."[198] The party's prestige grew thanks to these efforts, although its clashes with black political, social, and religious organizations—and its hostility to black nationalism—left many doubting its true commitment to the community.[199]

As Ellison would later demonstrate, some of this skepticism never fully dissipated, but 1934–35 marked a turning point in the party's campaign to organize Harlem. Responding to developments in Italy and

Germany, the party's Central Committee tempered its emphasis on doctrinal obedience, and instead contributed to the creation of a "Popular Front" (or "United Front") movement. This movement aimed at linking all progressive groups—Communist and otherwise—under an antifascist banner.[200] The Popular Front represented an ambitious, and important, political project: "Born out of the social upheavals of 1934 and coinciding with the Communist Party's period of greatest influence in US society, the Popular Front became a radical historical bloc uniting industrial unionists, Communists, independent socialists, community activists, and émigré anti-fascists around laborist social democracy, anti-fascism, and anti-lynching."[201]

Within Harlem, one effect of the Popular Front was the integration of the party's activities with those of civil rights organizations in the black community. Simultaneously, the party avoided conflict with black nationalists and tried "to adapt [party members'] behavior to the mores and traditions of the black population."[202] These changes in policy substantially improved the party's standing in Harlem. Its reputation was further enhanced following the Harlem Riot of 1935, when the party—during hearings on the riot's causes—drew attention to the economic inequalities devastating the community.[203]

Beyond Harlem, the party's support of the Popular Front resulted in overtures to artists sympathetic to its antifascist, antilynching, and pro-union politics. Prior to this time, the party had emphasized art focused on the experiences of the working class, by artists who were party members. The most famous of these efforts was the John Reed Club—a national organization whose chapters were devoted to developing revolutionary writers and popularizing proletarian literature. The Popular Front, however, caused the party to dissolve the John Reed Clubs and ally with leftist writers outside the party—especially those with established reputations in literary circles. To this end, members of the party drafted a "Call for an American Writers' Congress," an event that would be held in the spring of 1935 and would inaugurate a Popular Front organization for revolutionary artists: the League of American Writers.[204]

The First American Writers' Congress began on 26 April 1935 and consisted of two hundred official "writer-congressmen," with an audience of four thousand.[205] Given the impetus for the Congress, many of those attending were party members. Among them were modernists-turned-Communists like Malcolm Cowley—whose conversion to communism was symptomatic of Villagers' reactions to political developments in post-1920s America[206]—as well as former members of the John

Reed Clubs, including an aspiring black author named Richard Wright. Reflecting the inclusive intent of the Congress, the program featured men and women, blacks and whites, Americans and non-Americans, and writers sympathetic to (but not members of) the party—including Cowley's old friend Kenneth Burke.[207]

Since differences in allegiance translated into clashes over the importance of party doctrine, agreement among the participants was often difficult to obtain; as Cowley later described the event, there were "more recriminations and bruised feelings than one would infer from reading the official report of the congress."[208] Burke, famously, was wounded by response to his paper "Revolutionary Symbolism in America"; some charged that Burke's substitution of the "people" for "the worker" made him a "traitor" or "snob."[209] Wright, by contrast, mourned the dissolution of the John Reed Clubs—since, as an aspiring writer, the Congress seemed to cast him aside in favor of writers less committed, but more prominent.[210]

Despite these—and other—complaints, the Congress served its purpose: it brought together a range of left-leaning artists and created the framework of the new League of American Writers. Moreover, the disputes marring the First Congress did not always translate into exclusionary practices; for example, Burke was nominated, and approved, for the new league's executive committee.[211] Wright, similarly, was not wholly overlooked: despite his youth, he was elected to the league's National Council.[212] Thus, when the Second American Writers' Congress convened, in June 1937, Burke was on the program, and Wright was again in attendance—but this time he did not attend the meetings alone. Joining him was a transplant from Alabama named Ralph Ellison.[213]

Ralph Ellison, Author

Ellison had arrived in New York in July 1936 with little money and few connections—his only assistance a few letters of introduction provided by Tuskegee faculty.[214] However, soon after his arrival at the YMCA on West 135th Street in Harlem, he began to develop a network of friends and associates—a network that acclimated him to life in the North and oriented him to the city's intellectual and political circles. The rapid rise in Ellison's social standing was due, in part, to good fortune: on his second day in New York, he noticed Alain Locke conversing with another man in the lobby of the YMCA. When Ellison introduced himself, Locke recalled their brief meeting at Tuskegee; however, it was Locke's interlocutor, Langston Hughes, who captured Ellison's attention. Ellison immediately warmed to Hughes, who surprisingly (to Ellison) reciprocated; the two remained deep in discussion well after Locke departed. This chance meeting with Hughes was profoundly important; it would "change [Ellison's] life forever."[215]

By the end of their discussion, Hughes asked Ellison to do some secretarial work and agreed to assist Ellison in his artistic ambitions.[216] Thanks to Hughes, Ellison was accepted as a student (and, later, a roommate) by the prominent sculptor Richmond Barthé; thanks, in turn, to Barthé, Ellison was hired as a receptionist by the famous psychiatrist Henry Stack Sullivan.[217] In late December 1936, when these arrangements ended, Hughes helped find Ellison alternate housing, in a rooming house run by a friend's mother.[218]

But Hughes had another, more lasting, impact on Ellison; he provided Ellison intellectual guidance, especially regarding the relationship of art and politics. Following their initial meeting, Hughes supplied Ellison with leftist literature, including books by André Malraux, and introduced him to prominent Communists, black and white.[219] As a result of Hughes's influence, Ellison's politics shifted to the left; he likely also joined the party.[220] However, Hughes's most important contribution to Ellison's development was inadvertent. Before he left to join the fight against the fascists in Spain, Hughes helped Ellison meet the man who would continue his education and complete his change of vocation: Richard Wright.[221]

In some ways, Wright was an unlikely mentor. As Ellison later wrote, "Both of us were descendants of slaves, but since my civic, geographical and political circumstances were different from those of Mississippi, Wright and I were united by our connection with a past condition of servitude, and divided by geography and a difference of experience based thereupon."[222] Fittingly, though, the two men came together through art. Hughes had first introduced Ellison to Wright's poetry; as Ellison read Wright's work, he "found in it traces of the modern poetic sensibility and technique that [he] had been seeking."[223] Recognizing Ellison's enthusiasm, Hughes quietly wrote the poet on behalf of his young friend. Since Ellison was unaware of Hughes's actions, he was understandably (but pleasantly) surprised to receive a postcard from Wright proposing a meeting in May 1937—one day after the latter's arrival in New York.[224]

Wright was moving to New York from Chicago, where, as a result of his participation in the John Reed Club, he had become heavily involved with the party. However, unwilling to abandon his efforts to become a novelist, even when so directed by the party, Wright had clashed with his superiors—resulting in his resignation from the Chicago Communist Party.[225] Since Wright had not resigned from the party itself, and since the party was invested in the recruitment and organization of black Americans, he readily obtained an assignment in New York—as editor of the Harlem bureau of the *Daily Worker*. Soon after his arrival in the city, he received another assignment: revitalizing the literary magazine *New Challenge*.[226] But Wright was more excited by his new location than either post since working in New York gave him easy access to the city's many publishers.

Wright's novelistic ambitions—and his background in modernist literature—impressed Ellison. Moreover, Wright's perspective was unique among black authors, in Ellison's opinion: he united Marxist theory with a concern for the existential position of black Americans. Ellison recognized that, unlike many leftist writers, Wright's political commitments were not upheld at the expense of his artistic integrity. Since Ellison impressed Wright with his intellect and was eager to play the role of Wright's "legman," the two were soon inseparable—whether working in the offices of the *Daily Worker* or listening to Ernest Hemingway's address at the Second American Writers' Congress.[227] As a result, before long Ellison "had become [Wright's] closest friend in New York."[228]

This close contact with Wright was immensely beneficial to Ellison; "in talking with Wright," he later admitted, "my plans and goals were altered—were, in fact, fatefully modified by Wright's."[229] Wright reinforced Ellison's belief in the importance of artistic technique. In Wright, Ellison saw firsthand the discipline necessary for good writing; "Wright's intensity, his willingness to write and revise and then revise again, made an indelible mark on Ralph's understanding at last of how a serious writer works."[230] Just as important, however, Wright pushed Ellison to write for publication. To echo Ellison, it was at this moment that his plans and goals were irrevocably changed; Ellison would not return to Tuskegee, but would remain in New York and work at becoming a writer.

Ellison first attempted a book review, at Wright's insistence, for *New Challenge*. Although Ellison initially resisted Wright's request, insisting that he did not know enough to analyze others' work, he acquiesced, completing his review of Waters Turpin's novel *These Low Grounds* in August 1937. Wright was pleased with the results and next requested a work of short fiction. Overcoming his trepidation thanks to some advice (and a reading list) from Wright, Ellison crafted a short story, "Hymie's

Bull"—inspired by his harrowing, but successful, foray into the world of hoboing.[231] Although both were the efforts of a first-time writer, the experience of writing had a profound effect upon Ellison; as he later admitted, after completing these two pieces, "I was caught, hooked."[232]

After finishing "Hymie's Bull," Ellison received disturbing news: his mother was very ill. He immediately left for Ohio, but arrived only one day before her death, on 16 October 1937. Stunned at Ida's rapid decline, Ellison found out that his mother had been misdiagnosed earlier in the summer following a fall—and, by the time doctors recognized a cracked (and, then, tubercular) hip, it was too late to save her. Ellison was devastated; both his parents were gone. Even though "the loss of Ida Ellison Bell was the deepest hurt he'd experienced in his life," his brother, Herbert, was even more distraught—and needed the care of his reluctant older brother.[233]

Faced with the responsibility for the estate and for a grief-stricken Herbert, Ellison delayed his return to New York. Instead, both brothers moved to Dayton, staying first in a relative's house and then with a sympathetic friend. After difficulty with Ida's insurance company again prevented him from leaving, Ellison resigned himself to a longer stay in Dayton. However, determined to pursue the path he had so recently discovered, he found a typewriter and a patron—who supplied him with paper and, at a desperate moment, shelter—and began writing furiously. When he finally returned to New York, in the spring of 1938, he had more to show for it than his letters to Wright; he had a cache of four new short stories, the beginnings of a novel, and growing confidence in his own abilities.[234]

Ellison maintained this confidence upon his return, though Wright began to cool toward him—even accusing Ellison of copying his style, calling the work completed in Dayton "'*my* stuff.'"[235] Despite this growing distance between the two men, Wright still proved to be a valuable contact. Soon after Ellison's return to the city, Wright helped him gain employment in the federally funded New York Writers' Project.[236] Just as important, Wright's jealousy did not end their relationship altogether. Thus, as 1938 changed into 1939, Ellison continued to gain insight and inspiration from Wright—even reading the pages of Wright's new novel, *Native Son,* as quickly as Wright typed them. He also dutifully studied the literature that Wright recommended, including Malraux's just-published book, *Man's Hope,* and Miguel de Unamuno's *The Tragic Sense of Life.* Further, thanks to Wright, Ellison published a series of book reviews for *New Masses,* which kept him writing, and helped enhance his bank account—and his prestige in Communist circles.[237]

Ellison's success with *New Masses* did not, though, indicate an increasing allegiance to the party. As he explained in a 1967 interview, his work for the party never reflected his own views: "I wrote what might be called propaganda—having to do with the Negro struggle—but my fiction was always trying to be something else."[238] This "something else" was inspired by authors like Wright, Malraux, Unamuno, Dostoevsky, and Henry James—authors whose existential themes described humanity in its fullness, not simply as it related to party doctrine.[239] Influenced by such "decadent" literature, and by the sources he found working for the Writers' Project, by early 1939 Ellison had determined that, though they published his reviews, *New Masses* (and the party) championed an impoverished kind of art. Rampersad nicely captures Ellison's ambivalence: "He was eating the Communists' bread but nurturing opposite ambitions as a cultural worker."[240]

At the same time, Ellison's rejection of Communist literature was not also a rejection of radical politics or of Marxist thought. Rather than dismissing Marx along with the party, Ellison sought to fit Marx's concepts into a more comprehensive perspective that could guide and ground his fiction. Seeking a way to reconcile leftist politics with modernist and existential thought, he became "very curious," as he later wrote, "about how one could put Marx and Freud together."[241] Thus, in June 1939, when Ellison attended the Third American Writers' Congress, he was captivated by one presentation in particular—even though his friends Hughes and Wright were also in the program.[242] In its critique of the rhetoric of fascism, Kenneth Burke's "The Rhetoric of Hitler's 'Battle'" demonstrated to Ellison that a synthesis of Marx and Freud was not just *possible*, it was analytically *powerful*.

Burke's paper was occasioned by the February 1939 publication of two unexpurgated, English-language versions of Hitler's *Mein Kampf*. A host of hostile reviews had subsequently filled American magazines; but, to Burke's eyes, none had taken Hitler's text, and its appeal, seriously enough. As a result, the Writers' Congress presented Burke with a golden opportunity—an opportunity to bring his still-developing theoretical system to bear on a prominent (and dangerous) piece of rhetoric.[243]

Though few would have recognized this, the paper also represented a repudiation of Burke's early views on race—his youthful acceptance of the racial hierarchies common to East Liberty in 1900. Like many Americans, for Burke the Nazis' unabashedly racist politics had revealed the ugliness of anti-Semitism, whether in Europe or America;[244] as Burke would later admit, "some of my early stories show occasional pre–Reichstag Fire laxities. Since then, Hitler and his noxious Ism have made it hard even to remember the climate in which such laxities were taken for granted."[245] Indeed, although reaction to Nazism would not destroy racialist thinking—scholars' efforts to combat anti-Semitism typically naturalized racial binarism[246]—"The Rhetoric of Hitler's 'Battle'" fiercely challenged Hitler's efforts to make symbolic magic out of racial inferiority.

For Ellison, Burke's primary achievement was less his rejection of Hitler's racialism than his blending of Marx and Freud into one richly nuanced conceptual vocabulary. Displaying his commitment to Marxist criticism, Burke's essay describes the role played by material conditions in Hitler's rise to power; he emphasizes that the postwar devastation of Germany, and the rampant inflation in the period that followed, "made people *ripe* for a Hitler." Further, Burke links Hitler's rhetorical maneuvers to the interests of German industrialists. Through the Nazis' anti-Semitism, class differences within Germany could be deemphasized, in favor of Aryan unity: "By attacking 'Jew finance' instead of finance, [they] could stimulate an enthusiastic movement that left 'Aryan' finance in control." As a result, Burke contends, Hitler's doctrine of racial inferiority captured the German imagination because it "provided a *noneconomic interpretation of economic ills.*"[247]

But, as Ellison recognized, Burke's essay cannot be reduced to a materialist debunking of Hitler's book. Even as he underscores the importance of economic conditions in pre-Nazi Germany, Burke points out the *inadequacy* of a purely economic account of Hitler's rise to power. For this reason, Burke's essay relies as much on Freud as it does on Marx—as in his discussions of Hitler's sexual symbolism, of projection devices and symbolic rebirth, of curative and purifying imagery, and of Hitler's "symbolic change of lineage." More telling is Burke's Freud-tinged refusal to grant that Hitler's anti-Semitism was wholly deliberate—that it was a handy (if cynical) political-economic strategy. At the very least, Burke insists, we must "replace the 'either-or' with a 'both-and'" and recognize that "he could *spontaneously* turn to a scapegoat mechanism, and he could, by conscious planning, perfect the symmetry of the solution towards which he had spontaneously turned."[248]

Moreover, Burke's essay offers a second argument against a strictly materialist analysis of Hitler's book. Given the economic crises faced by Germany, Burke argues, Hitler's racialist discourse did something that no Marxist vocabulary could do—it satisfied the public's desire for certainty, dignity, and unity. By offering Germans one cure for their ills, his vocabulary addressed a need that Marxism did not recognize: "The desire for unity, such as a discussion of class conflict, on the basis of conflicting interests, could not satisfy."[249]

Burke concludes that the source of Hitler's power was not, primarily, economic—it was *symbolic*. Hitler gave the German people a unifying vocabulary, ordering their chaotic situation and infusing it with meaning; he insists that "Hitler provided a 'world view' for people who had previously seen the world but piecemeal." Since Hitler's appeal thus stemmed not from German inflation but from something more human, Burke's essay concludes not with self-righteousness, but with an urgent call to criticism: "Our job, then, our anti-Hitler Battle, is to find all available ways of making the Hitlerite distortions of religion apparent, in order that politicians of his kind in America be unable to perform a similar swindle."[250]

Ellison was so moved by this nuanced mix of Marx and Freud, theory and criticism, that he "pressed his way through the crowd to shake Burke's hand."[251] Six years later, Ellison still vividly pictured the event: "You were the only speaker out of the whole group who was concerned with writing *and politics*, rather than writing as an *excuse* for politics—and that in a superficial manner."[252] This moment, so decisive for Ellison, marked the birth of his connection to Burke. Nearly forty years after the Congress, Ellison could still recall how Burke's presentation both created "a meaningful fusion of Marx and Freud" and "provided a *Gestalt* through which I could apply intellectual insights back into my own materials and into my own life."[253] Thus, when Ellison stepped toward the podium following the presentation, he certainly could not call Burke a friend—but he could rightfully call him an ancestor.

2 / Antagonistic Cooperation

*Writers of different backgrounds and generations often disagree because
they seek to make unique works of art out of the subjectivity of diverse
experiences which are connected objectively by duration and by issues
arising from within the social scene in which they find themselves. If
friendships between writers are not strong enough to overcome these built-
in sources of conflict and competition, they fail, but if the relationship has
been fruitful it finds continuity in the works of art that came into being
during the quiet moments of antagonistic cooperation which marked the
friendship.*

—RALPH ELLISON, *CONVERSATIONS WITH RALPH ELLISON*

The Third American Writers' Congress proved a formative moment in
Ralph Ellison's intellectual life. In Kenneth Burke's address to the congress, "The Rhetoric of Hitler's 'Battle,'" Ellison found a model for his
own viewpoint—since Burke integrated the seemingly disparate insights
of Marx and Freud in the service of social critique. As a result, after the
congress concluded, Ellison wasted little time in tracking down copies of
Burke's published work. This detailed study of Burke's ideas produced no
small change in Ellison's perspective; as he recalled in a 1977 interview, "I
was just starting out as a writer, and as I went on struggling to understand
[Burke's] criticism, I began to learn something of the nature of literature,
society, social class, and psychology as they related to literary form."[1]

Ellison, in later years, took great pains to acknowledge Burke's influence on his art. At a 1964 meeting of the American Academy and Institute of Arts and Letters, for example, "Ellison ascribed his birth as
a writer to" Burke;[2] he similarly introduced his collection *Shadow and
Act* with a statement acknowledging "special indebtedness" to Burke,
whom Ellison credited as "the stimulating source of many of" its essays.[3]
Thanks to these testimonials, we know that Ellison was changed decisively by his encounter with Burke. Yet, Ellison's confessed indebtedness
to Burke has overshadowed another significant facet of their relationship: Ellison's influence on Burke.

Although less forthcoming than Ellison, in the early 1980s Burke contributed to a volume devoted to Ellison and his work. His essay included a short reflection on their friendship: "The demands local to your story [*Invisible Man*] ruled out that biographical strand in which not only did *we* back you, but you could and did get us to look for traces of unconscious Nortonism in our thinking."[4] Though tantalizingly brief, this passage is significant because it contains Burke's only published description of the "friendly nonracial 'we'" that connected Burke, Ellison, their spouses, and their mutual friends Stanley Edgar Hyman and his first wife, the novelist Shirley Jackson.[5]

Just as important, Burke's comment suggests that their relationship was more complicated than we might otherwise assume—that an account of their relationship cannot be confined to Burke's influence on Ellison. Burke's essay tells us that Ellison prompted him to engage in critical self-reflection, to ferret out some "unconscious" prejudice lurking within his own perspective. In other words, though short on details, here Burke alludes to a dialogue that took place between the two men regarding matters of race. Burke's essay provides no further insight into the nature of this dialogue. However, there appear to be hints of this exchange, clues to follow, in a key Burkean text: *A Rhetoric of Motives*.

In contrast to *A Grammar of Motives*, Burke planned for his second volume on motivation, the *Rhetoric*, to focus not upon universal "ways of placement," but "observations on parliamentary and diplomatic devices, editorial bias, sales methods and incidents of social sparring."[6] When the *Rhetoric* appeared in 1950, though differing from Burke's earliest designs, its approach to the subject proved revolutionary—and contributed to the creation of a "New Rhetoric."[7] However, in highlighting these commonly recognized aspects of the *Rhetoric*, we might overlook a smaller, yet significant thread woven into Burke's account: the subject of race. The *Rhetoric* was not Burke's first foray into this topic—indeed, as discussed in chapter 1, it plays a key role in "The Rhetoric of Hitler's 'Battle.'" The *Rhetoric*, though, is the only of Burke's published works to give consistent attention to race.[8] One reason for this seems clear; the *Rhetoric*, given its focus on conflict and identification, is well-suited to consideration of discourse surrounding racial difference and racist violence.

At the same time, Burke had another, less obvious, motivation for this treatment—one that had as much to do with the conditions surrounding the book's composition as with its subject matter. The contextual factor shaping Burke's discussion of race, I argue, was his friendship with Ellison. Indeed, the intimacy of their relationship spills over into Burke's text: it is the only one of Burke's books to cite Ellison. This was no accident; in November 1945, when Burke read Ellison's early essay "Richard Wright's Blues," he was only one month into serious work on his now-canonical text. Ellison's essay provoked a series of exchanges between the two men, exchanges that played a role in shaping Burke's thoughts on the rhetorical dimensions of race. In short, though the two men would formally meet in late 1942, they were closest—and in closest contact—during the period of time when Burke was planning and writing the *Rhetoric*. I thus believe that we can see within its pages traces of the dialogue on race referenced in Burke's late essay.

Since Burke and Ellison often met face to face, some of their exchanges were never recorded. However, I believe we can piece together this ongoing conversation, trace Ellison's influence on Burke's thinking—and thereby reconstruct the interaction that produced Burke's ruminations on race in the *Rhetoric*. As I discuss in the next chapter, their dialogue did not end with Burke's book; Ellison's *Invisible Man* profoundly shaped the relationship between these two men. However, we can grasp the significance of their discussion across and concerning the American "racial divide" only by attending carefully to its inaugural moment.

Ellison's Burkean Foundations

After hearing Burke deliver his paper on Hitler's *Mein Kampf,* Ellison was inspired to begin a systematic study of Burke's published work—to immerse himself in Burke's critical perspective. This was no easy task, since the 1930s had been productive for Burke, and since Ellison had little money to spend on books. Ellison soon managed, though, to borrow a copy of Burke's first book of criticism, *Counter-Statement.*[9]

Burke's text immediately resonated with Ellison's training as a musician, given its emphasis upon eloquence and technique, the path by which experience becomes art. At the same time, Burke emphasizes the links between artist, audience, and situation—focusing upon the rhetorical function, the appeal, of art. As a result, Burke's volume cannot be easily categorized; in its attempt to develop a synthetic approach to the problems of art, it appeals as much (or as little) to the formalist as to the Marxist.[10] Since Ellison had a foot in both camps, Burke's "counter-statement" was particularly powerful; as in his analysis of Hitler, Burke's rejection of the easy path, whether aestheticist or propagandist, promised a holistic, integrative perspective on the relation between the artist and society.

Convinced anew of the value of Burke's approach, Ellison turned to Burke's other books from the 1930s, *Permanence and Change* and *Attitudes toward History*.[11] By 1942, Ellison obtained personal copies of these books, which allowed him to pore over their contents, reading, marking, and rereading them.[12] These texts represent an extension of *Counter-Statement*'s aesthetic project, but—reflecting Burke's increased politicization—they also look critically at the symbolic processes constituting the American social order. In *Permanence and Change*, for example, Burke advocates a poeticized communism, but grounds this critique in a genealogy of perspectives; he argues that capitalism and technologism represent an unfit orientation toward the then-current situation. Burke thereby links symbolic "orientation" to revolutionary social change.[13]

Burke's companion work from this decade, *Attitudes toward History*, similarly displays his commitment to the creation of a new "orientation," but highlights the difficulties involved in radical social change. Through analysis of individual and collective frameworks of meaning, Burke joins Freud to Marx—demonstrating the interconnection of self and society by unearthing their common symbolic origins. Building a vocabulary around this insight, Burke directs revolutionaries to harness symbolic resources for the creation of social change, but also to remain vigilant, lest their movement solidify into another problematic orthodoxy. Grappling with these ideas, Ellison again applauded Burke's rebuttal of economic and psychoanalytic determinism. Ellison also embraced Burke's proposed alternative, the "comic corrective"—which, in its dialectical "broadening, or maturing" of perspectives, "enable[s] people *to be observers of themselves, while acting*. Its ultimate would not be *passiveness*, but *maximum consciousness*."[14]

Comic consciousness became a hallmark of Ellison's thought—demonstrating the impact of these early Burkean texts.[15] Yet, this encounter with Burke also had a more immediate impact on Ellison's perspective; as a result of his studies of Burke, "he was ready to embrace ideas that would supplant the influence of pure Communism, weaken the persisting distractions of black nationalism in his thinking, and give order to the impulses toward liberal humanism that he had suppressed in his radical writing."[16] The key was Burke's insistence upon the centrality of human symbolicity. In a later interview, Ellison recalled this as a transformative insight: after reading Burke's work, "I began to grasp how language operates, both in literature and as an agency of oral communication."[17] The result was a symbolic foundation for his perspective on art and society; as Ellison confessed in a letter to Burke, Burke's books provided a stable ground for the development of his own art: "Your method gave me the first instrument with which I could orientate myself—something which neither Marx alone nor Freud alone could do."[18]

Thanks to this disciplined study of Burke's work, Ellison was equipped to assert his artistic and critical independence—a fortunate development, since he was drifting away from familiar sources of support. For one, Ellison's relationship with Richard Wright was undergoing substantial change—due not just to Wright's jealousy, but to the success of Wright's 1940 novel, *Native Son*.[19] During this same period, Ellison also began to break free of his allies in the Communist Party.

Ellison had, as discussed in chapter 1, never been an orthodox Communist, but he had achieved some prominence with his articles in *New Masses* analyzing the oppression of black Americans. The party had thus contributed to the building of Ellison's intellectual reputation, despite his refusal to fully accept its doctrines.[20] Ellison's move away from it, then, signaled less a dramatic conversion than a rejection of the party's policies. The weakening of the Popular Front—a casualty of Stalin's 1939 pact with Hitler—had tested Ellison's allegiance, but the final straw was the party's response to Hitler's attack on the USSR. Reasoning that the fight against fascism was too important to jeopardize, the party endorsed the American war effort—and abruptly withdrew support for the struggle for civil rights.[21] Ellison, like many black Americans, was disgusted by the party's sacrifice of racial equality and refused to accept it as the price of Hitler's defeat.[22]

By 1942, with Wright's mentorship lessening and the party making concessions to antiblack racists, Ellison was primed for a change. As a consequence, when the activist Angelo Herndon invited him to edit a new journal of black intellectual culture, the *Negro Quarterly*, Ellison jumped at the opportunity.[23] This position proved an important one for Ellison since the "*Negro Quarterly*, the haven of 'intellectual democracy,' became the development ground for Ellison's experiments in new critical directions."[24] Further, his service as editor of the journal—indirectly—launched his friendship with Burke.

Ellison, Hyman, and Burke

After shaking Burke's hand at the Third Writers' Congress in 1939, Ellison encountered Burke only through his books—although the two may have crossed paths in 1941, when Ellison published an essay in the Burke-edited journal *Direction*.[25] All this changed in late 1942, when

Ellison was introduced to his "ancestor." Their friendship blossomed in the wake of this encounter, but much of the credit for this should be given to another close friend, Stanley Edgar Hyman—who helped ensure that this fortuitous meeting produced a friendship.

Ellison's work for the *Negro Quarterly* was the catalyst for his relationship with Hyman. As Ellison told the story, "Our friendship began with a postcard."[26] In June 1942, after reading an issue of the journal, Hyman sent the aforementioned postcard to Ellison, offering his services as a reviewer. Ellison, who had been stymied in his efforts to secure white critics' work for the journal, was overjoyed—and wrote back immediately.[27] Judging from the ensuing correspondence, the two instantly hit it off. Their connection arose from a mutual respect; not only had each read the other's work, but, more importantly, each had come away impressed. Ellison's first letter to Hyman maintained a professional tone, but admitted that "I have known of your work for quite some time. I have always thought it interesting."[28] Returning the compliment, Hyman's reply was even more effusive: "I have followed your stuff eagerly for quite a while, and thought your story, Mister Toussan, so good that I have it filed away in a little folder marked 'Ellison, Ralph.'"[29]

This mutual appreciation aside, it quickly became apparent that they had a great deal in common; their letters touch upon a variety of shared interests, from literature and criticism to the blues. Through an exchange over blues lyrics, however, they discovered another point of connection: their mutual admiration of Burke. Hyman was the first to confess his indebtedness, writing Ellison that Burke, "as you have probably guessed, is my critical hero and mentor."[30] Replying to Hyman, Ellison admitted his own Burkean influences: "No, I am not at all surprised that Kenneth Burke rates highly with you, having noticed similarities in your approaches to art. But, perhaps, most of all because he is also a hero of my own (I have just about exhausted myself in trying to obtain a personal copy of *Counter-Statement*), and I'm never able to understand critics who don't admire him."[31]

Thirty years later, following Hyman's sudden death, Ellison identified this conversation as the turning point in their relationship: "Along with trying to write fiction I was busy reading in Marx and Freud, trying to fit their ideas together in some sort of conceptual whole, and when I mentioned Kenneth Burke (whom I had heard lecturing on The Rhetoric of Hitler's Battle a few years before) as the critic most useful in this regard, a relationship of intellectual exchange began which continued from that moment until Stanley's death."[32] The realization of their common

Burkean roots rapidly melted the formality between them, and Ellison's friendship with Hyman—and Shirley Jackson—deepened. The men exchanged fewer letters, instead meeting face-to-face—by the fall of 1942, on a weekly basis.[33] Before long, their friendship expanded, to include their "critical hero and mentor."

Although not responsible for introducing Ellison to Burke, Hyman played an important role in shaping the nature of their first interaction. After learning that all of them were attending the same wedding, Hyman proposed extending their discussions beyond the confines of the event. He explained his idea to Burke a few days before the wedding: "My friend Ralph Ellison, with whom I have a weekly lunch devoted principally to expounding the revealed word of Burke, tells me that you will be in town Saturday at Harry Slochower's wedding, where he is to have the privilege of meeting you. I am very anxious to see you, not having done so in two years, and am hoping you will have some spare time Saturday either before or after the wedding to go out for a meal or some drinks with me and perhaps Ralph."[34]

The correspondence reports few details from this occasion, but it was apparently positive—with Hyman and Ellison playing the role of eager Burkeans. In March, Burke wrote Hyman: "Haven't forgotten about my promise to send you and Ralph the books. Shall send them soon. If you see Ralph, would you please ask him to drop me a card, saying where I should best send his?"[35] Burke was true to his word: a month later Hyman received a copy of Burke's early novel, *Towards a Better Life*, while Ellison received *Counter-Statement*.[36] Hyman was enthusiastic: "The books arrived today and I am delighted with the one for me and your kind inscription. I haven't seen Ralph to tell him about his yet (as you probably know, the Quarterly's phone was disconnected) but I will give it to him as soon as I can get to see him. I imagine he will write you."[37] He also passed on Ellison's address to Burke, in case "you have occasion to write Ralph."[38]

Ellison's letter of thanks was longer in coming, due to some significant personal trials. On one front, the impending demise of the *Negro Quarterly* was intensely disappointing—and consequential, since the resulting draft reclassification made Ellison eligible for military service. Just as pressing, between late 1942 and early 1943, Ellison's marriage was ending, and he suffered from a variety of ailments that consumed his remaining attention.[39] In May, hoping to regroup and recuperate, Ellison traveled to the Vermont home of friends John and Amelie Bates.[40] Since Burke's gift was one of the few things Ellison had brought to Vermont, he was moved to write Burke from his mountain retreat: "Here are my very belated, but no less gracious, thanks for *Counter-Statement*. When it came I was in the midst of a sick spell, which I am trying to shake off up here with maple syrup and fresh air. Sorry we were unable to get together before you went back to N.J. as I had many questions to ask you."[41] Ellison's letter also indicated that *Counter-Statement* was not the only Burkean text that he was reading. He offered an appreciative evaluation of Burke's work on Coleridge, as well as a published selection from Burke's forthcoming *Grammar,* focusing on the dramatistic pentad: "Am just beginning to grasp the implications of your five terms and am becoming impatient to get into your opus in progress. It promises something stable in a world too much in flux."[42] Burke did not reply to Ellison's letter, though the two stayed in contact through their mutual friend. In September, for example, Hyman reported to Burke that "I see Ralph regularly," and that "he sends his best regards." Hyman's letter also passed on news about Ellison's preoccupations: "He is on the verge of being inducted, detests the idea and is trying to get into the merchant marine, and is meanwhile working on some stories and waiting for Angelo to get the next issue of the Negro Quarterly out, if he ever does."[43]

Ellison, anxious to avoid the Jim Crow army, managed to arrange a position in the merchant marine in late September 1943—though he was not immediately sent to sea.[44] As a result, he was still in New York when Burke proposed an early October gathering. Hyman accepted on behalf of himself, Jackson, and Ellison: "This Monday dinner at the Farmfoods restaurant sounds fine. Ralph is particularly anxious to see you, since he expects to ship out to sea any week now."[45] In early November, when Burke was forced to postpone another reunion, Hyman replied: "I am sorry we can't see you until after Thanksgiving, since Ralph will have left by then. He goes in about a week, barring a break."[46] After Ellison's departure was delayed, Hyman wrote Burke that "Ralph has not yet gotten a ship, and is likely to be in town for another week or so. If you will be in town next Monday evening, would you care to come over to our place for dinner with him and perhaps the Schneiders? We might have a drink or two, kind of a mild farewell celebration."[47]

The early December "farewell celebration" was successful, and was, in fact, a farewell—since Ellison shipped out soon afterward. As Hyman reported to Burke in early 1944: "Ralph has been at sea for about a month now. He left suddenly one night without being allowed to phone us, and God knows where he is now."[48] Ellison returned a few days after Hyman's letter to Burke, but was physically and emotionally exhausted from the journey; he spent the next few months recuperating.[49]

Given the toll taken by the voyage, Ellison was happy to be on land and sent greetings to Burke via Hyman—though it is unclear whether they reunited before early 1945.[50] In part, this is because all three were quite preoccupied. Hyman was working on his now-famous book *The Armed Vision* and preparing to take a position at Bennington College.[51] Burke was continuing his own teaching at Bennington and finishing the *Grammar* manuscript.[52] Ellison's attention was divided between persistent stomach troubles, the prospect of a new tour of duty, and his new love, Fanny McConnell. This is not to say that he had abandoned his craft; in 1944, in addition to publishing three short stories, "Flying Home," "In a Strange Country," and "King of the Bingo Game," Ellison wrote book reviews and was offered contracts by at least two publishers for his first novel.[53]

Preoccupied by the need to finance his literary vocation, even as Ellison pondered the competing contracts, he sought other sources of revenue. In late August, he applied for a Rosenwald Fellowship, requesting support for a novel centering on a black American prisoner of war in Germany. Since the application required a recommendation, Ellison requested, and received, a letter from Burke. Ellison also applied for a Guggenheim Fellowship, although he viewed it as more of a long shot than the Rosenwald.[54] Finally, pushed to make a decision by his literary agent (and by his dwindling bank account), in September Ellison signed a contract with the publishing firm of Reynal and Hitchcock to deliver a novel in a year's time.[55]

This nascent novel was soon put on hold, since, early in 1945, Ellison's efforts to be declared ineligible for the draft were thwarted. Desperate to avoid the segregated army, Ellison shipped out again with the merchant marine in mid-February 1945.[56] Unlike his first voyage, this tour of duty was not as brief. However, two months into the trip fortune intervened, and in April 1945 a debilitating illness allowed Ellison to take recuperative shore leave—a product of "two months of drinking tap water so supersaturated with rust that it trickled from the taps as red as tomato soup."[57]

Reaching home, Ellison was reunited with Fanny and soon received two more pieces of good news. He learned that he had, in fact, been granted a Rosenwald Fellowship. The award provided nearly two thousand dollars to support his project—and earned him hearty praise from Hyman and Burke.[58] After hearing the news, Hyman sent an enthusiastic letter: "It is about time I wrote you, chiefly to congratulate you on the Rosenwald thing, which is the damn best news we have had. Stuff is finally turning your way, as it should, and all of us . . . are pleased as hell. Kenneth sends his congratulations, and he and I are planning to have calling cards made reading 'Early Ellison Fans.'"[59]

Ellison's second bit of news was less lucrative, but no less welcome. He was asked by the editor of a highly respected journal to write an essay reviewing Wright's newly published—and hotly debated—autobiography, *Black Boy*.[60] Ellison immediately accepted, recognizing that this review could dramatically enhance his literary reputation. Though he would have no way of knowing this at the time, the essay, published that summer in *Antioch Review*, would also spark his first significant exchange with Burke regarding race and identity.

A Burkean *Black Boy*

Ellison was ideally positioned to review *Black Boy*. He had long been a defender of Wright's in Marxist literary circles, and he was intimately familiar with Wright's life story—and with the text itself. Prior to his second tour with the merchant marine, Ellison had read a prepublication version and had prepared a review for the journal *Tomorrow*. However, in 1944 Wright's text was selected by the Book-of-the-Month Club and, essentially, cut in half; rather than continuing through Wright's time in Chicago, the book now ended with Wright's departure from the South. Since Ellison's review drew heavily on the now-expurgated material, and since publication of the book was delayed until March 1945, the review was never published.[61]

When *Black Boy* appeared, a month before Ellison's illness brought him home, it debuted to mixed reviews. Though some critics praised the work, many prominent figures (such as W. E. B. Du Bois) accused Wright of providing an unnecessarily harsh portrait of black Americans' lives. Wright's detractors objected to an early series of meditations upon the "absence of real kindness in Negroes," "the essential bleakness of black life in America," and "the cultural barrenness of black life."[62] Despite his increasing independence from Wright, Ellison was eager to defend his former mentor from these charges.

Ellison's review was also motivated by something more—a desire to display his critical talent to Hyman and Burke. Analyses of Ellison's essay have typically focused upon Ellison's relationship to his former mentor Wright.[63] Though the review owes much to their relationship, I believe it cannot be understood apart from Ellison's appropriation and application of Burke's insights. Ellison grounds Wright as an individual artist within the American society of his birth, an interpretation of Wright's "conflicting pattern of identification and rejection" that would be quite at home in *Counter-Statement* or *Attitudes toward History*.[64] Indeed, the latter delves heavily into the subjects explored in Ellison's essay: identity, identifications, and rituals of rebirth. Burke's discussion of the frames of acceptance and rejection could be a synopsis of Ellison's essay: "In the face of anguish, injustice, disease, and death one adopts policies. . . . Be he poet or scientist, one defines the 'human situation' as amply as his imagination permits; then, with this ample definition in mind, he singles out certain functions or relationships as either friendly or unfriendly. If they are deemed friendly, he prepares himself to welcome them; if they are deemed unfriendly, he weighs objective resistances against his own resources, to decide how far he can effectively go in combating them."[65] Similarly, Ellison's oft-cited description of art—"art [is] a ship in which man conquers life's crushing formlessness, reducing it to a course, a series of swells, tides and wind currents inscribed on a chart"[66]—is reminiscent of both *Counter-Statement* and *The Philosophy of Literary Form*. The passage echoes Burke's definition of poetry (or any form of art) as "the adopting of various strategies for the encompassing of situations."[67] Moreover, Ellison's use of the unusual term "chart" to describe Wright's achievement is almost definitely a Burkean allusion. Compare Ellison's text to Burke's distinction between dream, prayer, and chart—where the chart function is defined as "the realistic sizing-up of situations that is sometimes explicit, sometimes implicit, in poetic strategies."[68]

However, what is most striking about Ellison's essay is its discussion of "the interpenetration of human instinct with environment, through the process called experience, each changing and being changed by the other."[69] Such is the core of Ellison's argument: Wright, as a sensitive individual, artistically summarized the situation faced by one black man in the Jim Crow South. Ellison writes of the emergence of Wright's personality through the creative "encompassing" or "summing-up" of a situation, with a set of standards, roles, values, and norms; this reading of Wright emphasizes that his individual achievement cannot be reduced to a reflection of his group identity. At the same time, Ellison claims that this individual's sensibilities were structured by his society—and that, whether an artist is black or white, the materials for artistic expression are *always* and *only* drawn from the material and social environment within which the individual is immersed.

Ellison thus provides, in "Richard Wright's Blues," a strikingly Burkean account of Wright's biography. This is especially apparent if we recall Ellison's admiration of Burke's pentad—believing that, by 1944, Ellison had fully "grasp[ed] the implications of [Burke's] five terms."[70] Ellison emphasizes the interconnected nature of scene, act, and agent (central to Burke's definition of pentadic ratios), the sense in which "the scene-act ratio either calls for acts in keeping with scenes or scenes in keeping with acts—and similarly with the scene-agent ratio."[71] As presented by Ellison, the autobiography depicts Wright, as agent, rooted in a structuring scene, one whose importance cannot be overemphasized in evaluating his character and subsequent acts. According to Ellison "the drama of *Black Boy* lies in its depiction of what occurs when Negro sensibility attempts to fulfill itself in the undemocratic South."[72]

Through this skillful application of the scene-agent and scene-act ratios, Ellison's review rebuts Wright's critics. To those who would rail against Wright's depictions of black Americans' lives, Ellison emphasizes the restrictive nature of Wright's native South. Wright's point, Ellison emphasizes, is not that black Americans are incapable of culture, refinement, or kindness; on the contrary, the point is that Wright's environment simply did not foster these virtues. In other words, the text describes "the full extent to which the Southern community renders the fulfillment of human destiny impossible" for black Americans.[73] To act as though this environment would have no impact upon Wright is, Ellison argues, to equate black Americans with angels—to assume they are not human, that their nature is fixed, independent of context. Here Ellison echoes Burke's argument: when considering human motives, agents and their acts cannot be divorced from their scenic embeddedness.

To rebut another critique—that Wright's autobiography does not explain the origin of his art—Ellison again draws upon Burke's pentadic ratios. Just as one cannot simply derive acts (or agents) from scenes, Ellison argues that Wright's acts and character cannot be reduced to a reiteration of his scenic conditions. We thus see, in Ellison's analysis, the necessarily reciprocal relationship between Wright as an individual and the South's racist social system: "Wright is pointing out what should be obvious (especially to his Marxist critics): that Negro sensibility is socially and historically conditioned; that Western culture must be won, confronted like the animal in a Spanish bullfight, dominated by the red shawl of codified experience and brought heaving to its knees."[74]

Unwilling to accept the violence casually directed against him by whites—and his own family—Wright sought to escape the strictures of the South. By moving to the North and nurturing his intellect in a richer environment, Wright grew able "to endow his life's incidents with communicable significance, providing him with ways of seeing, feeling, and describing his environment."[75] By learning to symbolically transform, and thus transcend, his environment through the processes of art, Wright demonstrated his essential, archetypal humanity.

Although this autobiography can be read as an individual's salvation—like a blues song, which "offer[s] no scapegoat but the self"—Ellison suggests it can be something more.[76] Wright's story can also provide a critical tool, one used to refashion the social contexts and institutions that make it difficult for other black Americans to replicate Wright's efforts to "possess the meaning of his life in the United States."[77] Ellison therefore has another goal for his essay: "There is, as in all acts of creation, a world of mystery in this, but there is also enough that is comprehensible for Americans to create the social atmosphere in which other black boys might freely bloom."[78]

Despite its Burkean roots, this reading of "Richard Wright's Blues" is Ellison's own intellectual product. Ellison's essay draws upon Burke's vocabulary, but extends it into new territory with his defense of Wright. Consequently, far from being a simple repetition of Burke's ideas, the essay represents a unique contribution to the study of race in America. Yet, given its Burkean origins, it is not surprising that Ellison desired Burke's feedback on the essay. Thanks to their mutual friend Hyman, he soon received Burke's response—but likely not the response that he had anticipated. As a result, upon the publication of "Richard Wright's Blues," the dialogue between Burke and Ellison on matters of race truly commenced.

"What Would Ralph Say?"

Ellison was proud of his accomplishment in "Richard Wright's Blues," although he admitted to the editor of *Antioch Review* that "the essay was longer and 'much different from what I had anticipated.'"[79] He was quite energized by the endeavor, but remained committed to producing a work of fiction. As a result, in August 1945, as he awaited publication of his essay, Ellison again escaped to the Bates' Vermont farm; this time, he took Fanny with him. For Ellison, this second stay at the farm was even better than the first since it allowed him to spend some of his day with Fanny and some of his day alone, writing.

Soon after their arrival, as Ellison sat in the Bates' barn, an unexpected, unfamiliar voice uttered his famous opening words to Ellison: "I am an invisible man."[80] Excited by this emerging narrator, and by the appearance of "Richard Wright's Blues," Ellison wrote Hyman to share the news. The ensuing letter, however, admitted that this new character was more in control of the author than he of it: "This section of the novel is going very well—though God only knows what the hell it's all about. Of one thing I'm sure, any close symbolic analysis of it will reveal how completely crazy I am. Anyway, it's fun." He also reported the publication of his essay: "I started a letter to you just before we left the city but somehow it got left; perhaps because I was unable to get a copy of the current Antioch Review with my Wright piece, which I wanted you and Kenneth to see. Let me know if you haven't seen it, so that I can pick one up or order one when I return."[81]

Replying from his own Vermont retreat (near Bennington College), Hyman remarked upon Ellison's creative breakthrough and his newest publication. In response to the former, he offered encouragement; in response to the latter, he made a request: "I haven't seen the Antioch piece, and would be grateful if you would pick me up a copy when you get back to town, since I won't be in again until mid-October. I am very anxious to see the article." He also clarified an invitation which Ellison had previously declined: "The arrangement on Bennington is this: You are not coming up to speak to my class, but to the whole college."[82] In short, Hyman explained, Ellison was invited to deliver an address to the Bennington community, followed by an informal appearance in his freshman class. This was no small invitation; thanks to Hyman's efforts, Bennington was according Ellison a significant honor. Given this additional context, Hyman urged his friend to reconsider.

Ellison did not immediately reply, but, upon returning to New York, he sent Hyman and Burke copies of "Richard Wright's Blues." Afterward, finally accepting the invitation to lecture at Bennington, he confessed to Hyman: "I know only vaguely what the hell to say to a college crowd. But speak I shall and if you or Shirley have any ideas send them along."[83] Hyman retorted that Ellison would need little help: "If you can argue with me the way you do, you can talk to a bunch of students."[84]

A month later, Hyman confirmed both the date and the expectations for the lecture: "I am assuming that you will speak to the college Thursday evening on some aspect of Negro literature, but am waiting to hear definitely. I am also assuming, since you always do, that you will bring a speech and read it, rather than speaking off the cuff." Having disposed of the arrangements, Hyman turned to Ellison's essay: "I thought your piece on Wright, incidentally, was terrific, the best critical writing of yours I have ever read. I agree with almost everything you say, would have written it myself if I could." After offering objections that he hoped to address in person, Hyman added: "Almost the perfect pattern for your speech is the Wright article. That kind of thing, social and psychological analysis taking off from literary form and content, is precisely what they would want. . . . So just write a speech like the article, less specialized."[85]

Hyman's praise of "Richard Wright's Blues" was echoed in literary circles, with enthusiastic reviews appearing in the *English Journal* and the *New Republic*.[86] The essay was also a hit with Ellison's other friends, including Wright, who advised Ellison to continue as a critic, since the genre seemed to suit him.[87] Burke's wife, Libbie, wrote effusively to Shirley Jackson: "Ralph Ellison's pamphlet on Wright is positively the best, the most profound, the wisest thing I have ever seen on the black-white issue. And this is a subject I follow, having lived through all the stages of it myself. He is really seeing things from a higher level, and thereby seeing to a deeper level of the underlying set-up."[88]

The buzz surrounding Ellison's essay charged his visit to Bennington with additional significance, for both Ellison and Hyman. Since Burke had left his position at Bennington, Hyman attempted to convert Ellison's lecture into a makeshift reunion. Hyman disclosed his plan to Ellison: "I am writing Kenneth now proposing that he come up and the four of us tear the joint down, but I doubt that he will."[89] Hyman wrote Burke the same day, describing the occasion and asking him to come up for the weekend: "Ralph and his wife are coming up Thursday, Ralph to lecture to the college Thursday night on Negro literature and leave Friday. For you and me, it is the social highlight of the Bennington season. . . . Ralph would be overwhelmed, and we would have a high good time. Let me know as soon as you can."[90]

Two days before Ellison's lecture, Burke replied that he was unwilling to leave his typewriter for the event, even though "it does sound like a damned good several days." To justify this decision to decline, he cited the status of his follow-up to *A Grammar of Motives*: "For the last week or so, I've been smacking down what I think is the sort of thing I want for the beginning of the Rhetoric. And I'm afraid it would be bad magic for me to risk losing my Creative Grouch this early, before it has become more deeply ingrained, in the transcendent form of a working outline."[91] Because he had written so little, Burke explained, he was at a delicate phase of the project; he feared that a trip to Vermont might derail him, just as he was on the verge of establishing the organizational framework of the text.

Before closing the letter, Burke turned to Ellison's essay: "Tell Ralph I continue to ponder the article he sent me. Reading it again, I find myself beset by a whole new line of thought. I guess I didn't read it right the first time. Now it seems to suggest a paradox. I.e., Wright is able to protest fully as a *Negro* by separating himself out as an *individual*; but such a protest, by the nature of the case, resists *organization*. What would Ralph say? Tell him I do hope I'll see him before I leave for the south."[92] Two points from this passage stand out. First, Burke was reading Ellison's work on racial identity while he was outlining this project. Thus, at a pivotal moment in the composition of *A Rhetoric of Motives*—a work organized around the conflict between individual assertion and group membership—Burke indicates a serious encounter with Ellison's thought regarding the relationship between individual identity, racial identity, and the corresponding possibilities for communal action. This point is significant, for it suggests that Ellison exerted a heretofore unrecognized influence on Burke's writings about rhetoric—suggesting, again, that this friendship was important for both men, not simply for Ellison.

Second, Burke's question to Ellison reflects not only his interpretation of "Richard Wright's Blues," but also his perspective on the question of race. The text, on Burke's reading, boils down to a conflict between Wright's status as an individual and his status as member of a minority group. To reject the restrictive nature of his early life, Burke notes, Wright necessarily struck out as an individual. However, Burke argues, such an act is partly self-defeating for someone interested in protest since it removes the basis for rhetorical advocacy. In other words, since Wright's struggle is to emerge as an individual, how can he simultaneously be part of a movement protesting against racial injustice?

On Burke's view, by choosing the path of individual artist, Wright compromises his ability to organize, in order to protest racial oppression. Missing from Ellison's argument, Burke contends, is a meditation upon this paradox. Wright's story portrays a man emerging into individuality—but this achievement compromises his factional (racial) identity since he cannot simultaneously distinguish himself and submerge himself within the larger group. To the extent that he tries to make his individual protest the foundation for a group protest, Burke concludes, Wright will fail. His success must be either as a *unique* artist or as a *black* artist.

When read alongside Ellison's essay, we can see in Burke's query the emergence of a conversation between the men on matters of race—the dialogue that, I believe, years later helped Burke identify the "unconscious

Nortonism" in his thinking. We see, in "Richard Wright's Blues," Ellison's first attempt to harness Burke's writings for the purpose of alleviating racial oppression. We subsequently see, in Burke's letter to Hyman, evidence of his response to Ellison's position. However, Burke's question regarding Wright represents the opening, rather than the closure, of discussion; Ellison's essay represents the first published portion of their dialogue on race, but not the last.

Ellison's Unpublished "Counter-Statement"

By all accounts, Ellison's visit to Bennington was a rousing success. On the evening of 1 November 1945, he delivered a well-received address entitled "American Negro Writing—A Problem of Identity," and the next day, he spoke to Hyman's class about the similarities between Wright's *Black Boy* and Joyce's *Portrait of the Artist as a Young Man*.[93] His visit even made headlines, given the novelty of a lecture by a black speaker at a white campus—and was later voted "among the top three events at Bennington that year."[94] Hyman wrote later that month to share the positive reviews: "All the talk around here about your act is still very enthusiastic, the people who hadn't read your Antioch article before you spoke ran to the library and read it immediately after, and in general you were a wow."[95]

Hyman sent a similarly glowing report to Burke: "Ralph's talk went very well, and he made quite a hit, had a good time and enjoyed the place." He added, "It is a great shame that the old Burke stasis kept you from coming up those few days. You would have had a nice time." Moreover, the letter suggested, Burke's absence also prevented the staging of a great debate. According to Hyman, Burke's interpretation of "Richard Wright's Blues" had provoked an immediate response from its author: "I passed your message onto Ralph when he was here, he promised to write you anent it hotly, and then apparently forgot what you said. Anyway he called the other day when I was out and had Shirley read the paragraph to him over the phone. So you will probably be hearing from him, or may have already."[96]

Ellison's letter, as Hyman suspected, had already been posted; however, this is not to say that Ellison dashed off a hasty reply. On the contrary, he took great care in crafting his response, writing in longhand (filling eleven sheets of a legal-sized notebook) before committing them to the typewriter. The final, typed version of the response, dated 23 November 1945, resembles less a letter than a five-page, single-spaced essay—an essay that both responds to Burke's question and elaborates the theoretical agenda grounding "Richard Wright's Blues." Though conceived as a reply to the question raised in Burke's note to Hyman, Ellison's letter also reflects upon his relationship to Burke's ideas—and their relevance to the question of individual and racial identity.

In opening his lengthy reply, Ellison confessed that he had planned to send a letter simply expressing his gratitude for the Rosenwald recommendation—but that he had been forced to abandon his early drafts. The problem, he wrote, was that he was indebted to Burke for more than a letter of recommendation:

> I realized then that my real debt to you lies in the many things I've learned (and continue to learn) from your work, and that perhaps the greatest debt lies in your courage in taking a counter-position and making your "counter-statement." But then the problem arose of whether one really has the right to thank a thinker for having courage, and would not that be a misunderstanding and an embarrassment? For when a man, in battling for his life, has given birth to works which enlighten and inspire, is it not a mistake to confuse the matter and attempt to thank him? It's like thanking him for being a human being.[97]

As Ellison explained, he was not simply a "fan" of Burke; Burke's writings provided the foundation for his own perspective. Since a simple statement of gratitude would not be sufficient to cover this debt, he hoped that Burke would instead accept essays like "Richard Wright's Blues" as an alternate form of payment: "If in the little things I write from time to time you observe something of value, then to that extent am I able to express concretely my appreciation for what you have done."[98]

Following this one-page preamble, the letter shifts decisively. The transitional moment is rather abrupt, with Ellison combining a new paragraph with a new topic: "Which leads up to your preference for an ethic which is 'universal' rather than 'racial.'"[99] From this point forward, Ellison systematically addresses Burke's comment from the letter to Hyman and, perhaps, a separate, face-to-face conversation.[100] Tempering his enthusiastic praise of Burke's work, the subsequent pages of the letter constitute Ellison's own counter-statement—one directed against Burke's treatment of the differences between racialist and universalist perspectives.

Contesting the position staked out by Burke, Ellison argues that a "universal ethic" is not necessarily preferable to one based on race.

For black Americans in a culture founded on white supremacy, Ellison writes, the two ethics are not easily disentangled: "I certainly agree with you that universalism is desirable, but I find that I am forced to arrive at that universe through the racial grain of sand, even though the term 'race' is loaded with all the lies which men like Davidson warm their values by."[101] For Ellison, the problem is not the quest for the universal; rather, the problem lies in the attempt to disguise racial bias behind a "universal" ethic, in seeking to "transcend" racial identity by ignoring race-based privilege—and racial injustice. Though white Americans might be able to "transcend" race, Ellison argues that he does not have the same luxury: "I, for instance, would like to write simply as an American, or even better, a citizen of the world; but that is impossible just now because it is to dangle in the air of abstractions while the fire which alone illuminates those abstractions issues precisely from my being a Negro and in all the 'felt experience' which being a Negro American entails."[102]

Although the letter began with gratitude, this counter-statement signals a change in Ellison's relationship to Burke—and their first significant intellectual disagreement. Though Ellison quotes Burke to make his point, his letter articulates a position quite different from Burke's own. He thus offers an opposing perspective on the proper path toward the universal: "To throw away the concern with the racial . . . emphasis would for me be like cutting away the stairs leading from my situation in the world to that universalism of which you speak."[103]

Attempting to forestall objections from Burke, Ellison addresses the danger that such an approach would generate violent opposition between white and black Americans. Ellison simply argues that this opposition already exists; here he cites the damaged nature of the perspectives and motives of white Americans—a pathology reflecting the weight of antiblack racism and its impact on the development of white consciousness and identity. Though Ellison would more fully pursue this analysis in *Shadow and Act*, the letter provides an early glimpse of his perspective on the issue: "How well I understand that possibility of civil war that you mention! But don't you see the war exists already and its effects are in many ways more serious than any mere shedding of blood. It has warped our culture, truncated our ability to think deeply and broadly and schooled us to drop bombs on a defenseless city."[104]

Given these destructive psychic effects, Ellison suggests that the social unrest brewing within the black community might be therapeutic: "Perhaps what is missing from the American tradition is a major internal conflict of such a nature as to make us aware of the dangers of arrogant power and an over-simplified and contemptuous approach to human life." If a bloody conflict erupts, according to Ellison, it will reflect not black Americans' belief in victory, but the loss of alternatives. It will be because black Americans can no longer accept their second-class status; violence will simply represent "the explosion of outraged humanity against an oppression which it can no longer confront with hope or optimism."[105]

Following this bleak diagnosis of the divide between white and black Americans, his letter returns to Burke's question—on Wright as individual and as black. Rather than directly answering the question, Ellison disputes its basic assumptions. He argues that Wright's dilemma is not one of *organization*—as Burke suggested—but of *allegiance*. This problem, Ellison admits, is not restricted to any one racial group, but is instead an American problem: "When it comes to breaking worn-out allegiances we Americans have a gangster psychology. For even when an organization goes bad, or when it persecutes us or maims us spiritually, we feel a strange need to keep silent about it. . . . We are afraid to stand alone or to speak alone."[106]

Although intrinsically American, according to Ellison, the problem of allegiance is especially painful for black Americans—since their efforts to combat white supremacy have historically been undermined by organizations claiming to be allies. Ellison illustrates this point with a narrative; it is presented as archetypal, though its arc mirrors Wright's autobiography:

First the Negro breaks blindly away from his preindividual condition; next he discovers the organized discipline of communism, but naively believes that he has discovered a utopia in which blacks and whites are magically cleansed of their mutual antagonisms; then reality exerts itself and instead of revealing new forms of man he discovered the Negro communists wearing their psychological slave chains and the whites their psychological bull-whips, and a man like Wright begins slowly to discover that he has not escaped the nightmare which set him careening away from the pre-individual mass, but that he has found another of its many forms. At this point he must make a decision: Should he stay and accept the nightmare because it is more rational in this form than in the feudal shape it takes in the South—or should he denounce it. Should he remain loyal to a political party, accepting it for its stated aims, for its former rather than for its current action, or should he remain loyal to his people and to his own experience?[107]

Ellison contends that this narrative reflects both Wright's experiences and the underlying tension in his autobiography. Wright's struggle lies not in his organizing with other black Americans, but in his need to question inappropriate loyalties, to break unfit allegiances to a racist political organization.

Ellison counters Burke's description of Wright's paradox by reframing the question. Ellison claims that individuals must engage in collective activity—but they also must reject or re-create problematic aspects of the groups to which they belong. According to Ellison, this is the lesson contained within Wright's biography; Wright's rejection of the Communist Party signaled that any group claiming to be a haven from racism must deliver on this promise, or suffer the loss of its members of color. For Ellison, the central question is not whether individuals—taking responsibility for their lives and for their communities—*can* organize for racial protest. Rather, the question is how, as members of an oppressed group, they can critically *reflect* upon the nature of their current and future allegiances. Ellison's letter ends with his answer: "I'd say that since all of us who pretend to think have now the obligation to resist and reject even while we participate in organization. It is an ambiguous solution, but hell, so is the situation."[108]

Ellison's essay/letter offers a rich and nuanced position on the subject of race in America. Yet, Burke's response to it, and to Ellison's counterstatement as a whole, is just as fascinating a subject for analysis. Burke, upon receiving Ellison's letter, was evidently impressed; though enmeshed in his work on the *Rhetoric*, Burke wrote Hyman to discuss it: "Ralph wrote me. And a very good letter it was. So good that I'll have to write him an essay for an answer." At the same time, Burke indicated his disagreement with Ellison on some of the letter's points: "If he never yields more than half to his temptation (quite justified!) to become an intellectual Garveyite, he'll go on getting better and better. And he's damned good already."[109] We thus have two messages here; on the one hand, Burke expresses admiration for Ellison's work, while, on the other, his invocation of Garvey offers a racially charged, and rather negative, characterization of Ellison. His letter equates Ellison's position with racial separatism, a position he implies is understandable (given Ellison's racial identity) but suspect—an intellectual position that, while tempting for a black author, is best avoided.

Adding to the ambiguity of Burke's reaction, his promised response was slow in coming.[110] However, this temporal gap provides a convenient means of punctuating their interaction. Ellison's essayistic reply to Burke's question represents the second moment in their dialogue on race, the continuation of the discussion begun by "Richard Wright's Blues." Yet, even as this letter identified differences between Ellison's and Burke's perspectives on race, it helped lay the groundwork for Burke's *Rhetoric*—and thus generated the next moment in their dialogue.

Burke's Attempted, Abandoned Replies

Three weeks after receiving Hyman's report of the Bennington visit, Ellison sat at the typewriter, composing a reply. He attributed the delay to a hectic schedule but also admitted that he had deliberately waited, hoping for a letter from Burke: "As usual I'm late. Things here are still in an uproar, and I have been waiting to hear from Kenneth before I answered you. He hasn't, so I suppose that he has left for Florida."[111] Ellison was cheered by Hyman's reply—"Kenneth didn't get to Florida and didn't get to New York, but is right in Andover for the winter, mad"[112]—since it implied that he might still receive a response from Burke.

Despite remaining in the snowy Northeast, however, Burke did not write Ellison—nor, apparently, did he call. In late April 1946, Burke added a postscript to a letter to Hyman, suggesting that he still planned to reply to Ellison: "If you think of it, would you sometime send me Ralph's present address? I still owe him that letter. Also, I'd like to ask him out, now that the wrens are back (heard the first one this morning)."[113] Hyman sent Burke the address and phone number and urged Burke to call the next time he was in New York.[114] Burke, though, did nothing with this information. Since nearly six months had elapsed, as far as Ellison knew, Burke had forgotten the matter—or not deemed it worthy of reply. Yet, as Burke worked diligently on the *Rhetoric*, Ellison's essay and letter weighed heavily on his mind. Though Ellison had no way of knowing this, immediately following his receipt of Ellison's letter, Burke had attempted—but abandoned—two separate responses to it.

Since he had promised Hyman "an essay for an answer" to Ellison's letter, Burke had first planned an essayistic response. He started by marking passages and paragraphs from Ellison's letter; he used those markings, and his reading of "Richard Wright's Blues," to develop a page of notes entitled "Rhetoric of the Negro." Because Burke typed the notes in the form of an outline, some details of the argument are murky.

Nevertheless, the notes clearly position Ellison as Burke's interlocutor. The outline includes allusions to "his letter" and "his debunking of my views about [George Washington] Carver," both referring to Ellison's letter of November 1945.[115] Further, Burke's outline begins with the Davidson article mentioned in Ellison's letter and moves to Wright's *Black Boy* and *Native Son*—followed by "Ralph Ellison's article on Black Boy."[116]

Judging from these notes, Burke's examination of the "Rhetoric of the Negro" was to be divided into four or five parts. First, Burke would begin by contrasting the perspectives offered by Davidson and Wright on the subject of race in America. This discussion would set up Burke's central contention: that the differences between Davidson and Wright (and between Wright's texts) are best viewed "from [a] rhetorical angle."[117] Reading this today, we might be tempted to assume that Burke's "rhetorical angle" would revolve around identification—since that is regarded as the defining characteristic of Burke's approach to rhetoric.

In a letter to Cowley written during this same period (December 1945), however, Burke offered a different definition of the "rhetorical angle." Describing his manuscript, Burke wrote: "Because Rhetoric requires par excellence the 'strategy for handling a situation' approach, I find myself up against the problem of trying to state just what the situation is (using for this purpose a series of concentric circles, the widest of which states 'the situation' in the most general possible terms, 'the human situation' in the most universal or metaphysical sense, and then narrowing the scope gradually, at least down to a summary of what one considers to be the general politico-economic situation in contemporary U.S.)." This definition of rhetoric is more reminiscent of *Counter-Statement* or *The Philosophy of Literary Form*. Indeed, he told Cowley, one of the challenges of the *Rhetoric* was "the problem of trying to use the sort of stuff I had in Counter-Statement, without merely repeddling that book."[118] Rather than focusing upon symbolic identification, at this point in time Burke viewed rhetoric as a strategic summarizing of a situation, a symbolic naming of (and response to) a context of wider or narrower scope.

Given this definition of the "rhetorical angle," Burke planned to treat Wright in terms of one of the narrower concentric circles: the American racial situation. Judging from the notes, such an approach would lead naturally into the second section of the essay—a meditation upon "Negro responses to the problem of power."[119] Although Burke does not explain this title, he lists nine possible responses to the American racial situation—nine ways that black Americans strategically summarize their place within a white-dominated culture.[120] The notes indicate that the essay's third section would apply this typology to *Black Boy*, but drawing (in an indeterminate way) upon "Richard Wright's Blues."[121]

The outline provides more details regarding the fourth section of the essay, which again focuses upon Wright—and, specifically, upon *Native Son*. Based on the notes, Burke planned to approach the book as Wright's "response to the problem of power," his stylized naming of the race situation in America. Burke also suggests that Wright's naming gained additional rhetorical power because it combined racial with sexual symbolism—and thereby addressed the situation faced by its white audience. According to Burke, the novel's wide appeal is traceable to whites' fascination with "sexual corruption," the "surrender to the low," and "the mark of the guilty act."[122]

Burke's proposed essay turned, in its final section, to Ellison's long letter. The notes integrate Ellison's critiques of Burke's views with their shared admiration of Dostoevsky—and thereby suggest a new item for his typology: a "possible sacrificial type."[123] Burke planned to argue that such a type combined the rhetorical and symbolic dimensions of human life. A novel reflecting this "sacrificial type," according to Burke's notes, would be grounded in the narrative of an individual self, but it would have a broader resonance—since its "characters would also have rhetorical effect on Negro readers."[124]

At this point, Burke's notes break off; something prevented him from moving forward with the project. Despite completing a fairly robust outline on the "Rhetoric of the Negro," Burke did not produce an essay from this material—and it does not appear that he tried, given the absence of drafts in his archives. Yet, though Burke decided to abandon his essayistic response to Ellison's letter, he did not altogether abandon his attempt to address Ellison's concerns. Not quite a month after receiving Ellison's letter, Burke decided to craft another response—but this time, in the form of a letter.

Since nearly three weeks had elapsed, Burke's letter first apologized for the delay in replying. He attempted to reframe his silence, hoping that Ellison would not mistake it for indifference: "The better a letter is, the longer it waits for an answer. But I am violating that sound principle to answer yours in much less than a month." Before moving into the main thrust of his response, Burke also thanked Ellison for his praise—though he confessed his discomfort with Ellison's views. As Burke put it, "Thanks much for your kindly references to my work. But as regards the high percentage of indignation with which you apparently propose to write on the conditions of the Negro, I find it extremely awkward to reply."[125]

With this, Burke's letter quickly shifts gears, from prefatory statements toward a more sustained argument regarding race and identity. He begins, as Ellison did, with the distinction between universal and racial ethics. Taking a different tack than in their exchange over Wright, Burke grants the legitimacy of the perspective presented in Ellison's letter—but does not grant Ellison's conclusions. According to Burke, their differences on this topic reflect a more fundamental difference. Whereas, Burke states, his own writings define social life as a conflict between the individual and universal, Ellison defines it as a conflict between the racial and the universal. For Burke, experience is the key to this difference in viewpoints: "Whatever indignities and fears I have suffered, I have always had the feeling that I suffered them as an individual; hence that the problem of repair was primarily an individual problem. . . . The indignities and fears you suffer, you suffer not as an individual, but as member of a race."[126]

Burke's letter ascribes this difference in experience to their racial differences. Reflecting on his own racial identity, Burke confesses, "If I often forget that I am a white man, and burn merely from the sense of my inadequacies as an individual, it is only because I am not surrounded by a set of customs that continually reminds me of my color." Ellison, in taking up the question of race—and in "intensify[ing] racial thinking"— is responding to his experiences as a black man. The white intellectual, by contrast, must instead "do all that he can to mitigate the magic of race" by striving "to weaken the magic of any such classification" by skin color. The true dilemma, for Burke, is that these two tasks necessarily result in black and white scholars espousing contradictory positions on the issue of race. Even as the white intellectual attempts to "reveal some of the remoter magic of the classification by color," his "colleague on the other side of the issue must talk of 'carrying as many white folks with me as I can.'"[127]

As a result, according to Burke's letter, the American racial divide can only be addressed through complex artistic representations of whiteness and blackness. Returning to a theme developed in the "Rhetoric of the Negro" outline, Burke declares Wright's work, like any emphasizing the "power Negro," inadequate: "I can't see that any good can come of that for anyone, except perhaps that a few Negro intellectuals may make good money by selling a titillating book to a somewhat decadent though timidly sympathetic white audience."[128] Such literature flatters, or seduces, but does not lead to true understanding.

Although Burke judges Wright's aesthetic too simplistic to reflect "the true complexity of the Negro situation," he also criticizes Ellison's intellectualist redescription of Wright's autobiography. "Richard Wright's Blues," Burke argues, suggests that external conditions can stamp out universal human characteristics. This, Burke insists, is a mistake: "There is a different area still alive in every Negro mind. There is, because there is in everybody. At some points in your Antioch piece, you say as much. At other points you uphold a position almost in a way as bad as Davidson's. For you say in effect that many Negroes have been brutalized by their situation, and anybody who looks at them otherwise is being sentimental." Burke's letter urges Ellison to instead remember his literary hero: "There are no sheer brutes in Dostoevsky."[129]

Before ending the letter, Burke returns to the impetus for their exchange—his initial question about "Richard Wright's Blues." Burke warns of the conservative implications of Ellison's terminology of allegiance and critique of the party. Racialist critiques of communism, Burke writes, reduce the current situation to the narrow confines of race and ignore its broader sociopolitical dimensions. Burke acknowledges that, given Wright's experiences with the party, "there is something unsatisfactory about remaining silent. But there is something much more unsatisfactory in selling one's grievances to an audience which loves to hear of them for wholly reactionary reasons."[130] In short, Burke argues that Wright's (and, by implication, Ellison's) attacks on racism in the party simply provide ammunition to the defenders of industrial capitalism.

Perhaps to minimize his discomfort, Burke ended the letter apologetically: "If any of this sounds dumb, at least I meant well."[131] Yet, even this qualifier proved insufficient. Though Burke signed the letter—including, in the last paragraph, an invitation to Andover—he hesitated before placing it in an envelope. Ultimately, this three-page, single-spaced letter did not make the trip from typewriter to mailbox; it remained on his desk, unsent, and Burke resumed work on the *Rhetoric*.

Race and *A Rhetoric of Motives*: Burke's Long-Delayed Reply

Burke's protracted silence nearly ended in May 1946, when Ellison and Burke crossed paths at the American Academy of Arts and Letters. Ellison—in attendance with Langston Hughes—was only able to see Burke at a distance, through a crowd.[132] As Ellison reported to Hyman: "I dropped into the American Academy ceremony and saw Kenneth stand to receive the applause of the audience, but I had to leave before it was

over in order to leave town. Thus was unable to see him."[133] Responding to Hyman's suggestion that he and Fanny exchange wedding vows
at Andover, Ellison declined, confessing that "I'm afraid that it is a little
late now as we have taken care of the matter already. So let your mind
be at ease."[134] However, he suggested, "Why don't all of us get together at
Kenneth's anyway?"[135]

Hyman dutifully wrote Burke, proposing that he, Jackson, Ellison,
and Fanny descend upon Andover in August.[136] When Hyman later commented, "We will bring the Ellisons if we can, but I don't guarantee it,"[137]
Burke was dismayed. He wrote Hyman, emphasizing that the Ellisons
should reconsider. Burke clearly hoped to redress his failure to respond
to Ellison's letter: "We'll be expecting you both, and with the Ellisons.
Tell Ralph I'd write him in person; but have once again misplaced the address you gave me. (When he comes out, I'll show him how these things
happen, if you happen, like me, to equate a neatly ordered filing system
with death, and often don't want to be a-dying.)." At the end of the letter,
he underscored this point, adding: "Hope to be seeing you all soon. And
do impress it upon Ralph that we very much hope they'll come too."[138]

Burke's concerns were soon put to rest; by the time Hyman and Jackson set off for Andover, Fanny and Ralph had decided to join them. Ellison found the visit tremendously rewarding. His letter of thanks, written a month afterward, expressed sincere gratitude for the hospitality,
for the conversation, and for the living reminder of their time together:
"The plants are thriving and we suspect that the New Jersey soil in our
window boxes is about the richest earth on this, for the most part, barren
Harlem hill."[139] Ellison had something else to be thankful for; during the
visit, "Burke surprised Ralph by handing him a letter he had written to
him but decided not to mail."[140] Although Burke had opted against mail-
ing his letter to Ellison, he had not discarded or destroyed it. Instead, he
had apparently decided, during the visit, to deliver it personally—finally
giving Ellison the response to his letter and to "Richard Wright's Blues"
that he had so patiently awaited.[141]

Contact resumed between the two men in the aftermath of the visit.
Burke sent regards to Ellison (via Hyman) in early October, Burke and
Ellison met again in New York, and in early December, Ellison sent Burke
a list of works on "Negro writing."[142] The Ellisons made another trip to
Andover in late 1946 or early 1947, though this visit ended less amiably
than the previous one. Afterward, in a letter to Hyman, Burke reported
dissatisfaction with Ellison's manners: "Ralph and Frances E. were out.
Thought it was a good session. . . . But haven't heard a peep from him

since, which may or may not indicate vast preoccupation or vague disgruntlement, but certainly does not indicate vast graciousness."[143]

No more was said of this incident, but Fanny Ellison and Libbie Burke subtly worked to soothe hurt feelings. In April, Fanny sent Libbie photos of the Burke family that they had taken during their August 1946 visit—and Libbie wrote back that her only disappointment was "not to have any of those of Ralph and Kenneth—didn't any of them turn out?"[144] Perhaps alerted by Hyman to Burke's discontent, Ellison wrote Hyman in June and asked him to pass on a message: "Give my regards to Kenneth and tell him I hope to see him soon for a talk."[145]

In August, Ellison finally contacted Burke directly and offered an explanation for his silence: "Until quite recently I've found it next to impossible to write letters—which explains why you haven't heard from me. I did manage to use the telephone and was thus able to keep in touch with Stanley, but with you this wasn't possible; so I had to contend with my vain resolutions and bad conscience." The two had not spoken since the visit to Andover, so Ellison provided an update on his quickly evolving novel-in-progress. Though avoiding specifics on the plot or characters, he reported that his writing was going well, and that it reflected the influence of his change of scenery: "Here I have my nightmares at night and by eight in the morning after watching the thick mist sweeping before the swift rising of the sun, I've achieved enough of a precarious tranquility to turn in a rather successful day of writing." Despite his daily regimen of writing, Ellison still made time for his friend's work; he indicated that Burke's recent article "Ideology and Myth" had "set off a few bells in my head. When I return I plan to give it a careful study, as it reawakens my interests in a piece I planned concerning the relation between our 'science' of sociology and racial ideology."[146]

Over the next several months, Ellison continued to send greetings to Burke; Burke, in turn, proposed another reunion at Andover in late 1947.[147] Clearly the relationship between Burke and Ellison had rebounded from the long, mutual silences of 1945 and 1946. Yet, even with their relational issues apparently resolved, Burke had not forgotten his promise to "write . . . an essay for an answer" to Ellison's letter. Even as he labored over the *Rhetoric*, he continued to ponder the significance of his exchanges with Ellison on matters of race. Although Burke had abandoned the proposed essay on the "Rhetoric of the Negro"—and had only reluctantly delivered his reply to Ellison—as Burke worked on the *Rhetoric*, these reflections on race and identity never strayed far from his thoughts.

This was made evident in early 1948, when Burke paused from his writing and composed a note to Ellison. Although framed as an overdue reply to Ellison's August 1947 letter, its timing was no accident. Burke had been in possession of Ellison's letter for five months, but it had suddenly become quite relevant to his work on the *Rhetoric*—so much so that he had decided to solicit Ellison's opinion. Within his letter, Burke focused attention upon Ellison's reading of "Ideology and Myth": "I hope you have done something about that article on sociology and racial ideology you thought of writing. . . . I'd much like to see it worked out." Burke's words reflected more than idle curiosity; Ellison's perspective on ideology and race resonated with a recently completed portion of the *Rhetoric*: "The section I have just finished is hitting all around that business."[148]

The central insight developed in this part of the manuscript, according to Burke, was his identification of "The Mystery" as a concept central to the entire rhetorical tradition.[149] However, Burke wrote Ellison, there was something missing; struck by the relevance of race to this material, he wrote: "There is some stuff in this section which I want very much to talk with you about. I believe that if you brought the vividness of your own experiences to bear upon some of the formulations I am now working on, we could both profit." Indeed, Burke argued, the approach represented by the *Rhetoric* held great promise for the contemplation of the American racial situation: "In any case, I think it can be shown that rhetoric brings one quite near to the dropping-off place."[150]

Based upon Burke's correspondence, the portion of text mentioned in this letter is the end of the second section, "Traditional Principles of Rhetoric," and the beginning of the third, "Order." The day before, for example, a note to Hyman celebrated the completion of the second section—pages that had taken Burke so far into "The Mystery" that, he admitted, "it's just as well that I extricated myself."[151] Burke's correspondence with Ellison thus sheds new light on a central theme running throughout the *Rhetoric*—the mystery produced by the separation of classes, as well as the devices used to manage their estrangement. Given the content of this letter, it is not surprising that Burke's text frequently ties together the themes of race and mystery—especially regarding white southerners' doctrine of "racial superiority."[152] Such references are peppered throughout the *Rhetoric* and comprise a central element of Burke's treatment of race: race as a socially defined group identity that can be manipulated for a multitude of purposes.

However, the *Rhetoric* also features another, more sustained discussion of the subject—a discussion that includes Burke's citation of

"Richard Wright's Blues." This portion of the text focuses not upon the supremacists' efforts to create a black scapegoat, but upon the dilemma faced by black artists like Wright. Burke began writing these pages not long after his letter to Ellison, and, in them, he drew heavily upon the essay mentioned by Ellison: "Ideology and Myth."[153] Further, I believe that, in his discussion of positive, dialectical, and ultimate terminologies, Burke saw a way to finally respond to Ellison's 1945 letter—and to suggest an alternative reading of *Black Boy*.

Burke uses the distinction between these three orders of terminology in order to reinterpret Wright's central dilemma. Thus, Burke both revises his earlier views on *Black Boy* and responds to the objections raised by Ellison's long "counter-statement." According to Burke, vocabularies can be understood as falling into one of these three categories; positive vocabularies are built upon perception, dialectical upon opposition, and ultimate upon transcendence.[154] The transcending power of the ultimate leads Burke to place it atop his "hierarchy of terms" as the most complex of the three.[155]

Drawing upon this tripartite distinction, Burke asserts that the fundamental problem faced by Wright was one of allegiance, but only because his success led to a kind of transcendence: an "improvement in social status."[156] Though striving to achieve such improvement is a rational response to oppression, Burke argues that success produces a crisis within the individual whose status has improved. In one sense, Burke here echoes his initial response to "Richard Wright's Blues"; Wright's problem is that the attaining of higher individual status requires a concomitant rejection of racial identity. His success creates a crisis of identity because, in acquiring a new vocabulary and a new way of life, "he would in a sense be 'disloyal' to his class, in transcending the limitations traditionally imposed upon him as a member of that class."[157]

Burke therefore contends that Wright's struggles, as described in *Black Boy*, reflect something characteristically human: the drive for transcendence. Here Burke echoes themes first articulated in Ellison's essay.[158] Ellison had, in "Richard Wright's Blues," first broached the topic of transcendence in relation to Wright—characterizing the book as a blues-tinged form of transcendence, "an impulse to keep the painful details and episodes of a brutal experience alive in one's aching consciousness, to finger its jagged grain, and to transcend it . . . by squeezing from it a near-tragic, near-comic lyricism."[159] Yet, drawing upon the terministic orders, Burke broadens this analysis of Wright. For Burke, transcendence is not simply a question of art; the human condition is itself marked by transcendence because "there is in language itself a motive force calling man to transcend the 'state of nature.'"[160]

At this point, Burke specifically invokes "Richard Wright's Blues," noting the complicated nature of this situation. Any attempt to achieve transcendence will be met with resistance from other members of the community: "The Negro intellectual, Ralph Ellison, says that Booker T. Washington 'described the Negro community as a basket of crabs, wherein should one attempt to climb out, the others immediately pull him back.'"[161] Burke extends this citation, arguing that other minorities are not the only obstacles to such transcendence; the individual herself may also resist this transcendence of status. As Burke writes, an individual like Wright "may visit upon himself the antagonistic attitude of the whites; or he may feel as 'conscience' the judgment of his own class."[162] The central outcome of Wright's attempt to gain "improvement in social status" is, then, guilt regarding the transcendence of his racial identity— which leads to what is typically called an "inferiority complex."[163] However, Burke suggests this "complex" is better described as the rhetorical situation faced by a member of an oppressed group who would aim at transcending her oppression.

Confronted with this paradox, the individual is forced to formulate a strategy to mediate the conflict between her individual, group, and generic identities. Burke uses Wright to illustrate this phenomenon, citing *Native Son* and *Black Boy*.[164] By reading Wright's texts as responses to this paradoxical situation, Burke both develops themes sketched in the "Rhetoric of the Negro" and responds to "Richard Wright's Blues."

This argument, presented in a significant passage in the *Rhetoric*, gains new significance in light of Burke's exchanges with Ellison. Not only does it contain Burke's only citation of Ellison in his main body of work, but it also comprises Burke's long-awaited response to Ellison's arguments. First, and most obviously, we see Burke address the question of Wright's status as an individual and a black American, hearkening back to their exchange over "Richard Wright's Blues." In addition, though, we see the evolution of Burke's thought on the issue; though he originally defined Wright's as a problem of organization, Burke seems to have reconsidered in light of Ellison's reply, and his own aborted attempts to respond to Ellison's letter. Thus, Burke's *Rhetoric* constitutes a significant treatment of race, one developed in response to Ellison. For this reason, I see the text to be not only a canonical work of rhetorical theory, but also Burke's contribution to his dialogue with Ellison on race.

This is not to say, however, that Ellison was pleased with Burke's response—or with Burke's citation of "Richard Wright's Blues." In a letter following the publication of the *Rhetoric*, Hyman warned Burke of Ellison's disapproval: "I also saw Ralph, who wants to see you and talk over your butchery of him in Red Taurus. I said the three of us should get together in town (do you ever come in Fridays?) or he and I would drive out to Andover some day (he just bought a station wagon) and beard you. I would advise you to grow a quick beard."[165]

Though Ellison's critique was provided orally, his copy of the first edition of the text offers a clue about its general outlines. Responding to Burke's quotation of his essay on page 193, Ellison placed a question mark in the right margin, next to the line citing Wright's feeling as "'conscience' the judgment of his own class." He added, in black ink, "But what if he's novelist, scientist? a technician? artist?"

A 1957 letter from Burke to Hyman provides more insight into Ellison's critique. In it, Burke reported stumbling upon the work of "some Negro author who peddled to Kenyon the point you and Ralph bopped me for, on pp. 193–5 of the Rhetoric."[166] Based upon the arguments made by Richard Gibson—the "Negro author" referenced by Burke—we may conclude that at least part of the criticism involved Burke's identification of Ellison as "the Negro intellectual." In his essay, Gibson wrote: "Perhaps it should modestly and most humbly be suggested to the still uncorrupted Negro youth with an itch to write that he become not another Negro writer, that he become instead a writer who happens also to be a Negro; not because he is ashamed of being a Negro, but because he is more ashamed of not being human, of not being himself rather than a stereotype."[167]

Judging from Burke's reference to this essay (and Ellison's marginalia), a portion of Ellison's critique likely addressed Burke's relegation of him to the margins, Burke's definition of him as a "race man." His status as an intellectual need not be confined to the problems of race, as Burke's characterization of him in the *Rhetoric* implies.[168] As noted at the beginning of this chapter, Burke credited Ellison with spurring him toward greater racial sensitivity; however, Ellison's critique of the *Rhetoric* suggests that in 1950 this process had not yet been completed.

At the same time, drawing together the published and unpublished materials from the latter half of the 1940s, it is clear also that their exchanges on race represented the "moments of antagonistic cooperation" described in this chapter's opening quote. With Hyman's help, Burke and Ellison had constructed a friendship that could withstand, and even profit from, a decade of "antagonistic cooperation." Though at times difficult, this ongoing dialogue had helped both men create some of their most celebrated works. As we have seen, Ellison's Burkean reflections resulted in the provocative analysis of "Richard Wright's Blues," while Burke's attempts to draft an adequate reply culminated in a key section of *A Rhetoric of Motives.*

Thirty years later, Burke reflected on this period of their friendship, and on the *Rhetoric*'s citation of Ellison: "Those paragraphs I wrote in connection with your literary situation then were done, of course, when I had not the slightest idea of what you were to unfold in your (literally) 'epoch-making' novel ('epoch-making' in the strict sense, as a work that, by its range of stories and corresponding attitudes, sums up an era). I had heard you read a portion of the early section on the battle royal, and had vaguely sensed the introductory nature of your narrator's fumbling acquiescence to the indignities implied in the encounter. But the actuality of your inventions was wholly beyond any but your imagining."[169] With the publication of the *Rhetoric* in 1950, Burke provided his answer to Ellison's letter—citing Ellison's essay in the process. However, as this quote indicates, within two years of the *Rhetoric*'s appearance, Ellison produced a startling "counter-statement" of his own: the "epoch-making" novel *Invisible Man.*

In contrast to the exchanges of the 1940s, the success of Ellison's novel presented a new, and formidable, threat to the Burke-Ellison friendship. For this reason, the next chapter turns to *Invisible Man*—the final moment of Burke-Ellison dialogue on race—and focuses attention upon the novel's Burkean roots, as well as Burke's ambivalent response to it. By closely examining the relational strain created by the book's (and Ellison's) instant celebrity, we deepen our understanding of Ellison's famous novel and begin to glimpse the implications of this remarkable friendship for analyzing our characteristically American "racial divide."

3 / From Acceptance to Rejection: *Invisible Man*

P.P.S. I've always tried to turn your insights back to the necessities of fiction.

—RALPH ELLISON TO KENNETH BURKE, 7 NOVEMBER 1982

When Ralph Ellison's *Invisible Man* was published in April 1952, he and Kenneth Burke had been friends for nearly ten years—a span of time that had provided Burke a unique window into the painstaking creation of the novel. Burke had first learned of its existence from Ellison's letter of 23 November 1945, the letter that had deepened their dialogue on race and identity. Through correspondence and conversation spanning the next seven years, as the two continued their exchanges on matters of race, they also discussed Ellison's novel. In 1951, Ellison even read aloud the "Battle Royal" section to a gathering at Burke's home. As Michael Burke later recalled:

> He sat on the piano bench with the microphone for the recorder balanced in front of him on a tall kitchen stool. I sat on the floor and knew I had to be quiet. He read of a time in his youth when he boxed for the amusement of a jeering white audience. After the boxing the black youngsters, still in their trunks and sweaty from the fight, were led to an electrified carpet where they had to scramble for coins. Ralph described the convulsing bodies and the circle of reveling spectators, and I concentrated on the rag rug in front of the piano bench imagining a rich, red, ornamental Persian Carpet, with an electrical cord winding from the rug to the outlet on the wall by the bookshelf. I don't remember the Ellisons visiting often, or much of what went on, but I still have a clear picture of the boxers on our carpet.[1]

This vivid description nicely captures the personal dimension of their professional relationship, the intimate connections between Ellison's project and his friendship with Burke.

Immediately following its appearance in bookstores, Ellison's novel was hailed for its singular artistic achievement;[2] yet, the book's appearance held a personal significance for both Burke and Ellison, and represented a different kind of achievement. Recall that Ellison's 1945 letter had prefaced its counter-statement with extended reflections upon Ellison's indebtedness to Burke. Despite confessing his inability to repay Burke with more than "little things I write from time to time," Ellison added that he had might have hit upon something more substantial: "I am writing a novel now and perhaps if it is worthwhile it will be my most effective means of saying thanks. Anything else seems to me inadequate and unimaginative."[3] Since Ellison's narrator had "spoken" his first words a mere three months before this letter—and since his arrival had prompted Ellison to abandon all other projects—it is clear that the book mentioned was *Invisible Man*.[4] As early as 1945, then, Burke knew something that is now widely acknowledged by Ellison scholars—that Burke's work had played a vital role in the novel's composition. However, Burke also knew something rarely mentioned in the literature on *Invisible Man*. According to Ellison's own testimony, his celebrated novel not only drew upon Burke's terminology, but *was dedicated to him by its author*—as a means of repaying his intellectual debt to Burke.

It is not surprising, then, that a 1985 collection celebrating Ellison included a chapter from Burke, "Ralph Ellison's Trueblooded *Bildungsroman*." Since Burke was rather reticent about his friendship with Ellison, this piece is quite notable—indeed, it contains Burke's sole published acknowledgment of their relationship. Burke's essay offers a description of the "friendly nonracial 'we'" that joined him to Ellison, as well as his admission of some "unconscious Nortonism" that Ellison helped him expunge. This is not the only distinctive feature of Burke's chapter; it appears to be a personal letter from Burke to Ellison, opening with "Dear Ralph," and closing, "Best luck, to you and Fanny both, K. B."[5] The editor's prefatory note reinforces this interpretation: "This essay began as a short letter from Mr. Burke to Mr. Ellison and has been expanded for the present volume."[6]

Largely on the basis of this evidence, most scholars, even those focusing attention upon the Burke-Ellison relationship, have taken this essay at face value; they have interpreted it as a personal message from Burke to Ellison, later published as part of a celebratory volume. Eddy, for example, refers to it as a "letter to Ellison."[7] Pease, similarly, notes that "in 1985, Burke published a private letter to Ellison."[8] Even Rampersad's careful biography integrates it into his discussion of Ellison in the 1940s—tacitly presenting the letter as Burke's timely feedback on portions of *Invisible Man*.[9]

Such interpretations of "Ralph Ellison's Trueblooded *Bildungsroman*" have missed something crucial; this chapter contends that this letter is not what it seems despite its formal similarities to a "private letter." Examination of the correspondence indicates that the essay was written nearly forty years into the friendship; as a consequence, it cannot be taken as a faithful reflection of earlier stages of their relationship. More importantly, it was written specifically for inclusion in the collection—and thus was *never* intended to be a private document. Adding to its public character, the "letter" passed through a series of revisions (revisions by Burke himself, by Ellison, and by the editor of the collection) prior to its publication.[10] These situational factors make it impossible to take it at face value, as an unvarnished reflection on their relationship—or on Ellison's novel.

Yet, this is not to say that I would dismiss the essay as unimportant to the story of the Burke-Ellison friendship. On the contrary, if we read the essay within the context of their relationship, this late "letter" from Burke takes on a surprising significance: Burke's essay represents the long-delayed fulfillment of his promise to read *Invisible Man*. This interpretation explains why, more than thirty years after the novel's publication, the bulk of Burke's essay offers a dramatistic analysis of *Invisible Man*. However, this reading of Burke's "letter" requires that we look beyond its formal structure and place it within the context of the (truly) private correspondence among Burke, Ellison, and their mutual friend Stanley Edgar Hyman.[11] If we do so, we see Ellison's novel, and Burke's response to it, as a decisive moment in their relationship—one that halted their dialogue on race and, for a time, derailed their friendship.

Dueling Dostoevskys

Given Ellison's intensive study of Burke's work during the early 1940s, it is not surprising that his first major work of fiction drew on Burkean concepts. However, in an oft-cited 1955 interview, Ellison credited Burke with more than a few concepts; he claimed that Burke had provided the entire structural framework for the novel. Responding to a question about his planning of the book, he answered: "The symbols and their connections were known to me. I began it with a chart of the three-part division. It was a conceptual frame with most of the ideas and some incidents indicated. The three parts represent the narrator's movement from, using Kenneth Burke's terms, purpose to passion to perception. These three major sections are built up of smaller units of three which mark the course of the action and which depend for their development upon what I hoped was a consistent and developing motivation."[12] Following the appearance of this interview (and its subsequent inclusion in Ellison's essay collections), devotees of Ellison's work adopted his account of the Burkean structure underlying the book.[13] The anecdote might be exaggerated—more retrospective sense-making than faithful history—but this triad, taken from Burke's *Grammar of Motives*, undoubtedly played an important role in Ellison's work on the novel.[14] Rampersad testifies to this fact: "Although Burke's precise influence on the manuscript of *Invisible Man* is impossible to track, Ralph scribbled throughout his manuscript drafts, as a kind of inspirational mantra, the Burkean formula: 'Purpose to Passion to Perception.'"[15]

It is not clear when Ellison seized upon this Burkean "mantra," but his copy of the first edition of the *Grammar* contains a penciled notation inside the front cover, just below his signature: "Poiema, mathema[ta], Patheme P.39." Ellison's notation corresponds to a section entitled the "Dialectic of Tragedy."[16] On the page referenced by Ellison, Burke does not translate these three Greek terms into "purpose, passion, perception," but it appears from Burke's discussion that this is the original source of Ellison's formula.

Within this section of text, Burke analyzes the "'tragic' grammar" summarized in a Greek proverb: "'*ta pathemata mathemata*,' the suffered is the learned."[17] To apply this proverb accurately to tragedy, Burke writes, it must be altered—to include the vital role played by tragic action. Burke's reformulation of the proverb closely resembles the formula cited by Ellison: "If the proverb were to be complete at the risk of redundance, it would have three terms: *poiemata, pathemata, mathemata*, suggesting that the act organizes the opposition (brings to the fore whatever factors resist or modify the act), that the agent thus 'suffers' this opposition, and as he learns to take the oppositional motives into account, widening his terminology accordingly, he has arrived at a higher order of understanding."[18] Given Burke's dramatistic expansion of the Greek proverb, its relevance to Ellison's novel becomes even clearer.

Structuring his story according to this three-part sequence allowed

Ellison to combine narrative progression with the logical progression of "the act, the sufferance or state, the thing learned."[19] By faithfully following this Burke-derived formula, Ellison could thereby imbue his narrator with "tragic vision," a dialectical transcendence of the self through the "widening [of] his terminology"; this widening would be accomplished through the systematic confrontation with "oppositional motives." The result, the end of the narrative, would be the "higher order of understanding" achieved by the narrator as a result of his action and experiences.[20]

This structure was undoubtedly an ambitious one for a first-time novelist, but Ellison had become convinced that anything less was inadequate. For Ellison, the quest for "tragic vision" was both a problem of narrative structure and a pressing existential concern. He had become increasingly convinced that the development of adequate perceptions was the vital challenge faced by black Americans—himself included—as they struggled against the violence and inequality of American society. The situation, he explained to Burke in 1945, "demands an ever-alert consciousness, and not because you are full of neurotic anxiety but simply because reality itself demands that you approach it from second to minute with your eyes wide open."[21]

Further, he argued, such a task requires achieving a clarity of thought, a robust self-consciousness, unnecessary for white Americans. One need only look, he noted, to the racism of white men like Donald Davidson to see the contrast: "Davidson's kind have been consciously concerned with blinding my kind for over 300 years and while he can smugly embody an unconscious culture, prejudice etc., I must, if I am to survive and struggle against them, be conscious every second of every idea, insight and concept that I am able to grasp, as though they were spread upon a parapet like so many rifles waiting to be fired."[22] This struggle between black and white Americans represented nothing less than a struggle over the nature of reality—a struggle wherein he could leave no assumption or concept unchallenged.

For that reason, Ellison confessed, Burke's treatment of Dostoevsky held a special significance for him. In discussing *Crime and Punishment*'s Raskolnikov, Burke might have been describing the situation faced by black Americans: "Being a Negro is (once one becomes self-conscious) very much like being a criminal. It 'produces a kind of "oneness with the universe" in leading to a sense of universal persecution whereby all that happens has direct reference to the criminal.' I could continue quoting this passage of yours endlessly without once violating the parallel."[23] In citing the "communion between inner and outer" felt by Raskolnikov, Ellison underscored the complexity of living with racism, the sense in which "there is no 'impersonality' in the environment," that "much of the world that would be otherwise neutral is charged with personal reference."[24] This oppressive "communion between inner and outer" is why, he argued, black Americans' efforts to interpret reality are simultaneously efforts to achieve self-consciousness.

Given this perspective on race and identity, Ellison admitted aiming—as a novelist—to accomplish more than Wright did with *Native Son*. This is not to say that he saw nothing of value in Wright's work; on the contrary, he wrote, "I do think that it contains a fundamental approach based upon a self-acceptance which Negroes seriously need." Yet, Ellison agreed with Burke that Wright's approach was insufficient. He added, "In my own work . . . I am aiming at something I believe to be broader, more psychological, and employing, let us say, a scale of twelve tones rather than one of five."[25] Just as a complete musical scale includes, but is not reducible to, the blues scale, Ellison sought an alternative to Wright's "esthetic over-simplification"—an approach that did not reduce human existence or experience to one portion of it. As he put it in a later essay, "Wright could imagine Bigger, but Bigger could not possibly imagine Richard Wright."[26] Instead of limiting black humanity to Bigger Thomas, he told Burke, "I should like an esthetic which restores to man his full complexity."[27]

The trick, for Ellison, was building a narrative around such a representation of black life—while also speaking to a white audience. Their privileged social position, Ellison wrote, leaves "whites unable to see Negroes as the reincarnation of any of the values by which they live." The resulting clash between blacks' heightened self-consciousness and whites' unconscious prejudice means that "the two racial groups in this country lack the accord of sensibilities" that would lead to understanding. As a novelist, he admitted that this conflict placed him in a difficult situation, generating the haunting question cited in chapter 1: "How will a Negro writer who writes out of his full awareness of the complexity of western personality, and who presents the violence of American culture in psychological terms rather than physical ones—how will such a writer be able to break through the stereotype-armored minds of white Americans so that they can receive his message?"[28]

Ellison's was not a rhetorical question. He opened the paragraph with, "But now let me ask you a question," and ended it by restating the appeal: "This is a crucial problem with me just now and I would like to have your opinion."[29] The question was clear—as was his desire for a reply. Burke, though, proved unable to provide the desired answer. In part this is because, as discussed in chapter 2, Burke struggled to formulate *any* response to Ellison's letter. After beginning to outline an essay on the "Rhetoric of the Negro," he stopped before completing it; he composed a three-page, single-spaced letter of reply, but chose not to mail it. Burke's reluctance to respond spawned a nine-month silence, only broken when Burke hand-delivered his letter to Ellison during the latter's visit to Andover. Even then, however, Ellison's question remained unanswered. Rather than addressing Ellison's concern over whites' openness to complex representations of black existence, Burke expressed mistrust of what he called Ellison's "out-and-out battlecry kind of literature."[30]

Burke did not challenge Ellison's citation from the *Grammar*; on the contrary, he noted, "Your identification with Dostoevsky seems to me quite justified." The problem, according to Burke, was that Ellison's focus on Raskolnikov had blinded him to a more relevant comparison: "You must some day tell me how you can make any sense out of Dostoevsky without placing his Alyoshas and Myshkins at the very centre of his scheme."[31] Here Burke called Ellison's attention to characters (from *The Brothers Karamazov* and *The Idiot*) symbolizing innocence and unconditional love.[32] Indeed, Dostoevsky introduces Alyosha by describing how "the gift of making himself loved directly and unconsciously was inherent in him, in his very nature, so to speak."[33] For this reason, he is typically described in absolutes: "A Christ-like figure . . . He turns the other cheek; loves, forgives, and suffers for his fellows; takes no thought for worldly matters."[34]

Returning to the "possible sacrificial type" that he had proposed in his notes on the "Rhetoric of the Negro," Burke suggested that such a character provided a much better base for Ellison's novel than that proposed by its author. Burke fleshed out his alternative, a narrative organized around Dostoevsky's Alyosha and Myshkin: "To my way of thinking, the *ideal* Negro book contributing to the emancipation of the Negro would contain a character who was trying, right in the midst of the harshnesses of the white-black opposition, even to recover the spirituality of the spirituals." Rejecting Wright's Bigger in favor of Dostoevsky, Burke argued, meant envisioning "a figure who is struggling always to picture some little island of green, right in the midst of squalor." Such a character would not be forced into simple dichotomies—he would neither reject the black church nor automatically embrace it, neither reject his family nor wholly accept it. Burke consequently offered advice to Ellison on such a protagonist, describing him as "a figure who is beset even by the temptations of his own words, who finds that an attempt to improve himself is by implication a treachery against his people, that attempts to quiet his people are mainly serviceable to white landlords, indeed, who finds a contradiction at every turn. He would be ashamed of being tough, and ashamed of being tender. He would do far less than he wants to do; and whatever he does do, his motivations are distrusted not only by those whom he would help, but even by himself. He would, let us say, be a kind of figure off to one side." Only a novel built on such a character, he concluded, could "contribute to the *humanization* of the issue (in contrast with a character like Bigger, whose rapist power contributes dubiously to the *humanitarianization* of the issue)."[35]

Though pleased that Burke had finally broken his silence, Ellison found Burke's long-delayed answer unsatisfactory.[36] In a letter to Wright, sent after his return from Andover, Ellison complained that Burke had "attempted to set down a formula for a Negro character who would incorporate all the contradictions present in the Negro-white situation in this country and yet be appealing to whites," but had "arrived pretty much at a Dostoevskian *Idiot* type, aware of contradictions, but clinging to the spiritual element of the Spirituals."[37] Further, the months-long delay between question and response meant that Ellison had already begun to solidify his approach within the novel—making Burke's advice, from a practical perspective, unappealing. By the time Burke had set aside his letter of reply, Ellison had developed portions of the narrative; by the time Burke hand-delivered his letter, Ellison was "uncertain as to the body of the book" but "clear about its spine."[38]

From Ellison's perspective, what was most troubling about Burke's letter was the dissonance between Burke's view of his project and his own. "I've always preferred another Dostoevsky type," he told Wright, "the Ivans, or Dmitris, rather than the Aloyshas or Myshkins."[39] As he awaited Burke's reply, Ellison had begun to envision the novel as a dialectical progression from action to heightened vision, rooted in the Burkean terms of purpose, passion, and perception. Burke, by contrast, was suggesting a character built strictly upon suffering, upon passivity— an Aloysha rather than a Dmitri, a "figure off to one side." The novel, on Burke's view, would thus focus not upon the narrator's evolving perspective, but upon the less-than-idyllic world around him: "The central story could be the realistic life of battle, as poolroomy as the fashion requires."[40] After reading the letter, Ellison recognized that he clearly shared Burke's views about human symbolicity. Even more clearly, though, he saw that he did not share Burke's vision of the "*ideal* Negro book contributing to the emancipation of the Negro."

Thus, when Ellison needed to provide "a clear outline of the novel from start to finish," in order to complete a shift in publishers (from Reynal and Hitchcock to Random House), he turned not to Burke, but to Hyman and Jackson.[41] Holed up in their Vermont home, Ellison leaned upon his friends for advice—even soliciting a list of key authors from Hyman—in order to produce a document describing his vision for the novel.[42] Writing Hyman following his return to the city, Ellison reported the results of these efforts: "Just so you won't think I wasted my time up there, Random House thought the outline that I worked on there was quite a piece of writing—which it isn't—and that was an amusing surprise to me."[43] With his friends' help, Ellison had secured a new publisher and "hammered out a coherent statement about the novel he was now calling 'The Invisible Man.'"[44]

Though this was likely the first time that Hyman and Jackson contributed to *Invisible Man*, it was not the last. From its inception until publication, Hyman served as an important reader of portions of the narrative. Ellison escaped regularly to the Hyman-Jackson residence, where, manuscript in hand, he worked on the revision of existing sections and the creation of new ones.[45] Given his familiarity with the book, as Ellison neared its final pages Hyman was one of two friends whom Ellison trusted to help edit his manuscript.[46] Ellison even credited Hyman and Jackson with helping him complete the novel, writing Albert Murray that "I was having a little difficulty about that time . . . but I got over it and went on to turn in the book during April, having finished most of it at Hyman's place at Westport. I went there just about the time Shirley was doing the page proofs of *Hangsaman* and it was just the spur I needed."[47]

Given these contributions to *Invisible Man*, Ellison would later describe Hyman as "invaluable to me" during the process.[48] Yet, though Burke had a much less direct role in Ellison's creative process, this is not to say that Burke played little role in the novel's development. I believe that, in a sense, Ellison *was* in conversation with Burke as he worked on *Invisible Man*—that the text reflects the continuation of their dialogue on race, begun by "Richard Wright's Blues" and continued in *A Rhetoric of Motives*. As a result, I would read Ellison's novel as his published response to Burke, his award-winning (even "epoch-making") contribution to their ongoing conversation.[49] It is common for scholars to cite the Burkean structure of *Invisible Man*, and to point to the Burkean themes in Ellison's novel.[50] However, I believe that the narrator, especially in the prologue and epilogue, is doing more than alluding to Burkean concepts. Instead, I would describe him as speaking a kind of Burkese. To put it simply, I believe that the "vision" of Invisible Man, the "systematically widened" terminology displayed in his speech, betrays him as a black American Burkean.

Invisible Burke

"I am an invisible man," the narrator tells us—a sentence that represents the opening of the novel, and its birth.[51] Yet, upon first hearing this now-famous voice, Ellison was not inclined to listen; after typing the words, his impulse was to discard the page. But he hesitated: "Who, I asked myself, would make such a statement—and out of what kind of experience?"[52] He reflected upon "that pseudoscientific sociological concept which held that most Afro-American difficulties sprang from our 'high visibility'"; this character suggested instead that "'high visibility' actually rendered one *un*-visible."[53]

These first words from Invisible evoked a central theme, the seen and the unseen, the visible and the invisible—a theme that resonated with the black American experience, and with Ellison's own experiences. Ellison's Invisible Man is no science-fiction character launched from H. G. Wells's imagination; his invisibility is a social, not supernatural, product. Thus, following the narrator's first words, Ellison immediately offers a clarification: "I am invisible, understand, simply because people refuse to see me."[54] As Ellison sought to build a narrative from this opening line, he turned to many sources of inspiration—but few were as important to him as was Burke.[55]

Examination of Ellison's library indicates that, as he drew forth the implications of his narrator's opening line, he leaned upon Burke's work, but especially upon *Attitudes toward History*—that it played a vital role in the design and development of the narrator and his narrative. Ellison's detailed study of this text explains why, as Genter remarks, "Ellison's idiom [in *Invisible Man*] directly parallels the conceptual framework Burke constructed in his 1937 *Attitudes toward History*."[56] On a dog-eared page of the book, for example, Ellison placed a check mark next to a passage: "The eyes are the 'remotest' of the senses. They lack the immediacy that goes with experiences of taste or contact. They have been called a protrusion of the brain."[57]

This passage is dramatically brought to life in the novel's central character. In the opening of the prologue, Ellison's Invisible Man diagnoses the central cause of his invisibility. It has nothing to do with him—nothing, that is, that physiologically would cause invisibility: "That invisibility to which I refer occurs because of a peculiar disposition of the eyes of those with whom I come in contact. A matter of the construction of their *inner* eyes, those eyes with which they look through their physical eyes upon reality."[58] In other words, the narrator explains, his invisibility stems not from his own body, but from the perspectives animating others' eyes; they see him as an idea, not a person, composed of their assumptions and conceptions, not his flesh and blood. At one point he includes the reader among those responsible for his invisibility, "since you never recognize me even when in closest contact with me" (13).

What he means by this is quite specific; others' eyes create the conditions for his invisibility. They do not *take in* his image, but *project one onto* him—their vision functioning, in Burke's terms, not receptively but actively, as a "protrusion of the brain." Invisible uses this point to explain a recent encounter with a (presumably white) man, when an accidental jostling nearly led to bloodshed. After they collided, the man uttered an invective, provoking a violent response from Invisible. On the verge of killing the man, Invisible recalled his invisibility and realized the absurdity of the situation; he remembered that the man had not, in fact, *seen* him. Or, rather, what the man had seen was the product of his own imagination, imposed onto Invisible's body. "Then," the narrator wryly notes, "I was amused: Something in this man's thick head had sprung out and beaten him within an inch of his life" (5).

Invisible uses this episode to offer a broader claim about social life; he compares such studied misperception to a dream state. This point is reemphasized at the end of the prologue, when Invisible comments that the man he nearly killed "was lost in a dream world. But didn't *he* control that dream world—which, alas, is only too real!—and didn't *he* rule me out of it?" (14). Invisible describes the man as less awake than asleep; for such a man, his eyes do not perceive the world as it is, but as refracted through the peculiar internal logic of his dream. Invisible thus calls the man a dreamer, a sleepwalker, but one who may never awaken—he may even, Invisible muses, be asleep at the moment of death. Invisible sadly reflects that this episode is not an isolated incident; entire communities, like the man, spend their lives asleep—a point he keeps in mind since "there are few things in the world as dangerous as sleepwalkers" (5).

In these moments from the prologue, Ellison's narrator echoes Burke's comment about the active, projective nature of eyesight. However, Burke does not simply argue that the eyes sculpt their objects of vision to fit a particular conception of the world; he also emphasizes the necessarily limited nature of the resulting perspective. In *Permanence and Change*, Burke writes: "A way of seeing is also a way of not seeing—a focus upon object A involves a neglect of object B."[59] In *Attitudes toward History*, Burke extends this point, contending that "people are *necessarily* mistaken, that *all* people are exposed to situations in which they must act as fools, that *every* insight contains its own special kind of blindness."[60]

Drawing upon these Burkean meditations, Invisible explains his point about the prevalence of sleepwalkers, singling out white Americans as blind to their privilege and prejudice—and to him. Late in the novel, Invisible describes his shattering recognition of the perspectival similarity shared by all of the white men he had encountered. Despite their apparent differences, "Jack and Norton and Emerson merge[d] into one single white figure. They were very much the same, each attempting to force his picture of reality upon me and neither giving a hoot in hell for how things looked to me. I was simply a natural resource to be used" (508).

Yet, according to *Invisible Man*, white Americans are not the only ones afflicted with this Burkean blindness; just as the novel contains a glass-eyed-Jack, it also contains a sightless Rev. Barbee. Thus, Invisible eventually expands his equation of Jack, Norton, and Emerson to include the central black figures in his life, including his college president, Dr. Bledsoe; Bledsoe is indistinguishable from these white men, Invisible concludes, given their identical "confusion, impatience, and refusal to recognize the beautiful absurdity of their American identity and mine" (559). Similarly, when confronted by Ras the Destroyer's men at the end of the novel, Invisible laments their blindness and longs for "a few simple words, a mild, even a meek, muted action to clear the air. To awaken them and me" (557, 559).

In Burke's terms, sleepwalkers, black or white, are wedded to one way of seeing—wedded so fully that when something falls outside their narrowed visual field, they fail to see it. They are blind to that which they are not trained to perceive; the penalty for this consistent, partial insight is the life of the sleepwalker. The guidance for action provided by the sleepwalker's dreams comes at a price: the loss of direct contact with others, and the world. Not only, then, does Invisible find himself unseen, invisible to others' eyes, but also uniquely aware of the conditions that render him invisible. By claiming that he is, as he says, "aware of my invisibility" (5), he indicates that he is able to recognize what the sleepwalkers are not, the limited nature of their perspective. Invisible confesses that he, too, was once a sleepwalker: "I myself, after existing some twenty years, did not become alive until I discovered my invisibility" (7).

The two realizations are linked; Ellison's narrator awakened to his invisibility by recognizing the narrowed perspectives of those he encountered—and vice versa. Further, he describes this breakthrough with a decidedly Burkean phrase. Late in the novel, the jarring news of his (and Harlem's) betrayal by the Brotherhood shreds Invisible's comfortable view of others, and thus of himself: "It was as though I'd learned suddenly to look around corners; images of past humiliations flickered through my head and I saw that they were more than separate experiences. They were me; they defined me. I was my experiences and my experiences were me, and no blind men, no matter how powerful they became, even if they conquered the world, could take that, or change one single itch, taunt, laugh, cry, scar, ache, rage or pain of it. They were blind, bat blind, moving only by the echoed sounds of their own voices" (508). The novel repeatedly invokes this theme; in the prologue, Invisible suggests that seeing around corners "is not unusual when you are invisible," and, following a drug-fueled encounter with Louis Armstrong's music, even suggests the possibility of *hearing* around them (13).[61]

Ellison's appropriation of this phrase is deliberate; his copy of *Attitudes* indicates that he focused a great deal of attention upon it.[62] On a page bearing the marks of Ellison's careful study, Burke defines the power to "see around the corner" as the ability to step outside the familiar boundaries of one's perspective, to refuse the easy limitations of a particular way of seeing. Rather than remaining within a single perspective, someone able to "see around the corner" of their perspective sees what lies behind and beneath it; she primarily glimpses not the object of perception, but her perceptual framework itself. Gaining perspective upon her customary perspective, such a person is "seeing from two angles at once."[63] This escape from restricted perception, Burke writes, marks the person as "'prophetic,' endowed with 'perspective.'"[64] In the prologue, Ellison's narrator announces that he has achieved such insight, that he now has the ability to see around corners. Blind and asleep before, he tells us, "Now I see. I've illuminated the blackness of my invisibility—and vice versa" (13). Yet, seeing from "two angles at once," he muses, means more than this; it also means, "I now can see the darkness of lightness" (6).

According to Burke, this prophetic insight, characteristic of one capable of "seeing around corners," is generated through a process of rebirth—since "change of identity (whereby he is at once the same man and a new man) gives him a greater complexity of coordinates."[65] In a passage heavily marked by Ellison, Burke explains this point further: "Rebirth is a process of socialization, since it is a ritual whereby the poet fits himself to accept necessities suggested to him by the problems of the forensic. It will also, as regression, involve concern with the 'womb-heaven' of the embryo, and with the 'first revolution' that took place when the embryo developed to the point where its 'shelter' became 'confinement.' Hence, when you examine this ritual, you find such symbols as the 'pit,' a symbolic return-to and return-from the womb."[66] Echoing Burke, Ellison traces Invisible's "greater complexity of coordinates" to a process of rebirth. When the novel opens, its central events have already unfolded; he is living underground, in a space reminiscent of Burke's "pit." The narrator takes great pains to distinguish it from a grave—and to emphasize the womblike character of his shelter. His hole, he insists, does not signify death, but life; he reminds the reader that "there are cold holes and warm holes. Mine is a warm hole" (6). This hole is not a grave but a place of rebirth, he explains, calling himself a hibernating Jack-the-bear—whose emergence will be "like the Easter chick breaking from its shell" (6).

Given this imagery, we are already prepared for the moment of rebirth, the return from the womb/pit that will display the breadth of insight characteristic of one newly capable of seeing (or hearing) "around the corner."[67] However, when the novel begins, Invisible is still in the process of building this new, broadened perspective. As a result, he assures the skeptical reader that his hole functions as a space of illumination, not rest or confinement—or, as he says, it is a place of light, not darkness: "Yes, full of light. I doubt if there is a brighter spot in all New York than this hole of mine, and I do not exclude Broadway. Or the Empire State Building on a photographer's dream night" (6). Ellison's narrator means this literally. He has wired the ceiling, and at least one wall, with 1,369 lights, which he uses to illuminate his home, thanks to an illicit link to an electrical line. In part, this project offers a concrete indicator of his progress toward rebirth; when the novel opens, he still has some walls and the floor to wire before he will have completed his project of self-illumination.[68]

The prologue suggests the Burkean significance of this Edisonian installation: "Nothing, storm or flood, must get in the way of our need for light and ever more and brighter light. The truth is the light and light is the truth" (7). As he filled his hole with light, Invisible writes in the epilogue, he began "trying to look through myself" (572). The result was insight, not only into the production of his invisibility, but the creation of reality itself: "Step outside the narrow borders of what men call reality and you step into chaos . . . or imagination. That too I've learned in the cellar, and not by deadening my sense of perception; I'm invisible, not blind" (576). He describes this as a revelation accompanying his changes of identity: "I've come a long way from those days when, full of illusion, I lived a public life and attempted to function under the assumption that the world was solid and all the relationships therein" (576).

Thanks to his immersion in the hole—the process of renewal producing his newfound awareness—he is able to see what others do not: the symbolic constitution of reality. This is the illumination cast within the hole, the light missing from those who blindly plot their course according to their customary coordinates; this is the insight that distinguishes the brightness of his hole from the darkness of New York. Invisible's light-saturated hibernation has given him a more complex set of coordinates, a broadened terminology for the "charting of human relationships."[69]

Interestingly, in the prologue, Invisible indicates that he enlisted an ally in this project. His quest for light, he explains, required the help of another to amass the necessary supplies: "A junk man I know, a man of vision, has supplied me with wire and sockets" (7). I believe this is Ellison's nod to Burke—a characterization of him as the bricoleur who provided assistance in the construction of Invisible's light-filled womb.[70] I would further suggest that these wires and sockets, the raw materials of Invisible's illumination, represent the components of Burke's comic frame from *Attitudes toward History*.

In this text, Burke famously advocates the comic frame for the charting of human relationships; he characterizes it as the foremost of the "frames of acceptance," the "'strategies' for living" that provide "the mental equipment (meanings, attitudes, character) by which one handles the significant factors of his time."[71] Burke's contention is that human beings symbolically equip themselves to engage their social and natural environment. Our acts of naming carve the world in particular ways, and thereby suggest attitudes we should take toward it—thus also creating our character. Since a symbolic framework is a "more or less organized system of meanings by which a thinking man gauges the historical situation and adopts a role with relation to it," one's choice of framework is quite consequential.[72] The comic represents the most "well-rounded" of these symbolic frameworks, Burke's "attitude of attitudes."

The comic frame is the most "well-rounded" because unlike the (all-too-common) tragic frame, the comic does not center upon victimage, but upon the limitations endemic to symbol use. "The process of humane enlightenment," Burke argues, "can go no further than in picturing people not as *vicious*, but as *mistaken*."[73] Because human action relies upon symbolic structures that are necessarily partial, error—or "blindness"—is an inevitable result. The comic frame calls us not to vengeance against those whose perspectives differ, but to the ironic appreciation of our common symbolic finitude, and a cooperative attitude toward the amelioration of conflict. At the same time, comedy is quite unlike humor, with which it is often confused. Burke argues that humor seeks to dispel dissonance in favor of sentimentality or blithe unconcern; as a result, humor "does not make for so completely well-rounded a frame of acceptance as comedy, since it tends to gauge a situation falsely."[74] By contrast, Burke writes, the comic frame is "charitable, but at the same time it is not gullible"; it aims at a realistic assessment of a situation "by astutely gauging situation and personal resources."[75]

Ellison's introduction to the thirtieth-anniversary edition of *Invisible Man* suggests that both the novel and Invisible's character were constructed upon a comic foundation; early on, he decided that the narrator "would be one who had been forged in the underground of American experience and yet managed to emerge less angry than ironic. That he would be a blues-toned laugher-at-wounds who included himself in his indictment of the human condition."[76] Here, Ellison acknowledges choosing irony over victimage, human finitude over human viciousness—comedy, in short, over tragedy in his depiction of American life.[77] Not surprisingly, terms associated with the comic frame are echoed throughout Ellison's novel, but especially in the prologue and epilogue, as Invisible describes his newfound awareness—the product of his immersion in his light-filled hole.[78]

We can, for example, see Burke's comic ideal—*"maximum consciousness"*[79]—in Invisible's claim to have "illuminated the blackness of my invisibility—and vice versa," and in his confession that "I love light . . . need light, desire light" (13, 6). Burke indicates that comic consciousness requires, and is signaled by, heightened self-awareness, another point linking the comic frame with Ellison's narrator. The comic frame, Burke tells us, "promotes the realistic sense of one's limitations," by "making a man the student of himself."[80] Invisible embodies this ideal thanks to his illuminating hibernation, since he now is "aware of my invisibility," concluding that "the world is just as concrete, ornery, vile and sublimely wonderful as before, only now I better understand my relation to it and it to me" (5, 576). Invisible's descent into the depths of Armstrong's music, his ability "to hear the silence of sound," and his unsettling experience of both seeing and hearing around corners, testify to the—sometimes unbearable—degree of consciousness that he achieves in regard to his social existence (13).

Similarly, in the epilogue, Ellison's narrator articulates the broadened nature of his perspective, the comic insight gained through his rebirth—in Burkean terms. *Attitudes toward History* opens by contrasting the "'*voluntary* alternatives' between which 'in a given case of evil the mind seesaws'": "To 'accept the universe' or to 'protest against it.'"[81] Ellison's narrator confesses to such an attitudinal swing in his journey toward illumination; Invisible admits that "like almost everyone else in our country, I started out with my share of optimism. I believed in hard work and progress and action" (576). He describes this as "being 'for' society"—the choice to accept the universe, to pledge allegiance to the symbols of authority comprising one's culture (576).[82] However, his struggles with the stubbornness and violence of racism alienated him from these dominant symbols, turning him "then 'against'" them (576).

Invisible's development reflects a typical progression, according to Burke: "'Rejection' is but a by-product of 'acceptance.' It involves primarily a matter of emphasis. It takes its color from an attitude towards some reigning symbol of authority, stressing a shift in the allegiance to symbols of authority. It is the heretical aspect of an orthodoxy—and as such, it has much in common with the 'frame of acceptance' that it rejects."[83] Rejection is a common response to disillusion with "symbols of authority." Yet, since rejection and acceptance differ in emphasis, not in kind, a rejection frame does not represent a real break with symbols of authority. To reject an "authority" is to acknowledge its sway. This is why, I believe, Invisible sees his life to have consisted of uncritical acceptance—until "I became ill of affirmation, of saying 'yes' against the nay-saying of my stomach—not to mention my brain" (573).[84] Since rejection frames "tend to lack the well-rounded quality" characteristic of an adequate charting of society, Burke contends that the "partiality of negation" must be replaced by "the completeness of acceptance"—but a different order of acceptance than the first, a frame that "'negates the negation,'" and thereby makes possible a new social order.[85]

It is this comic acceptance, I contend, that Ellison's narrator achieves in the epilogue. After accepting, then rejecting, the reigning symbols of authority, he now embraces a different attitude; he has attained a Burkean "equilibrium":[86] "after first being 'for' society and then 'against' it, I assign myself no rank or any limit, and such an attitude is very much against the trend of the times. But my world has become one of infinite possibilities" (576). This Burkean mash-up of counter-statement and comic frame is, Invisible suggests, the attitude necessary to confront the fact that, for black and white Americans, "life is to be lived, not controlled; and humanity is won by continuing to play in face of certain defeat" (577).

Combining irony, humility, and insight into the symbolic constitution of reality, Invisible's perspective aims at an accurate charting of American life. Ellison's narrator revisits the puzzling advice of his long-dead grandfather, and muses: "Could he have meant—hell, he *must* have meant the principle, that we were to affirm the principle on which the country was built and not on the men, or at least not the men who did the violence" (574).[87] In part, this reflects Invisible's growing belief that a solution to social ills requires black Americans' affirmation of both the promise and the viciousness of America—or the promise in the face of the viciousness, "the plan in whose name we had been brutalized and sacrificed" (574).

Invisible's comic affirmation seeks not to divide white from black— to seek a tragic victim for punishment—but to recognize our common (symbolic *and* nonsymbolic) substance. Given our shared investment in American democracy, and rootedness in "the loud, clamoring semi-visible world," Invisible points out that white and black Americans are indissolubly linked (574). Further, this connection underscores the irony of whites' segregationist efforts: "Hell, weren't they their own death and their own destruction except as the principle lived in them and in us? And here's the cream of the joke: Weren't we *part of them*, as well as apart from them and subject to die when they died?" (575).[88] Invisible's new perspective emphasizes the symbolic production of reality, the unity of opposites—and the possibility of uniting black and white Americans under a broader, comic form of acceptance. "Our fate," Invisible asserts, "is to become one, and yet many—This is not prophecy, but description" (577).

Even as he recalls that whites have "violated and compromised [American principles] to the point of absurdity," Ellison's narrator cites the symbolicity uniting black and white Americans, the shared condition that inevitably generates error and blindness (574). He thereby announces the complex frame of acceptance cultivated by his time underground: "Now I denounce and defend, or feel prepared to defend. I condemn and affirm, say no and say yes, say yes and say no" (579). Recognizing white Americans' acts as premised not upon criminality but upon human limitation—a response to "the human greed and smallness, yes, and the fear and superstition that had kept them running"—Invisible displays

Burke's charitable, but not gullible, comic consciousness. (574). "I sell you no phony forgiveness," he remarks, "but too much of your life will be lost, its meaning lost, unless you approach it as much through love as through hate" (580).

Having adopted this Burke-fueled comic vision, Invisible finds himself called back to the world. He expresses misgivings about this next, uncertain stage of his journey; he both echoes and questions Burke, asking, "Yes, but what *is* the next phase?" (576).[89] At first, he admits, "the next step I couldn't make," and so "I've remained in the hole" (575). By the end of the epilogue, however, he embraces this phase—and ends his time underground. His shelter now a space of confinement, Invisible declares that the time has come for rebirth: "The hibernation is over. I must shake off the old skin and come up for breath" (580).

Invisible recognizes that he will emerge from his hole looking no different than when he entered; his comic consciousness will render him "no less invisible" than before (581). Nonetheless, he tells us, he will emerge transformed. He will be reborn as Burke's "poet-plus-critic," one who "both acts and observes his act."[90] As poet-plus-critic, Invisible's next phase necessarily involves action; he assures us, "I believe in nothing if not in action" (13). Yet, this will not be the selfish, blind action of a sleepwalker or dreamer. Equipped with an adequately complex set of coordinates, he realizes that "even an invisible man has a socially responsible role to play" (581).

Burke gives us a clue to the nature of this role, in a passage heavily marked by Ellison. Imagine, Burke says, a man who meets "new people, not on their merits, but on the basis of some likeness they suggest to people he met in the past."[91] The social function of the comic frame is to provide a vehicle for the transformation of a limiting (dreamlike) structure of meanings: "Were this man, by critical conceptualization, to locate the particular set of conditions that thus negatively incite him, he would be prepared to 'discount' them."[92] Invisible offers a strikingly similar account of the role that he is now prepared to play aboveground, thanks to his time below. In fact, he suggests at the novel's end, the narrative is his vehicle for transformation—a transformation of both the reader and himself. The epilogue, and *Invisible Man* itself, thus closes with his comic call to wakefulness, self-illumination, and clarity: "Being invisible and without substance, a disembodied voice, as it were, what else could I do? What else but try to tell you what was really happening when your eyes were looking through? And it is this which frightens me: Who knows but that, on the lower frequencies, I speak for you?" (581).

Speaking to Burke

Given Ellison's creative appropriation of *Attitudes*, it is tempting to twist the famous question at the end of *Invisible Man*—and ask whether Ellison's narrator does not simply "speak for" Burke, but speak *as* Burke. *Invisible Man* borrows more from Burke than the "'tragic' grammar" of purpose, passion, and perception; the book offers a Burkean narrator whose words reflect Ellison's adoption and adaptation of the comic frame. But the Burkean influence on this work is not limited to the novel's prologue and epilogue; the episodes between these famous bookends display a distinctly Burkean emphasis on the "ritualistic naming and changing of identity," a process carefully constructed to imbue the narrator with an appropriately complex level of insight into American life.[93]

Yet, Ellison's novel also includes implicit critiques of Burke; we might wonder whether Ellison's "speaking for" Burke might equally be a speaking *to* Burke. As Eddy indicates, the novel certainly contains "hints that Ellison is speaking to Burke personally."[94] One example appears in the prologue, when Ellison takes issue with Burke's "curve of history" from *Attitudes*. "Beware of those who speak of the *spiral* of history," the narrator warns, since "they are preparing a boomerang. Keep a steel helmet handy" (6; original emphasis).

However, given Burke's late reference to "unconscious Nortonism in our own thinking," one character may have hit especially (uncomfortably) close to home.[95] Though not solely a comment on Burke, there are clues that Burke is one of the figures symbolized by the figure of Mr. Norton.[96] Norton, the rich white philanthropist whom Invisible is fatefully asked to chauffeur, is described as short in stature, and having "a face pink like St. Nicholas', topped with a shock of silk white hair," a description that could easily apply to Burke (37).[97] Ellison similarly alludes to Burke's *The White Oxen* when he points out to Norton a "team of oxen hitched to a broken-down wagon" (40).[98] Like Eddy, I find it significant that, though assisted by Invisible, "Norton can see neither the oxen nor the people laboring alongside them for the trees."[99] Perhaps a comment on Burke's inability to recognize Ellison as different from Wright, on Burke's inability to answer Ellison's November 1945 letter, or on Burke's stereotype-laden description of the "ideal" novel about black Americans, this moment in the novel seems a clear indictment of Norton's—Burke's—lack of vision.

Later episodes also display Norton's blindness, the reverse of his insight. Inside the Golden Day, for example, "the vet" rebukes Norton for his paternalism toward the young narrator; to Norton, the vet remarks, Invisible "is a mark on the scorecard of your achievement, a thing and not a man; a child, or even less—a black amorphous thing. And you, for all your power, are not a man to him, but a God, a force" (95). Similarly, at the novel's end, when Norton unexpectedly appears in the subway, Invisible finds the man still unable to recognize Invisible. Norton's indignant confusion prompts Ellison's narrator to render a pentadic judgment: "Mr. Norton, if you don't know *where* you are, you probably don't know *who* you are" (578; original emphasis).

Just as Invisible uses the scene-agent ratio against Norton, it appears that Ellison, in *Invisible Man*, turned his Burkean gaze upon Burke himself—distancing himself somewhat from his friend and ancestor. Indications of Ellison's increasing ambivalence appear not just in his manuscript, but also in his correspondence. Writing Hyman in mid-1948, for example, Ellison was more critic than disciple—especially regarding Burke's newest publication, a selection from *A Rhetoric of Motives*. "There's little news here," he reported, adding that "I've read Kenneth's piece in the Hudson, finding it o.k., small o, small k. I expected something more exciting, being involved in my own imagery of killing, which I hope is more complex and the kind that giveth life and light."[100] Significantly, he did not offer this judgment to Burke, but to Hyman. Though Ellison asked Hyman for Burke's address a year later,[101] no letter ensued—and the publication of *A Rhetoric of Motives* would only drive them further apart.

As described at the end of chapter 2, Burke's citation of "Richard Wright's Blues" generated a quick rebuke from Ellison. Although Ellison and Hyman proposed a visit to Andover to discuss this passage, the visit fell through when Hyman's son was injured in an accident.[102] They had more luck the following summer. It was agreed that the Ellisons would visit Andover on Saturday, 25 August, that Hyman and Jackson would arrive on Sunday, and that all four would leave on Monday.[103] The visit was partly designed to give Ellison and Hyman an opportunity to dispute Burke's characterization of Ellison in the *Rhetoric*—and so was motivated by concerns both personal and professional.

Though the reunion took place, afterward Burke indicated his dissatisfaction with the weekend—not because of the debate over the *Rhetoric*, but because the Ellisons left Andover earlier than expected. Burke displayed hurt feelings in the postscript to a letter to Hyman: "The Ellisons were presumably disgrunt! Livnlearn!"[104] Hyman did not share Burke's assessment since he made light of Burke's complaint: "I don't understand what you mean by the Ellisons being 'disgrunt.' Not so far as I know. Please explain. Poor old Burke, he was quite a gay fellow until these general delusions of persecution caught up with him."[105]

Resisting Hyman's diagnosis, Burke retorted that his delusions were not the problem: "I want to help you somewhat modify or subtilize your notions about me and my sense of Persecyoosh. It does, I admit, keep dodging in and about. And if I lost it, I'd be as frightened as if I had lost my shadow (for like a pursuing shadow, it depends upon my substance). But in the main, I think, it is 'socio-anagogically' rather than individually motivated."[106] Burke's efforts to justify his discontent are enlightening. He explains his irritation with the Ellisons by referring to a term from the *Rhetoric*, the "socioanagogic": "Even the world of natural objects must have secret 'identification' with the judgments of status. . . . By 'socioanagogic' interpretation we mean the search for such implicit identifications."[107]

Based upon this explication of the term, it seems that Burke's "delusions" derived from the link between social hierarchy and his faculties of perception. In other words, Burke here indicates that his delusions are not idiosyncratic, but instead involve the imposition of social categories upon the world of experience. Thus, his letter suggests, his perceptions are grounded not in personal bias, but in the implicit identifications that unite things, places, and persons with the hierarchies of identity and rank. His belief, then, that the Ellisons were disgruntled appears to have a racial component to it; he was disposed to read their actions in light of their socially engendered differences, and to respond accordingly.

Perhaps alerted by Hyman to Burke's discontent, Fanny Ellison sent a conciliatory letter to Libbie. She emphasized that their early departure had a perfectly innocent explanation, and that it did not indicate any hostility toward the Burkes: "We would have liked to have stayed out for the remainder of the week we were there, but as I explained, Ralph had to return to the city and as it turned out it was good that I did too." Fanny's letter also underscored the importance of their friendship: "There aren't many places that we go, nor many people whom we see—six families in all—but these six, among whom are you and Kenneth, are very important to us and it is always a joy to see you and share in your hospitality and friendliness."[108] Though these apologies seemed to suffice, the tensions generated by the visit to Andover were soon compounded by the long-delayed arrival of *Invisible Man*. After its publication, Ellison found Burke a far less receptive audience than he had hoped—a development that had additional repercussions for their personal and intellectual relationship.

Jealousy, Injury, Ambivalence: *Invisible Man*

In April 1952, nearly seven years after its birth in a Vermont barn, Ellison's *Invisible Man* finally appeared in print. Its debut was no small affair, thanks to the overwhelmingly positive reviews it received from established literary figures—and especially from white critics.[109] It was an instant success, by any measure: "From the moment *Invisible Man* arrived in the nation's bookstores in April of 1952, it was an American literary classic. Within three weeks it was number 14 on the *New York Times* best-seller list."[110] Yet, one voice was conspicuously missing from this chorus of praise. Despite the distance that had crept into their relationship, Ellison cared a great deal about Burke's opinion; after all, the novel had originally been dedicated to Burke, and was built on a Burkean foundation. Ellison, as a result, was quite disappointed when Burke did not celebrate the novel's release—or even take note of it.

In a letter to Burke soon after the publication of *Invisible Man*, Hyman entered a plea on Ellison's behalf. "I saw Ralph Monday," he commented, "and he was awaiting Delphic word from you."[111] Given Burke's ancestral status and the Burkean framework of the novel, Hyman's invocation of the Olympian gods does not exaggerate the importance Ellison placed on Burke's opinion. When a few days passed, Hyman concluded that Burke had not taken the bait. His next message to Burke again broached the subject: "Ralph says he still hasn't had word from you."[112]

Prodded into action by Hyman's letters, Burke sent his belated congratulations to Ellison—although, even then, his remarks were restricted to a postcard. Burke apologized, explaining that he "had time only to find that you have a *very* effective beginning"—one familiar from early excerpts—and that "your treatment of the Light theme is a basic discovery." Burke deferred further judgment until later, ruefully stating, "Am in a jam at the moment, but hope to write you fairly soon about your book."[113] In a scrawled postscript at the bottom of the card, he avoided comment on the novel's racial dimensions, but complimented Ellison on its rhetorical insight: "From what I see by looking around here and there, I feel sure you really do have the solid stuff to contribute on the basic concerns with idea and image. (If I may speak 'generically'!)."[114] He also commented that, though he had not finished the book, the publicity effort pointed to "a very friendly press."

Buoyed by Burke's note, Ellison waited for another letter, one containing Burke's final pronouncements on the novel's merit. Months later, Burke's promised follow-up still unsent, Ellison expressed disappointment, though not to Burke. Writing a mournful letter to Hyman, Ellison closed: "That's about it. I haven't heard from that Kenneth; hope I didn't offend his sensibilities. Probably up to *his* ass in symbolics."[115] Ellison here again links Norton and Burke; his words echo a passage from *Invisible Man*, when Invisible explains Jim Trueblood's transgressions to Mr. Norton: "His face reddened. I was confused, feeling ... fear that I had talked too much and offended his sensibilities" (49). Moved by Ellison's letter, Hyman tried once more to spur their reluctant friend to action, telling Burke in late November that he had received "a long sad letter from Ralph."[116] Burke proved impervious to Hyman's hints and did not write the promised letter.

Burke's silence persisted into the new year, even as the accolades for Ellison's novel continued to mount. In January 1953, Ellison won the National Book Award Gold Medal for fiction—which provided a substantial cash prize, an opportunity to meet heroes like William Faulkner, and a launch pad for his ascent into the world of literary celebrity.[117] Upon receiving the award, he later reported feeling as though "lightning [had] struck me, leaving me standing amazed."[118] He wrote Hyman almost immediately, with an invitation to the award ceremony: "If you and Shirley happen to have to be in town around Tues. the 27th, wear your good clothes as I am supposed to be one of the important figures in a national ceremony about which I am not supposed to tell. Should you guess what I mean (there's a coin involved, I'm told) keep it to yourself."[119] Recognizing the significance of this honor for their friend, Hyman and Jackson replied by telegram: "Just heard news. Ten million congratulations."[120] From Burke, Ellison heard nothing.

Hyman, concerned for the fate of the friendship, again urged Burke to break his silence: "Today Ralph receives the Nat'l Book Award gold medal for 1952 fiction, and I hope you will write him a letter. He is still quite hurt that you never wrote more than a postcard on his novel."[121] Hyman even wrote Ellison's address in the margin, in a less-than-subtle attempt to goad Burke into action. Burke did not heed Hyman's advice, but he was quite aware of Ellison's successes; in a subsequent letter to Hyman, Burke indicated that his silence was not a simple oversight: "Heard Ralph's phonogenic voice on radio the other day. Missed first part—but from point at which I tuned in, he seemed to be faring quite well. In his joyous world of T. S. Eliots and Harvey Brights and Irving and Hows, he doesn't need the likes of me to say him yea. (Incidentally, the situation being what it is today, I think he has a good chance of being 'groomed' for a role of considerable politico-cultural importance. I say this in all seriousness.)"[122] Burke's silence, in other words, stemmed from his belief that Ellison had graduated to celebrity status—that, given the literary figures lining up behind him, and his novel's "fit" with political trends, Ellison no longer required Burke's affirmation.

Burke's letter deflected attention from his silence to Ellison's rising fame, but Hyman would not desist: "I am glad to see all the mists vanish, except the one about Ralph, where I still think you are wrong, and losing a good friend for reasons of disagreement that can be peaceably handled in the community of honest men. As for your unconcern with the forms of rejection, what kind of symbowelic actionist are you?"[123] This Burkean appeal—or the prospect of the end of the friendship—touched a chord. Burke's reply included a contrite aside: "(Psst. I'll be good, and write to Ralph. My aloofness has been due not to grouch, but to fact that I still haven't done my lessons. And if you knew how I have been beset, you'd know why I haven't done my lessons. Also, you'd know that I'll be quite some time yet. But I'll get around to it, that I will.)"[124]

Receiving Burke's letter, Hyman expressed relief, remarking, "It is good news that you are . . . not really unralphed, and have at least a throat left to lump."[125] Though Hyman made no further comment, hidden in Burke's apologia is a startling revelation—*a year after its publication, Burke had not read Ellison's novel*. Several months later, in another exchange with Hyman, Burke again confessed that he had not finished the text.[126] Celebrating the publication of Jackson's *Life among the Savages*, Burke promised a report, when he had time; of course, he coyly informed Hyman, "I can give the report much more quickly if you and Shirley allow me to read this book before I finish the second two-thirds of Ralph's. Or is that too obviously political a move?"[127] Hyman replied, with good-natured disapproval: "Finishing Shirley's book before Ralph's may not be political, but it certainly shows a discouraging preference for large type and wide margins."[128]

At this point, the interpersonal storm over *Invisible Man* had apparently blown over. Ellison had been hurt by Burke's silence over the novel but was able to move beyond it, especially as his own schedule filled in the wake of the novel's success. Libbie and Fanny exchanged friendly letters in 1954, discussing a trip to Andover that never transpired.[129] Ellison indicated interest in reuniting with Hyman and Burke—just as in the previous decade—before he left to spend six weeks in Austria, teaching in the Salzburg Seminar in American Studies.[130] Later, a lengthy letter to Hyman, sent during his yearlong residency at the American Academy in Rome, was notable for Ellison's warm reminiscences about Burke: "The talk here ain't very good, until some character like Roethke, or R Penn Warren (with whom I had a most interesting talk about KB, whom he admires) and I make up for the dead spots.... It was, by the way, very pleasant to learn that Warren was as stimulated by *Counter Statement* as I was. He thinks K. is a great man, as do I. Eight months with dry as dust scholars foaming at the mouth whenever some amateur writes about Rome or makes a classical allusion, has given me even deeper appreciation for that old rascal than ever before. I only wish now that I had his books here with me."[131] Though Ellison seems to have forgotten the dispute, Burke remained somewhat ambivalent about their friendship, and about Ellison himself. Burke continued to display admiration for his friend's abilities, as when he helped secure a grant for Ellison from the National Institute for Arts and Letters. Burke was modest in discussing the award with Hyman—"I can take no greater credit than the claim to have been Among Those Present. I'm just on the Membership Committee"—but this modesty hid his efforts to ensure Ellison received the grant.[132]

At the same time, Burke's letter to Hyman is not altogether supportive of Ellison. His characterization of Ellison, for example, was not exactly flattering: "one s. of a b. for whom I plugged in the litry dept. is being handsomely granted this year." Burke apparently had second thoughts about this characterization, adding a typed correction: "and a good friend of ours, unless he mushrooms into the stratosphere, as he might." This was apparently insufficient, and so he amended his description further, adding below his first correction a parenthetical: "(I say 's. of a b.' endearingly)."[133] Burke drew lines and arrows between these three lines, endeavoring to soften the initial sentiments. Hyman's response mocked the tortured prose and conflicting emotions in Burke's letter: "Are the s.o.b. you refer to, and the good friend, two people (your prose is more than usually ambiguous) or are they both Ralph?"[134] Burke gloomily replied, "I might have known you'd know about Ralph before he did."[135]

Though the issues raised by *Invisible Man* disappeared from the surface discussion related to the relationship, as this letter demonstrates Burke seems to have had difficulty reconciling himself to Ellison's success. His characterization of Ellison—as a friend, as long as he does not "mushroom into the stratosphere"—demonstrates that the shock of *Invisible Man's* success had not worn off, three years after its release. The subject quietly disappeared from Burke's correspondence after this exchange with Hyman, but reappeared in a 1957 letter from Burke to another literary scholar, George Knox.

Within the letter, Burke thanked Knox for sending along some recent articles. Since one of the essays discussed the work of several contemporary black writers, it also prompted Burke to offer a jarring reflection on his relationship with Ellison: "You should send an offprint of the Negro one to Ellison, if you haven't already. I don't have his present address, but I think I can get it for you if you want it. I used to see him on and off; he and his wife have been out here a few times; but I got so irritated with an ass-kissing job he did on Eliot in an interview, I still haven't finished his Invisible Man. (Mainly, of course, it was a matter of being busy. But I think I'd have finished it anyhow had I not felt prima-donnishly irritated by the Eliot line.) Incidentally, on our recorder we have his reading of the free-for-all episode (battle royal), which is quite effective."[136] Two points are notable in this letter—one sharply different in tone than those written to their mutual friend, Hyman. First, Burke fails to claim Ellison as a current friend—he does not even have Ellison's address, he says, though he thinks (but does not know) he could get it. His language relegates the relationship to the past and classifies it as superficial, a surprising development in and of itself, given their (at that point) fifteen-year relationship. Burke also admits in the letter—*more than five years after its publication*—that he never finished reading Ellison's novel. When we consider that this book was initially dedicated to Burke, this admission is simply astonishing. Moreover, since Burke read every word written by Hyman and Jackson (regardless of his workload), Burke's abandonment of *Invisible Man* seems no accident; as he implies in the letter to Knox, it was most certainly a deliberate act.

Though the evidence indicates that Burke intentionally halted his reading of the novel, the motive behind this decision is less clear. Distance had begun to creep into the relationship between Ellison and Burke—and the Ellisons' visits to Andover seemed only to damage the relationship further. However, several letters from Burke suggest that his act was motivated, at least in part, by feelings of jealousy and abandonment. Their relationship began with Burke serving as Ellison's cherished mentor, his ancestor; a few years later, Ellison achieved an almost overnight celebrity, making Burke's continued guidance (Burke feared) unnecessary. He felt that Ellison, having achieved success, was leaving him behind. This would have hurt even more because Burke's own work was then receiving only a fraction of the attention given Ellison's—and any attention that it did receive was quite unwelcome.

In the early 1950s, when McCarthyism dominated American politics, Burke was one of those caught in its grip—as an example of the

"Communist sympathizer" with whom "patriotic" Americans were at war. This framing of Burke proved consequential when a 1952 appointment as a visiting professor in Washington State was revoked. That sudden reversal was a result of his 1930s membership in suspected Communist organizations, making him "an object of strong political fears."[137] His prominence in the League of American Writers, and associations with members of the Communist Party, no longer looked innocuous in the harsh light of the "Red Panic" sweeping the nation.[138] Burke converted the episode into bitter verse:

Now things are getting turned around,
As turned around as things can be.
And the social conscience of '35
Becomes the treason of '53.[139]

Fears of a similar reaction led Burke to alter the text of *Permanence and Change* for its second edition, issued in 1953. The excised passages were those that advocated (or seemed to advocate) communism. Burke's explanation for the deletions indicated his concern that they would be used against him by McCarthyites: "Since, under present conditions, the pages could not possibly be read in the tentative spirit in which they were originally written, the omissions help avoid troublesome issues not necessary to the book as such."[140] Thus, between his own clashes with anticommunists, and his comparatively meager book sales, it is not surprising that Burke would feel some jealousy regarding the success experienced by his former mentee.

In his 1953 letter to Hyman, Burke hinted that this was the source of his discontent, citing Ellison's appearance on the radio as a sign that "he doesn't need the likes of me to say him yea."[141] The reference to Ellison's "politico-cultural importance" suggests that Burke was reacting more to Ellison's celebrity profile—and its connection to the civil rights movement—than to the artistic achievement represented by the novel. Additionally, Burke indicates that he was most hurt by Ellison's statements of indebtedness to Eliot—an account of his artistic development that glossed over Burke's role entirely. In other words, although Burke's letter to Knox seems extreme, given his characterization of Ellison's interview as "ass-kissing," he was responding to what he saw—and did not see—in Ellison's public statements from the 1950s.

In many of the interviews appearing after the publication of *Invisible Man*, Ellison identified Eliot as a central influence. Burke's name, by contrast, was mentioned only occasionally during these interviews, and never in the same breath as his pantheon of heroes: Eliot, Joyce, Hemingway, Faulkner, Twain, and Dostoevsky. Burke certainly did not take the perceived slight lightly; I believe jealousy and hurt explain a significant portion of Burke's silence regarding Ellison's novel and its author.

Subsequent correspondence from Burke reinforces this interpretation. In 1964, Hyman wrote Burke that he had reviewed Ellison's *Shadow and Act*, and that his review had "credited it all to you, including things you might want credited to someone else."[142] Burke's reply revealed his feelings of rejection: "I'd be much amused to see what I get credited and discredited for, in re R*lph *ll*s*n—for I'm morally (in a nasty way) certain that said Asterisks will be furious."[143]

Even more surprising than the tone of these sentiments is the timing of this letter. A month before this letter to Hyman, Burke had written Ellison, reporting that he had received his copy of *Shadow and Act*.[144] As a result, he would certainly have seen that Ellison introduces the text with a statement acknowledging "special indebtedness" to Burke, and credits him as "the stimulating source of many of" the essays in the book.[145] Given his "nasty" certainty that Ellison denied such indebtedness, Burke ignored these statements and focused instead on the publisher's decision not to use a quote Burke had supplied for the book's cover. In his letter to Ellison, Burke expressed displeasure with the decision to replace his statement ("my *moody-and-intelligent* angle") with another; "but," he sarcastically noted, "I can see how the testimonial of a great thinker like Dan Aaron might better serve the purposes of publicity."[146] Even when thanked by Ellison, then, Burke clung to his belief that his influence on Ellison's work had been ignored—even repudiated—by Ellison himself.

Writing Ellison a year later, seeking to cosponsor Hyman's membership in the American Academy of Arts and Letters, Burke's jealousy reappeared: "I rejoice to see you getting so much acclaim; but I could rejoice even more if I were getting some too."[147] A month later, Ellison proposed a visit to Andover as part of a television documentary on his life and work. Burke's reply was less than enthusiastic. Though he told Ellison that "we're delighted to learn of further developments in Ellison Year," Burke had initially attempted to dissuade the producer from the visit to Andover.[148] Only when the producer insisted did Burke finally acquiesce and agree to the interview.

Since he feared the producer would reveal their earlier conversations, in a letter to Ellison, Burke attempted to reframe his actions. Though he still displayed a measure of envy (references to "Ellison Year" and "thy glory"), Burke tried to soothe any hurt feelings: "I write these words, to assure you that my droopings represented not lack of joy in your advancement, but fears lest the project at this point fail to meet the Producer's expectations." In other words, he explained, the Andover house would not be a suitable location for a show honoring Ellison—and "the thought that I might make still greater blunders (involving thy glory), leaves me considerably scairt."[149] After agreeing to host the event, he glumly wrote Hyman of the impending event: "Ralph Ellison is coming here today with a TV crew. Channel 13 is doing a show in which he is the primus donnus."[150] Although the visit was a success,[151] Burke's strained tone reappeared soon after, in a letter congratulating Malcolm Cowley on an award: "Jeez, I thought that this was to be Ralph Ellison Year."[152]

When read together, Burke's letters from the ten-plus years following the publication of *Invisible Man* reflect disappointment, hurt, and jealousy over Ellison's success. Although Burke's work began to receive more recognition in the late 1950s and early 1960s (partly thanks to Hyman),[153] he never experienced the *instant* success that Ellison achieved with his first novel. Further, Ellison's seeming abandonment of his mentor did not sit well with Burke. Ellison's post–*Invisible Man* interviews—celebrating the influence of Eliot, Hemingway, and Twain on his work, but omitting Burke's name—only cemented Burke's suspicions that he had become disposable.

In 1966, though, Ellison took steps to heal the rift between them. The first indication of this came when Burke was granted a Rockefeller Foundation Fellowship.[154] Burke happily reported the news to Hyman: "I am also, demure as I am, being tempted with the proffer of Ten Grand, to the ends of self-expression, and without the need to sleep with anybody (which is fortunate in the case of a sixty-nine year old insomniac)."[155] He was even more surprised to learn the identity of his champion on the committee; he had received the award, he learned, thanks to Ellison. Upon learning of Ellison's efforts on his behalf, Burke was moved to thank him in a handwritten note—a letter that helped spark a renewed relationship between the two men.[156]

Three months later, Ellison sent Burke a copy of the *New Leader* containing his article "Harlem's America." Burke was again moved, not simply by the contents of the article, but by Ellison's gesture of friendship. His reply displayed genuine warmth: "As I read the report of your sayings, I continued to recognize and to admire your competence. You have a role, and it's quite real." More importantly, though, Burke's appreciation extended beyond Ellison's "competence"; he added, "I'm happy to think that I might have affected it somewhat."[157] Burke, apparently, saw something that he felt was missing from Ellison's interviews of the 1950s: an acknowledgment of Burke's importance in Ellison's artistic development.

Over the next few years, Burke and Ellison resumed regular correspondence, and they again saw each other socially in New York—both at literary events and informal gatherings hosted by the Ellisons.[158] Fanny and Burke exchanged heartfelt letters after the death of Libbie in 1969, and all of them shared in the grief over the sudden death of Hyman in 1970.[159] This continued contact set the stage for the final act of acceptance: Burke's late essay "Ralph Ellison's Trueblooded *Bildungsroman*."

Burke's Promise Fulfilled

At first glance, Burke's contribution to the collection of essays in honor of Ellison, *Speaking for You*, seems relatively straightforward: a letter from Burke to Ellison discussing the significant elements of *Invisible Man* from a dramatistic perspective. This description alone should puzzle the reader; why, thirty years later, would Burke craft a letter analyzing the plot of his friend's novel? One answer might be that the letter was written just after the novel's publication. However, there is nothing in the chapter to suggest that the letter dates from the 1950s; on the contrary, Burke stresses the time elapsed since then, the "book's way of carving out a career" for its author.[160]

Moreover, the correspondence between Burke, Ellison, and Hyman suggests that this "letter" could not possibly date from the 1950s. Recall that Burke claimed in 1957 not to have finished *Invisible Man*—so Burke's detailed assessment of its plot and structure must have been completed well after the novel's publication. Judging from the correspondence, in fact, it appears that the letter was written between 1982 and 1983, and not before. After receiving an invitation from the editor, Kimberly Benston, Burke apparently conceived of structuring his contribution as a letter to Ellison. Benston, overjoyed to have Burke as part of the project, told him that "I've sent on your idea for the letter to Ralph—I expect you'll be hearing from him soon."[161] Ellison wrote Burke soon thereafter, correcting one of Burke's statements about the novel, but expressing gratitude to Burke for "taking time out from your important work in order to give a wider dimension to the Yale boys' project."[162]

Burke's contribution did not arrive as quickly as Benston had hoped. In late December 1982, Burke wrote Ellison and explained that he had misplaced his draft of the first few pages of the "letter." Several months later, he again wrote Ellison, resolving that "if it ain't too late, and your backers at Yale care to send me a copy of those pages I sent, I'll still try to finish my piece."[163] Ellison's reply was warm and understanding, and held out hope for a contribution from Burke in the published volume: "I hope by now that you've heard from Benston, the Yale prof who's editing the collection. I called him right after I heard from you and he said that he'd get in touch."[164] Benston subsequently contacted Burke, and, in 1987, *Speaking for You* appeared, complete with Burke's reflections on *Invisible Man*. However, having established that Burke composed this essay in the early 1980s—thirty years later than is often assumed—we are left with another question. Burke apparently hit upon the "letter" device almost immediately upon receiving the invitation to contribute to the celebratory volume—but why? In other words, since "Ralph Ellison's Trueblooded *Bildungsroman*" was an essay written long after the novel's publication, why did Burke write it in the form of a letter?

This question, I believe, can be adequately answered only if we place the essay back in the context of the unpublished correspondence among Burke, Ellison, and Hyman. Burke's chapter is the letter that Ellison waited for, and Burke never wrote: the letter offering Burke's detailed assessment of the artistic merits of *Invisible Man*. The essay therefore represents Burke's offering to Ellison, the fulfillment of a thirty-year-old promise to read and respond to his friend's novel. Burke provides support for this thesis in a note to Ellison penned when the essay was completed: "'Tis done. I'm shipping it to Yaley-Waley tomorrow. It's not too good—and it's not too bad either. But I owed it to you, and I dare hope you'll like it."[165] Burke clearly felt that he had an obligation to Ellison, and that the essay could discharge that obligation. As Hyman pointed out several times during the early 1950s, Burke had promised to write Ellison "soon" about *Invisible Man* but had never delivered on this promise—and, worse, he had failed to celebrate his friend's success. I believe that Burke's essay thus represented a form of symbolic redemption. Only by writing an essay devoted specifically to Ellison's novel could Burke prove to Ellison that he had read it, and that he found it to be powerful, intelligent, and worthy of its acclaim. The letter that Burke should have written about *Invisible Man* in 1952 became the 1983 "letter" he *did* write, devoted to the novel, and published in a volume honoring Ellison's life and work. "Ralph Ellison's Trueblooded *Bildungsroman*" thus signals Burke's approval, and his acceptance of Ellison's artistry, thirty years later than expected; its form and content attempt to make up for Burke's earlier symbolic rejection of Ellison and his work.

Though intended to commemorate their relationship, *Invisible Man* had instead placed a great strain upon it. The book's success, Ellison's desire for independence, and Burke's jealousy had conspired to disrupt their friendship—and halt their ongoing dialogue on race. Yet, with a series of small gestures, the distance between the two men was gradually lessened, the friendship resumed. Burke recognized Ellison's efforts to acknowledge him, and he reciprocated; finally, presented with the perfect opportunity to address the debt he owed Ellison, Burke acted. Having missed the opportunity to write Ellison privately about the novel, he made his approval and admiration public.

With the publication of Burke's "letter," then, the dispute over Burke's silence was finally, and fully, put to rest. Yet, a portion of the underlying conflict remained. Writing Ellison in 1983, Burke noted, "Your book sums up an era when black mayors in cities like Chicago or Philadelphia were *unthinkable*."[166] Ellison's reply, though addressing Burke fondly, was direct: "As for my old novel and its *summing up* I have no opinion. But I do know that while it dealt with a period when black mayors of cities like Detroit, Chicago and Philadelphia were impossible, the *idea* of their being such was not."[167]

Though Burke's published "letter" declared that Ellison had helped eliminate "traces of unconscious Nortonism in our thinking," "Ralph Ellison's Trueblooded *Bildungsroman*" begins with Burke's treatment of Ellison in *A Rhetoric of Motives*, without comment—or reframing.[168] In fact, a 1982 letter to Ellison indicated that he remained "wholly satisfied" with his citation of Ellison in the *Rhetoric*[169]—a citation that, as we have seen, provoked an immediate and negative reaction from both Ellison and Hyman. The two men might have come to terms over *Invisible Man*, but they had not reached a similar accord over its central concern: America's "racial divide."

4 / Was Kenneth Burke a Racist?

The complete disappearance of the snow, meanwhile, has done wonders for my peace of mind. I hate snow. After the first virginal exaltation of its falling, it makes me crazy. It gives me a white mind. "Now that the first snow is down, giving me a white mind" . . . etc. And just, if you have an odd moment, look at the whites in [Towards a Better Life] to see the magic I always have to struggle against when there's too much white around. Or in The White Oxen, *for that matter.*

—KENNETH BURKE TO MALCOLM COWLEY, 19 JANUARY 1946

When the correspondence between Burke and Ellison ended—in 1987, six years before Burke's death—the relationship inaugurated by "The Rhetoric of Hitler's 'Battle'" was midway through its fifth decade.[1] Despite the peaks and valleys of the years following the Third American Writers' Congress, in the 1980s the friendship was very much alive. In some respects, as described in chapter 3, the relationship was on surer ground than when it first began. Ellison was sending fond letters to his "old friend and mentor," writing that "it was a real pleasure seeing you at the Academy. In fact you're the main reason we try not to miss the meetings, and when you don't show both Fanny and I are disappointed."[2] As Ellison typed these sentences into his word processor, he was proud that his connection with Burke had survived the volatility of literary trends, the sweeping changes wrought within American culture as a whole, and—more tragically—the deaths of Shirley Jackson in 1965, Libbie Burke in 1969, and Stanley Edgar Hyman in 1970.

Yet, though these men crafted a friendship they could be proud of in their later years, any complete account of this relationship cannot ignore the points of tension and conflict that mar this narrative arc. As we have seen, their friendship had, throughout the 1940s and 1950s, been disrupted by pronounced awkwardness, reluctant replies, even prolonged silences. In light of the positive tone of the 1980s correspondence, it is certainly tempting to overlook these uncomfortable disruptions, in favor of a more hagiographic narrative about this literary friendship.

However, Burke himself asks us to attend to such moments, to use them as a means to delve more deeply into the nature of a particular relationship. Reading these moments as signs of "embarrassment or self-imposed constraint," Burke's *A Rhetoric of Motives* suggests their rhetorical significance, since "we interpret any variants, however twisted or attenuated, of embarrassment in social intercourse as sign of a corresponding mystery of communication."[3] Here Burke argues that we should read awkward moments, large or small, as evidence of "the 'mystery' of courtship" within a relationship—the rhetorical situation generated when "'different kinds of beings' communicate with each other."[4]

In chapter 2, I pointed to one of the ways in which the "'mystery' of courtship" relates to the Burke-Ellison connection: Burke had Ellison on his mind while writing this portion of the *Rhetoric*. However, I would argue, we can also fruitfully apply this concept to unpacking the silences disrupting their friendship. To this end, we might recall the origins of the relationship, and the ancestral role that Burke, the established writer, played for Ellison, the aspiring writer. In light of their generational differences, we certainly could interpret Burke's mentorship of Ellison as interaction involving "'different kinds of beings'"—and, therefore, necessarily involving a degree of mystery, embarrassment, or awkwardness.

Not only would this framing of the situation make sense, but one of Ellison's interviews appears to support this interpretation of their friendship. In response to an interviewer's question, Ellison explained the necessarily courtly relationships established between older and younger writers: "What Kenneth Burke terms 'courtship' is implicit in friendship, which is a relationship between, shall we say, two consenting adults who 'woo' one another. In such relationships there are risks for both participants. For [although] the older writer might consider it flattering to be elected the 'father' of a gifted symbolic 'son,' there is also the possibility that he might be repelled by the responsibility of that role."[5] This reflection had originally been prompted by a question about Richard Wright, but Ellison's invocation of Burke is also quite appropriate. In many ways, these words offer an apt description of the differences in status characteristic of their early relationship.

To be sure, the "mystery" of age can be quite powerful, but I do not believe that chronological difference adequately accounts for the critical moments of embarrassment in the Burke-Ellison relationship. It would be one thing if the signs of courtly mystery were linked solely to the developmental stages of Ellison's career, his time as Burke's "apprentice"—but that is simply not the case. There is, instead, a quite different pattern to their appearance: every significant instance of awkwardness in their friendship was linked to the subject of race.

The first sign of such mystery, as we have already seen, was Burke's aborted reply to Ellison's lengthy letter of 23 November 1945. Uncomfortable with his answers to Ellison's questions on matters of race—whether he framed them as an essay or as a letter—Burke avoided response for several months. Recall also that, following his receipt of Burke's hand-delivered letter, Ellison seemed hesitant to discuss his novel with his friend; their differences on "the ideal Negro book" led to restricted communication over Ellison's developing narrative. But perhaps the clearest sign of mystery in their relationship was Burke's thirty-year silence in the wake of *Invisible Man*'s publication—and the illuminating, ambivalent comments about Ellison's "social role" within Burke's correspondence from the 1950s and early 1960s. When placed in the context of the *Rhetoric*'s treatment of courtship, these episodes suggest that there was something more than jealousy at work in Burke's reaction to Ellison's success. Burke's awkwardness over *Invisible Man* may instead signify a deeper discomfort over the issues raised by the book, the "unconscious Nortonism" that he later acknowledged.

A rhetorical reading of these moments of hesitation—of "self-imposed constraint"—marking the Burke-Ellison friendship suggests that we cannot ignore a second sense in which the two men were "different kinds of beings," at least according to the American racial hierarchy. In other words, rather than looking merely at their generational differences, we should instead focus critical attention upon the "'mystery' of courtship" produced by their racial classifications, the socially generated embarrassment that accompanied, and strained, their interracial relationship. As Ellisonian scholarship has grown exponentially since the early 1980s, it is now common to find acknowledgment—and, occasionally, systematic treatment—of the Burkean themes in Ellison's work on race and identity. However, this scholarship has rarely inquired into their divergences of opinion on these issues, or discussed the impact of race upon their relationship. In part, I believe, this is because of the potentially threatening implications of such a move. To emphasize their differing racial identities might easily lead to, or be confused with, a harsh judgment of Burke—a denunciation of racism in his thought or actions.

Eddy's discussion of the Burke-Ellison connection exemplifies the delicate treatment of this subject in the scholarly literature. Her book offers a detailed comparison of the published writings of both men, even making the argument that "Kenneth Burke was a major, perhaps *the* major, intellectual influence on Ralph Ellison."[6] At the same time, she avoids discussion of their racial differences or the contrasting attitudes generated by them. Her book, then, differs from the overwhelming majority of Ellisonian scholarship only in the explicit acknowledgment of her choice: "Obviously, the two men have racial identity differences. But to notice a profound intellectual resemblance between the two men is not to whitewash their racial differences. It is instead to make both the differences and the similarities all the more highly charged with importance and moral ambiguity."[7] Following this statement, except for a brief treatment of *Invisible Man*, she offers little explicit reflection upon the significance—rhetorical or otherwise—of these "racial identity differences."[8]

Donald Pease offers the most notable—and, indeed, the only sustained—attempt to redress this oversight in the literature, and to systematically address the interconnected differences of opinion and identity between Burke and Ellison. Drawing heavily upon his reading of race within the Burkean system, Pease describes "a transaction between Ellison and Burke that, in disclosing what could not be accommodated within Burke's theory of symbolic action, effected a profound transformation in the basis of their relationship."[9] In many respects, Pease's discussion of race in this relationship therefore offers a necessary corrective to the literature focusing upon the similarities in outlook and approach between these two men.

At the same time, his approach closely approximates the rather simple critique described above: Burke's disagreements with Ellison, Pease essentially argues, are a product of his unacknowledged white privilege, and of his racist theoretical system. Further, this argument is built principally upon examination of three published texts: Ellison's "Richard Wright's Blues," Burke's *A Rhetoric of Motives*, and Burke's late "letter," "Ralph Ellison's Trueblooded *Bildungsroman*." As should be clear from the preceding chapters, an account of this friendship based solely upon published texts can offer only a fragment of the story of the Burke-Ellison relationship. The ideas and arguments presented within these texts have a more personal, relational history—a history that can only be seen when they are read within a more holistic context.[10]

Consequently, drawing on the unpublished correspondence between and concerning Burke and Ellison, the remainder of this chapter links these public texts to the private debates from which they grew—and uses this analysis to highlight the significance of race within the Burke-Ellison friendship. Thus, although my account necessarily contests Pease's argument about Burke's racist tendencies, such a critique is not my goal. On the contrary, I believe that a complete account of the Burke-Ellison friendship requires us to properly articulate the significance of race within it.

I do not agree with Pease's (or any scholar's) simplistic denunciation of Burke; one cannot so easily dispose of the disagreements between these two men on matters of race and identity. Instead, as I argue later in this chapter, the signs of "social mystery" in this relationship suggest a more nuanced interpretation of the source of their disagreements. By the 1980s, Burke had recognized the "unconscious Nortonism" lurking in his thinking, but I believe that he was terministically prevented from eliminating it. That is, although Burke served as a source of inspiration to Ellison, Burke was unable to transcend a dialectical vocabulary of race, one built around an unquestioned and privileged white identity; Burke failed to critically reflect upon the racial binarism that, by the end of the 1940s, had become the dominant American discourse on race.

As a result, despite his dialogue with Ellison, Burke did not achieve an ultimate vocabulary for approaching the drama of race in America. By applying Burke's terministic hierarchy to the subject of race, we can see Ellison's perspective as, in some respects, more fully Burkean than Burke's own. The unpublished correspondence between Burke and Ellison thus challenges us to take a fresh look at the Burkean resources—including those not recognized by Burke himself—available for the contemporary analysis of race and identity.

"Public Disagreements": Pease on Burke, Ellison, and Race

Pease's discussion of Burke and Ellison represents a refreshing addition to the literature on their relationship since it attempts to account for more than the points of agreement or conceptual convergence between the two men. What he finds more interesting than the many terms Ellison borrowed from Burke throughout his life, in other words, is where their agreement ends. His essay consequently offers a very different account of their relationship: "Throughout most of his literary career, Ellison was involved in a dialogue with Burke that emulated the structure of call and response of the Negro spiritual."[11] However, this "call and response," he claims, was far from benign.

Drawing on Ellison's essay "Hidden Name and Complex Fate," Pease argues that Burke's vocabulary was vital in Ellison's development because it offered him "a mandated identity within an alternative symbolic world. . . . Burke's heterocosm also appeared to resolve Ellison's uncertainty about what the symbolic order wanted from him."[12] Pease views Ellison's early essays as attempts to harness the power of the Burkean vocabulary for broader analytical purposes, to deepen our understanding of race and identity in mid-twentieth-century America. For Pease, the most significant of these Burke-fueled offerings is the essay "Richard Wright's Blues," which, he claims, marked the highest degree of Ellison's involvement in the Burkean perspective; even as it recast the terms by which *Black Boy* was understood, the essay simultaneously (symbolically) reconstituted Ellison's social world and his place within it.

According to Pease, however, Ellison's identity project was fatefully undermined by *A Rhetoric of Motives*. Pease claims that Burke's book denied Ellison's bid for reidentification, and instead attempted to recapture Ellison within the safe confines of the white, liberal American social order. As evidence, Pease cites Burke's controversial quotation of Ellison in the text: "The Negro intellectual, Ralph Ellison, says that Booker T. Washington 'described the Negro community as a basket of crabs, wherein should one attempt to climb out, the others immediately pull him back.'"[13]

Pease questions not only this choice of quotation, but also Burke's relationship to the "crab basket" mentioned within it: "What subject position did Burke occupy when he verified Washington's description? Did Burke speak as a black? Did he speak as the secondary addressee of Washington's metaphor? . . . His representation of this scene could not take place within the crab basket but lay outside its frame. But if this is the case, had Burke taken up the position of the bearer of the crab basket that Washington's metaphor tacitly projected?"[14] Rather than recognizing Ellison's efforts to escape the racial strictures placed upon him, Pease contends, Burke instead reaffirmed his own privileged position, and tried to recapture his mentee within the dominating, silencing structures of white liberalism.[15]

Pease's critical focus on the Burke-Ellison relationship is certainly admirable, but at times he seems to overlook the fact that Burke and Ellison were not simply colleagues, but also friends; his invocation of Burke as Ellison's "ideal interlocutor" ignores the ways in which he was also Ellison's *real* interlocutor.[16] As I have argued over the course of this book, we must examine the entire record of the Burke-Ellison relationship, and especially the letters exchanged between the two men. The same is true in regard to Pease's essay; the correspondence demonstrates that Pease's chosen texts are not in direct conversation with one another. Rather, they are part of a larger dialogue between these two men on the relationship between race and identity.

As detailed in chapter 2, for example, the two men were in fairly close contact when Burke was doing the vast majority of the work on the *Rhetoric*.[17] In the letters leading up to the book's publication, both men continued to describe their projects as more similar than different, in content and in perspective. Writing Burke to express dismay over missing him at Bennington, for example, Ellison reported reading Burke's "Ideology and Myth" with great interest—and suggested an essay on the sociology of race built upon its insights.[18]

Consumed by his work on the *Rhetoric*, Burke did not immediately reply—but when he did, he likewise indicated the relevance of Ellison's work to his own: "I hope you have done something about that article on sociology and racial ideology you thought of writing. . . . I'd much like to see it worked out. The section I have just finished is hitting all around that business." In addition, Burke expressed a desire to discuss his evolving manuscript with Ellison: "There is some stuff in this section which I want very much to talk with you about."[19] Significantly, the section referred to in Burke's letter includes the beginning of the third part of the text, "Order," which contains his controversial citation of Ellison.[20]

The correspondence thus shows that this text was composed when the two men were quite close—that, if anything, collaboration with Ellison was Burke's dominant motive in writing these controversial pages. Consequently, reading the *Rhetoric* in light of the Burke-Ellison correspondence, we can see this text as simply another entry in their extended, public *and* private conversation on issues of race and identity. Moreover, with this context in mind, we can arrive at a more nuanced view of the disagreements between these men on matters of race than that offered by Pease. Their racial identities, I would argue, *did* have an impact on their relationship; however, in order to grasp how these differences made a difference, we need to turn once more to this problematic portion of the *Rhetoric*.

A Second Look at the *Rhetoric*'s "Crab Basket"

To fully understand Burke's use of the "crab basket" metaphor, we must first, as described in the previous section, place this passage from the *Rhetoric* back within the broader dialogue on race begun by "Richard Wright's Blues." In addition, however, we *also* must note the placement of the passage within Burke's text as a whole; it appears directly after his explication of the differences between the positive, dialectical, and ultimate orders of terminology. Although I return to these terms in the next section of this chapter, an initial summary is necessary in order to understand the relationship of the "crab basket" to Burke's overall argument within the book.

According to Burke, all vocabularies can be classified as falling into one of these three terministic orders. As described by Burke, the positive order is comprised of words that designate the visible things of the world; its terms center on, or are used to identify, the world of sensory perception. The dialectical order, by contrast, identifies the realm of principles, those terms that do not strictly indicate one particular thing within the realm of the visible (e.g., "capitalism"). Since dialectical terms are thus abbreviations for an infinite set of particulars, he explains, they are best understood as summarizing "titles." Further, since all such titles oppose other titles—terms that differently summarize the same set of particulars—this type of vocabulary tends to produce binary, Manichean logics, such as "capitalism" vs. "communism" (183–84). Given this structural incitement toward opposition, competition, and debate, according to Burke "terms of this sort are often called 'polar'" (184).

However, Burke cautions us not to limit ourselves to these two orders when classifying terminologies. A third order, the ultimate, contains terms that differ substantially from both positive and dialectical terms because they do not merely describe or oppose—they arrange. In essence, an ultimate vocabulary differs from both positive and dialectical terms because it provides an overarching symbolic structure that harmonizes, or orders, both dialectical and positive terms.

As Burke explains, "The 'dialectical' order would leave the competing voices in a jangling relation with one another . . . ; but the 'ultimate' order would place these competing voices themselves in a hierarchy, or sequence, or evaluative series, so that, in some way, we went by a fixed and reasoned progression from one of these to another, the members of the entire group being arranged developmentally with relation to one another" (187). An ultimate order sharply diverges from a dialectical order, then, in that it does not simply oppose one term (or title) to another; it instead provides the organizing principle for the evaluation and ordering of all titles and terms.[21] In this way, an ultimate order represents the transcendence of both the positive and dialectical orders because it symbolically resolves all oppositions—through the hierarchical placement of these other terms within a larger, more synoptic whole.

This treatment of the transcendence of dialectical conflict is what leads Burke to his controversial discussion of Ellison—by way of Marxism. Burke describes Marx's work as one of the most successful modern attempts to create a vocabulary for the transcending of social division. The Marxist vocabulary closely resembles an ultimate vocabulary since, within it, "the various classes do not confront one another merely as parliamentary voices that represent conflicting interests. They are arranged hierarchically, each with the disposition, or 'consciousness,' that matches its peculiar set of circumstances, while the steps from feudal to bourgeois to proletarian are grounded in the very nature of the universe" (190). As a vocabulary promising ultimate transcendence, Burke argues, Marxism is structurally quite persuasive; for members of minority groups, he adds, this appeal is only magnified.

Oppressed individuals, according to Burke, are even more likely than those in dominant groups to adopt a Marxist framework precisely because of its ability to order all aspects of social existence—thereby providing a symbolic "way through" the bitter struggles of the dominant and the oppressed. Fragments of transcendence appear throughout American culture, but Burke claims that for oppressed individuals, the Marxist vocabulary is superior to most such alternatives—because its symbolic bridging of division provides a systematic and rhetorically potent vision of a future beyond the current, divided social order (190–91, 194–97). This explains why, Burke suggests, Richard Wright was drawn to Marx; beset by conflicts on all sides, Marxism seemed to provide the perfect symbolic framework for the transcending of entrenched dialectical oppositions.

Delving further into this portion of the *Rhetoric*, we see that Burke's controversial quotation of Ellison ties this discussion of ultimate vocabularies to the arguments about universality first presented in their correspondence. Burke prefaces his invocation of "Richard Wright's Blues" by explicitly linking the subject of race to his discussions of transcendence and the ultimate order, observing that "any improvement in social status is a kind of transcendence" (193). However, the transcendence he identifies in this sentence is not that of an ultimate vocabulary; far from a solution to dialectical struggles, this form of transcendence simply intensifies these struggles, and thus calls for a further transcendence.

By way of explanation, Burke points out that oppression produces predictable dilemmas for an individual seeking (or achieving) higher status: "Where one is a member of an extremely underprivileged class, as with the Negro in America, an individual attempt at the transcending of inferior status gets increased poignancy from the fact that, atop all the intensity of such effort in itself, there is a working at cross-purposes" (193). Here Burke remarks that, for black Americans (or members of any minority group), success necessarily produces a limited kind of tran-scendence—since it offers an escape from the oppressive restrictions affecting other members of the group. But, returning to a theme from their correspondence, he contends that this subsequently creates a crisis of allegiance, a clash of identifications.

Burke illustrates this point through his citation of the "crab basket." Ellison's original use of Washington's quote emphasized the protective traditions of the black community. For Burke, the reverse of this group phenomenon is the guilt experienced by any black American achieving transcendence through individual efforts: "He may feel as 'conscience' the judgment of his own class, since he would in a sense be 'disloyal' to his class" (193). In these pages of the *Rhetoric*, Burke attempts to explain why Marxism is attractive for those, like Wright, who have experienced both oppression and individual success: "Clearly, the rhetorical appeal of the Marxist terminology in such situations is that it can allow for an ultimate order" (194).[22]

In this quote, Burke specifically addresses the *rhetorical* appeal of Marxism; as a result, I would emphasize that Burke is not mandating Marxism for black Americans, but viewing it through the lens of his three orders. Throughout these pages of the *Rhetoric*, Burke emphasizes not that an individual's racial identity should be rejected in favor of her class, but that the vocabulary of Marxism promises a kind of transcen-dence not easily achievable in the face of an entrenched social hierarchy. As Burke argues, the Marxist vocabulary, given its ultimate design, "per-mits the member of a minority to place his problem in a graded series that keeps transcendence of individual status from seeming like disloy-alty to one's group status" (194–95). Marxism, then, presents a rhetorical solution to this conflict of identifications since "it allows the member of an underprivileged minority, for instance, to confront the world at once specifically and generically" (195).

In other words, Marxism allows for the integration of all levels of identity, individual, racial, and universal; it promises a reordered world, one produced through the transcending of conflict. Since an ultimate terminology involves such an arrangement of parliamentary voices, it makes sense that Burke would discuss Marxism in relation to this third terministic order. As Burke writes, "The worker whose understanding becomes infused with this doctrine . . . sees himself as *member of a class,* the proletariat, which is designed to play *a crucial role in the unfolding of history as a whole*" (196; original emphasis). Yet, despite phrases such as these, Burke's discussion of Marxism casts strong doubt on the truly ultimate nature of its vocabulary.[23] On Burke's analysis, Marxism bears a close resemblance to an ultimate vocabulary, but does not, in the end, pass muster; it fails to achieve the transcendence of partisanship that is required of this third order.

Since Marxism fails to reach the top level of his terministic hierarchy, I believe that it cannot be equated with Burke's own perspective; by pointing out its inability to achieve ultimate transcendence, he introduces a distance between his own perspective and that of Marx. Burke's categories place the greatest value upon ultimate vocabularies, not those, like Marxism, simply deemed "'ultimate' enough to meet at least the preliminary requirements" (194). Note here that Burke describes Marxism not as ultimate, but ultimate "enough." In these pages, Burke points out that one can reject Marxism's particular hierarchical arrangement—denying that it is *the* ultimate order—but one cannot underestimate the rhetorical appeal of a *seemingly* ultimate vocabulary to oppressed individuals.

Judging from the content of his 14 January 1948 letter to Ellison, Burke wrote this section of the text with Ellison in mind—and even hoped for Ellison's assistance and advice on it. Since there is no record of Ellison responding to the text prior to its publication, I believe that Burke ultimately relied on the next best thing: Ellison's own words, taken from his correspondence with Burke. Although the quote attributed to Ellison in the *Rhetoric* comes from "Richard Wright's Blues," I would assert that, in these pages, Burke is primarily in conversation with Ellison's letter of 23 November 1945. Far from a condescending and aggressive attempt to "speak for" Ellison, Burke was simply trying to provide, and then respond to, Ellison's position on race and identity. Lacking direct feedback from Ellison, he drew on Ellison's letter as a substitute. As a result, these pages are best understood as Burke's attempt to incorporate Ellison's perspective into—not exclude it from—his rhetorical account of race and identity.

This claim might seem counterintuitive, on first reading statements from Burke such as this: "Striving for freedom as a human being generically, he must do so as a Negro specifically. But to do so as a Negro is, by the same token, to prevent oneself from doing so in the generic sense" (193). At the same time, compare this quote from Burke to a sentence that he marked within Ellison's letter: "I certainly agree with you that universalism is desirable, but I find that I am forced to arrive at that universe through the racial grain of sand."[24] Unlike Burke, here Ellison does not champion the universal over the racial—but, at the same time, he does not reject universalism out of hand. I believe that Burke interpreted these words as Ellison's declaration of interest in the universal, not as a critique of it; he saw Ellison as struggling not against universalism per se, but against his allegiances to others sharing his experiences of an all-too-present racism. By agreeing with Burke that "universalism is desirable," Ellison failed to signal the extent of his disagreement with Burke over the importance of race in American culture.

In the passage quoted above, then, Burke was simply trying to present—as he understood it—Ellison's position on race and identity. Burke translated Ellison's discussion of universalism and the "racial grain of sand" into the clash of identifications produced by an individual's experience of transcendence. Moreover, placing Burke's text back within the context of the correspondence, I believe that the same holds true for Burke's citation of "Richard Wright's Blues." Burke's use of the "crab basket" metaphor in the *Rhetoric* was an attempt to summarize, and then apply, the results of his dialogue with Ellison to his evolving perspective on rhetoric.

This controversial passage from the *Rhetoric* is prefigured in his 16 December 1945 letter to Ellison. Though "Richard Wright's Blues" interpreted the "crab basket" as the impulse to shelter the individual within the group, Burke's *Rhetoric* (like his December 1945 letter) suggested its reverse operation: the tug of loyalty, or allegiance, that the individual feels toward her group. Compare again Burke's text to Ellison's letter: "I, for instance, would like to write simply as an American, or even better, a citizen of the world; but that is impossible just now because it is to dangle in the air of abstractions while the fire which alone illuminates those abstractions issues precisely from my being a Negro and in all the 'felt experience' which being a Negro American entails."[25] Burke, I believe, stressed the "just now" in Ellison's "impossible"; he read these words not as a critique of universality, but as an expression of Ellison's own, conflicted, allegiances. Burke's subsequent use of the metaphor represented his extension of the concept of allegiance to the rhetorical dimensions and implications of black Americans' experience of transcendence.

Recall from chapter 2 that Burke originally proposed writing an essayistic answer to Ellison's letter; I contend that Burke, not satisfied with (or, perhaps, spurred on by) his initial attempts to reply to it, provided an additional, published, response in the *Rhetoric*. Given the sentiments expressed in his 14 January 1948 letter, it seems clear that these pages were composed with Ellison in mind; in them, I believe that Burke tried to translate Ellison's letter into the vocabulary central to Burke's own project. Accepting Ellison's reading of allegiance in *Black Boy*, Burke offered rhetoric as the key to both Ellison's discomfort with universalism and Wright's autobiographical crises; these pages in Burke's text are best read as an attempt to provide a *rhetorical* solution to the problems identified by Ellison. In short, Burke's invocation of the "crab basket" metaphor was simply his attempt to respond to Ellison's 23 November 1945 letter.

Evidence from the correspondence supports this reading of Burke's text. Writing Ellison of his work on this section of the *Rhetoric*, Burke remarked first that the section's content would benefit from the inclusion of Ellison's individual experience with oppression; he even opined that the exchange of comments on the subject would assist both of their intellectual projects. Most important (for present purposes), Burke claimed that rhetoric was the key term previously missing from their earlier exchanges over race: "I believe that if you brought the vividness of your own experiences to bear upon some of the formulations I am now working on, we could both profit. In any case, I think it can be shown that rhetoric brings one quite near to the dropping-off place."[26] With Ellison's help, in other words, Burke felt that his theory of rhetoric could isolate "the dropping-off place" for the contemplation and amelioration of racial conflicts in America.

In sum, to say that Burke cited "Richard Wright's Blues" in the *Rhetoric* is not to say that he was solely, or even primarily, responding to this essay. Further, to say that Burke's text did violence to Ellison's words is not to say that this was his intent; we can recognize that the two men had different perspectives on these issues without echoing Pease's charges against Burke. At the same time, to claim that the correspondence contradicts Pease's account of the Burke-Ellison relationship is not also to dismiss as illegitimate a focus on race within it. In the final sections of this chapter, consequently, I reexamine the significance of race within the Burke-Ellison relationship. Drawing upon the material presented above, I suggest the possibility of another, more appropriately complex, account of race and/in this friendship—one centered in the distinction among Burke's three terministic orders.

Race Matters in the Burke-Ellison Friendship

Throughout the preceding pages, I have focused specifically on the unpublished correspondence linking two key texts, "Richard Wright's Blues" and *A Rhetoric of Motives,* and thereby tried to contextualize Burke's controversial citation of Ellison's early essay. But I want to make my overall position clear; I do not hold that Burke's discussions of race (either in his letters or in his published texts) match Ellison's—nor would I expect Ellison to recognize himself in Burke's words. Given Hyman's 1950 letter to Burke, indicating that Ellison saw the *Rhetoric* as a "butchery" of his ideas, I think it much more likely that Ellison had serious reservations about his role within Burke's text.[27] Moreover, recall that, in a 1982 letter, Burke specifically told Ellison that "Ralph Ellison's Trueblooded *Bildungsroman*" was *not* a retraction of his position in the *Rhetoric*: "I didn't mind missing my first draft [of the essay] because I didn't like merely commenting on what I had written in my *Rhetoric of Motives,* though I'm wholly satisfied with what I said *then.*"[28]

As a consequence, I would dismiss the simplistic critique of Burke's racism—like the one offered by Pease—but would support a more nuanced claim: that race was very much a part of the conflicts and differences of perspective disrupting this friendship. In other words, rather than discarding Burke's system as a racist edifice, I would harness it for the exploration of the "'mystery' of courtship" that emerged in the Burke-Ellison relationship. If we do so, I argue, we see that Burke himself shows us the limited nature of his vocabulary of race.

Drawing specifically on the *Rhetoric,* we can use Burkean concepts to identify a fundamental fault in Burke's own perspective: unable to consider the issue in ultimate terms, *Burke was never able to fully transcend a dialectical vocabulary of race.* In other words, I believe the root of the conflict between Burke and Ellison was not Burke's desire to remaster his young mentee, nor his system's exclusionary foundations, but the terminology underlying and generating Burke's understanding of race. However, in order to flesh out this argument, let us return to the difference between ultimate and dialectical orders of terminology—and apply this distinction more specifically to Burke's published and unpublished writings on race and identity.

According to Burke's tripartite scheme, a dialectical term transcends the sensory particulars of the positive order. Rather than naming, it instead summarizes (entitles) a host of such particulars—which necessarily brings this dialectical term into conflict with other, competing titles for the same particulars. To picture what this means, Burke tells us, imagine dialectical terms as strident parliamentary voices raised against each other. If these dialectical disagreements are allowed to proceed unchecked, the situation will devolve into little more than an unproductive cacophony of fierce, seemingly unresolvable opposition.

Burke points out that dialectical paralysis can be avoided through the creation of compromise. However, given the discord of the dialectical order, Burke warns, this may not be an appealing solution to any of the parliamentarians involved: "It being the realm of ideas or principles, if you organize a conflict among spokesmen for competing ideas or principles, you may produce a situation wherein there is no one clear choice. Each of the spokesmen, whose ideas are an extension of special interests, must remain somewhat unconvinced by any solution which does not mean the complete triumph of his partisan interests. Yet he may have to compromise, putting through some portion of his program by making concessions to allies whom, if he could get his wishes absolutely, he would repudiate" (187). As a consequence of their investment in a chosen title (or principle), Burke writes, the voices raised in heated dialectical debate often equate any type of "compromise" with "demoralization." The result, at best, is a tense stalemate, with few possibilities for resolution; in such a situation there is little, if any, hope of progress beyond the level of dialectic since the representatives of these opposing titles "confront one another as somewhat disrelated competitors that can work together only by the 'mild demoralization' of sheer compromise" (187).

Within the *Rhetoric*, Burke used his citation from Ellison's essay to illuminate the rhetorical limitations of this second terministic order, the pitfalls of using a dialectical vocabulary to address the transcendence of social inequality. We can also, though, see these pages as providing a clue to the relevance of race in the distinction between dialectical and ultimate orders. Rather than offering an *external* critique—asking how Ellison might have been excluded from Burke's white-dominated symbolic order—we can generate an *internal* critique. That is, we can ask how Burke's vocabulary of race measures up to the standards set by his own system. Since Burke argues that all vocabularies fall into one of the three orders identified in the *Rhetoric*, we are justified in asking which best "fits" the vocabulary of race that he drew upon in his exchanges with Ellison.

If we begin by applying Burke's discussion of the three terministic orders simply to the *Rhetoric* itself, we find that—within the text as a whole—Burke's treatment of race falls squarely into this second terministic order. In the portion including his citation of Ellison, for example, Burke builds his argument upon a clear opposition between black and white Americans. Explaining the "rhetorical appeal" of Marxism for someone like Wright, Burke identifies whites as "antagonistic" others to black Americans, as blacks' "opponents" within the social arena—opponents whose "conspiracy" logically inspires blacks to form a race-based "counterconspiracy" (193, 194). Even looking beyond these pages, we see that *all* of Burke's references to race in the *Rhetoric*—whether they involve a discussion of "white supremacy" (32, 104, 117, 126, 285, 300, 313), or of the "class" or "factional" divisions represented by racial identity (34, 115)—describe a fundamental opposition between white and black Americans.

One might logically infer that this way of framing the issue merely reflects Burke's project in this text, since he explicitly described the *Rhetoric* as an attempt to treat "the ways in which individuals are at odds with one another, or become identified with groups more or less at odds with one another" (22). We might even extend this logic to cover similar language in Burke's late essay "The Rhetorical Situation." In it, he recognizes "racism" as an example of identification through antithesis, "particularly some pressing expressions of the black-white issue that have come to the fore, along with earlier morbidities that were latent in our social structure."[29] Burke then adds an aside, the wording of which underscores this racial antithesis; citing a 1965 piece in the *New York Review of Books*, Burke comments that "its data on the history of laws against freed black men in the North and West will astound you."[30] This essay's positing of race as "the black-white issue," as in the *Rhetoric*, could thus arguably reflect nothing more than Burke's exploration of the divisive realm of rhetoric.

Yet, this argument fails, on two counts, to offer an adequate explanation for Burke's terministic choices. First, it fails to justify the implied white auditor of this last comment, a point which cannot be so easily set aside. Second, it also fails to account for the appearance of this same framing outside of these explicitly rhetorical texts. If we expand our focus beyond them, we find that this pattern of thought in regard to race is not limited to Burke's work on rhetoric. It is also, for example, reflected in his meditations on whites' "faulty means-selecting," rooted in "the distinction by color," in *Permanence and Change*.[31]

In fact, digging further, we can see that this pattern of thought is not even limited to Burke's *published* work. Similar language recurs throughout Burke's letters from the 1940s and 1950s, suggesting that

Burke typically, even habitually, drew upon a dialectical vocabulary when discussing racial identity. Witness his December 1945 letter to Ellison, where he characterized race in starkly oppositional terms: "Whenever I am with a Negro, I think of myself as white; so I do not see how I could reasonably expect that a Negro should similarly consider our culture in any but racial terms." Burke implied that the chasm between the two races was so wide that blacks' wholesale rejection of white America was understandable: "The situation itself invites you to be a kind of sophisticated Garveyite." To see the situation in nonracial terms, Burke concluded, a black American would essentially have to adopt a white perspective—to engage in "an intellectualized mode of 'passing.'"[32]

This binaristic treatment of race is a consistent feature of Burke's correspondence from the 1940s onward; in his letters to Ellison, Burke regularly described race in terms that posited an absolute divide between black and white Americans. In 1966, for example, Burke wrote Ellison in response to the publication of the essay "Harlem's America." Burke's letter included both a harsh judgment of New York and an implicit racial antithesis: "I grant you: Human beings can humanize damned near anything, even battlefields if need be—and the Negroes in Harlem have done wonders along those lines. *BUT LET THEM GET OUT IF THEY CAN.* Don't make a ghetto all over again."[33] Here Burke's language erects a clear divide between "us" and "them," reflecting strongly dialectical assumptions about race. Though possibly invoking a more inclusive "us," a 1967 letter from Burke to Ellison likewise positioned race as a conflict between two American opponents: "Currently, I see us confronting three major problems: Man and his machines, Black and white, Vietnam."[34]

Burke's antagonistic framing of race in these letters is not simply a reflection of their addressee; comparable language can be found in letters sent to Burke's white correspondents. In the early 1960s, for example, Burke wrote to Malcolm Cowley regarding a recent address that Burke had given to a group of local Unitarians. Since an area newspaper had mistakenly titled the talk as "Language and Race" (rather than "Language and Religion"), Burke reported that he had spontaneously opened the lecture with some advice to the assembled crowd: "Any time the issue of race comes up as regards our role as a world-power it's good to remember that we of the white race are decidedly a minority—and we might well keep that thought in mind with regard to our treatment of racial minorities in the U.S."[35] Here, as in his letters to Ellison, Burke's admonition to the audience posits race as a dialectical divide between "us" and "them."

Suggesting the depth of Burke's acceptance of this dualistic framing of race, these assumptions were not limited to Burke's public discourse, or even his comments on political news; they also appear in descriptions of his personal life. Writing Ellison about meeting Ellison's friend (and Tuskegee classmate) Albert Murray, Burke noted: "All the time we were exchanging views, my black son-in-law kept warning him against me. But that's par for the course."[36] Nearly a decade later, Burke similarly described a household divided by binaries of identity: "As for Injustice, my anthropology daughter is now mostly steamed up about the cause of feminism. Her husband, being a black man, agrees with your emphasis. I agree with both, though thinking that the Indians got the worst deal of all. And with my five-feet-four, I consider my sickly Selph [sic] a member of an aggrieved minority."[37]

Recall that a central characteristic of the dialectical order is that its polarities are not productive; on the contrary, the sheerly oppositional nature of dialectical terms tends to generate stalemates, standoffs, and—even if compromise intervenes—"mild demoralization." Here again the characteristics of the dialectical order match Burke's own discourse on race since the signs of stalemate are interspersed throughout Burke's correspondence. To put it bluntly, his discussions of race invariably display the frustration produced by dialectical opposition; whenever the topic of race emerges within it, his letters paint a bleak, demoralized, and paralyzed portrait of racial conflict.

Such a view is evident in many of the above quotations, but an especially powerful instance of dialectical framing appears in his 1945 reply to Ellison: "This much I am sure you will agree with: that so far as a white intellectual is concerned, *his* job is to do all that he can to mitigate the magic of race. Yet ironically, precisely at that same time, his colleague on the other side of the issue must talk of 'carrying as many white folks with me as I can.' Whereat I am in a muddle."[38] Using the professionalizing language of "colleagues," in this passage Burke positions black and white Americans on two different "side[s] of the issue," a turn of phrase explicitly highlighting the divisive, parliamentary nature of race. Moreover, he confesses his inability to envision a way out of this dialectical cacophony—that vituperation, separatism, and violence appear, to him, the inevitable results of the black-white struggle. Burke finds himself at a loss (or "in a muddle") about how to avoid such an eventuality, how to transcend this dialectical opposition.

Though these sentiments were written in late 1945, Burke drew similar conclusions in letters from subsequent decades; since these were not all addressed to Ellison, we can again assume that this linguistic pattern was not dependent upon audience or topic, but was simply characteristic of Burke's customary vocabulary regarding matters of race. For example, in a letter to the white sociologist Hugh Dalziel Duncan—who had expressed a desire to teach at an Historically Black College (HBC)—Burke saluted "your resolve to patch up your anti-lilywhite conscience."[39] Yet, Burke cautioned Duncan about this decision, stating that the move to an HBC would not thereby allow him to escape the dilemmas of the American racial hierarchy. Burke offered two examples as evidence in support of this claim.

First, drawing on the experience of an unnamed female white friend, he noted that, at such institutions, classism often substitutes for the racism of white-dominated institutions—that, in fact, black students from the upper classes are often more hostile "with regard to less educated Negroes than most white supremacists are with regard to Negroes generally."[40] However, Burke's words of warning also drew upon a second anecdote: "A Negro friend of ours happened to be at our place when the Faubus fuss first started. I was excited, and began saying that all liberal whites should offer to teach some of the time in Negro schools. Our Negro friend was decidedly glum about this noble project. He said, simply: 'Yes, whites teach in Negro schools, and do Negro teachers out of jobs!' Wadda woild!"[41] Burke's letter to Duncan is dated twenty years after his reply to Ellison, but it features a remarkably similar set of assumptions about race; just as in 1945, Burke here posits race as a clash of opposing positions, white and black, with irreconcilable interests. Further, in both instances, Burke's words display the "demoralization" characteristic of an irreconcilable opposition. His letters both end in a verbal shrug—with "wadda woild" and "in a muddle" sighing resignation to the gridlock of a contentious racial parliament.[42]

Given this particular framing of race, and its consistent use throughout Burke's published work and unpublished correspondence, I believe that we cannot focus simply upon the *Rhetoric*'s quotation of Ellison. Without question, this text uses Ellison's words to present a view of race that differs from that articulated in Ellison's own work. At the same time, the *Rhetoric* should not be abandoned because of this problematic citation. In fact, as demonstrated in the preceding analysis, *the text itself* points toward the larger fault in this treatment of race, and in Burke's vocabulary as a whole.

Burke's substitution of a dialectical for an ultimate order of terminology is no mere triviality. On the contrary, it is significant for understanding and developing the role of race in the Burke-Ellison relationship;

there are consequences, as Burke would tell us, to our vocabularies. Since any insight carries with it a corresponding blindness—and since the dialectical order is not atop the "hierarchy of terms"—I argue that Burke's dialectical terminology of race prevented him from generating an adequately complex account of race and identity. Drawing this critique together with the first chapter of the present book, I would point out that this terministic fault is not unique to Burke—it says as much about *American* racial discourse as it does about *Burke's*.

Burke's American Inheritance

In his 14 January 1948 letter to Ellison, Burke exuded the confidence of someone who had stumbled upon something of immense value in his final section of the *Rhetoric*; he clearly believed that his rhetorical analysis had produced an important insight into the workings of race in America. We might, with Ellison, question this confidence—especially given the resulting treatment of Ellison's "Richard Wright's Blues" within the published text. However, I believe that Burke was, perhaps inadvertently, correct: the *Rhetoric*'s distinction between positive, dialectical, and ultimate terminologies does provide great insight into discourse, including Burke's own, about race. Burke's engrained tendency was to treat race in dialectical terms since he consistently framed the issue as a struggle between two polar opposites; when forced to confront his own racial identity, Burke could only locate it in opposition to the black American "other." As befitting this racial "terministic screen," Burke thus found himself at a loss when contemplating possible solutions—the "mild demoralization" of compromise, not the possibility of transcendence, was the best he could summon.

Yet, this limited vocabulary should not be understood simply as an individual flaw, as the "smoking gun" that damns Burke as a reactionary or racist. Burke's dialectical terminology of race, in other words, is symptomatic of something more consequential than a personal failing. Burke's vocabulary reflects the quintessentially American discourse on race that continues—even today—to reinforce the "hypnotic division of Americans into black and white."[43] Rather than offering an indictment of Burke as a human being, we should thus reexamine the broader set of assumptions funding this vocabulary of race, the assumptions that continue to reinforce and reproduce the unproductive struggle of "black vs. white."

Burke's writings on race, in short, expose not only the history and limitations of his perspective, but also our own. Shifting focus in this way, from individual to cultural discourse, underscores the contemporary significance of the Burke-Ellison relationship. Burke's friendship with Ellison arose at a crucial moment in American history, as popular, political, and scholarly treatments of race transitioned from pluralism to polarity. As a result, by unpacking the dialogue between Burke and Ellison on matters of race—and by attending carefully to the moments of awkwardness or "mystery" between them—we gain new insight into a powerful discursive construction: the American racial divide.

Reflecting Burke's childhood in turn-of-the-century Pittsburgh, his earliest writings devote little, if any, attention to black Americans. The "bumpy passages" Burke later apologized for within *The White Oxen* instead are populated by Jews and Italians—and, to a much lesser extent, by the Irish, Polish, and Chinese.[44] Since the stories collected in it were written between 1918 and 1925, they display a racial hierarchy topped not by a monolithic white identity, but by the "Nordic," the "Old Stock" American. The unflattering depictions of racial "others" in these stories are not stereotypes of black Americans, but of these "problematic" immigrant populations.

This makes sense, since Burke's correspondence from the period was similarly peppered with racial epithets—but, again, primarily directed against these non-Nordic immigrants, with very few references to blacks. In short, these early works display a conception of race far different from that contained in the *Rhetoric*. During this period of his life, Burke, like this entire "generation of Americans *saw* Celtic, Hebrew, Anglo-Saxon, or Mediterranean physiognomies where today we see only subtly varying shades of a mostly undifferentiated whiteness."[45]

It was only a complex and volatile combination of factors—the Johnson-Reed (National Origins) Act, the Great Migration, and the rise of Hitler—that produced a decisive shift in Burke's, and America's, conception of race. By the 1930s and early 1940s, the dramatic reduction of immigration had eased popular hysteria about non-Nordic Europeans, and reports of Hitler's atrocities had begun to reframe the racial distinctions that, during Burke's childhood, had seemed so salient. When combined with the exponential increase in the North's black population, American racial discourse began to collapse "the so-called minor divisions of humanity" into a unified whiteness—creating a racial identity whose sole other was the black American or "Negro."[46] "The result," as we have seen over the course of this book, "was a culture of racial thinking . . . which encouraged Americans to focus on race-as-color and almost solely on whiteness and blackness, leaving them increasingly unable, or unwilling, to deal with national 'race questions' other than the purportedly peculiar conundrum posed by 'the Negro.'"[47]

In Burke's writings from these decades, we can observe the quiet construction of this racial binary, and his growing acceptance of race as a question of black and white. For example, his two books from the early 1930s, *Counter-Statement* and *Towards a Better Life*, omit the anti-Semitic and anti-immigrant slurs of his earlier volume *The White Oxen*—in favor of meditations on the personal and social function of such stereotypes.[48] Similarly, though the figure of "the immigrant" appears in an essay in *The Philosophy of Literary Form*, this figure is not racialized, but simply juxtaposed to "the kind of citizens" who can boast of "middle-class status."[49] Despite a passing reference to the "southern races," then, the majority of this text—published in 1941, but composed of essays written during the 1930s—instead reflects the transition to a new conception of race.[50]

In its pages, we see Burke largely dissociate himself from his previous conception of race; the book contains both a passing critique of Nordicism and, in "The Rhetoric of Hitler's 'Battle,'" a systematic and relentless unraveling of Hitler's anti-Semitism.[51] Illustrating the deeper significance of these critiques, in the latter, written in the last part of the 1930s, Burke specifically calls into question the racial distinction between Jews and Aryans—signaling his rejection of the racial discourse of the previous decades.[52] Moreover, another essay in this text contains a sign of the racial binarism then beginning to saturate American culture. In a review of the 1933 *Run, Little Chillun!* Burke contrasts the characteristics of the play's "Negro" characters with those of the "Caucasians," who display a "White ethic" rooted in industrial capitalism.[53] This essay presaged Burke's slightly more detailed discussion, in 1935's *Permanence and Change*, of "the distinction by color"—according to Burke, "a simple perception of a difference in color"—relied upon by "Poor Whites" in their scapegoating of blacks.[54]

As Jacobson points out, over the past seventy years Americans have become accustomed to thinking of race in such terms—accepting, that is, the obviousness of the visual differences between "white" and "black" persons. But this evolution in Burke's own treatments of race parallels "the waning of the paradigm that had produced the Johnson Act, and the emergence and consolidation of a new, binary racial arrangement that would come to dominate American political culture for the balance of the twentieth century."[55] What began, in *The White Oxen*, as a panoply of

races had become, by *Permanence and Change*, a clear—even "simple"—
"distinction by color," a demarcation of black and white, "Caucasian"
and "Negro." Thus, by the time that Burke met Ellison, in late 1942, he
had learned, and accepted, an entirely different vocabulary of race than
that taught him by his East Liberty peers. Out of an array of races had
emerged two; Burke talked about, and perceived, race in binaristic terms,
as a matter of "black and white."

One of the consequences of Burke's adoption of this dualistic vocabulary—as seen in the correspondence from the 1940s, 1950s, and
1960s—was his inability to adequately address the racial conflicts roiling
American culture during this period. Admittedly, these were no small
events; this period witnessed early struggles over Jim Crow practices in
the military and defense industries, the fight over segregation (and the
landmark *Brown v. Board* decision), as well as some of the prominent
early successes of the civil rights movement. Nonetheless, after Burke
learned to describe race as a binary opposition between whites and
blacks, we might say, his selection of terms functioned as a consequential
deflection.

Since demoralization—or, at best, unhappy compromise—is the hallmark of dialectical conflict, no solution appeared capable of resolving
these racial struggles unless one group was prepared to "lose." Burke
was trapped in such a terminology, both in his correspondence and in
the *Rhetoric*. As a consequence, he could only point to local strategies to
cope with the "black-white" problem, and could identify no real solution
to the antagonisms generated by it. Burke's dialectical terminology made
this inevitable, since he was prepared to address matters of race only as
dialectical discord; *there was no tenable solution to racial conflict, given
Burke's vocabulary, because black and white Americans were necessarily—by definition—opposed to one another.*

This insight represents the central argument of this book, the relevance of the Burke-Ellison relationship for the analysis of race in
America. The years spanned by the Burke-Ellison friendship included
the birth, propagation, and acceptance of racial binarism, but not its end.
This binaristic vocabulary of race is still prevalent in the public discourse
of our twenty-first century. If we, like Burke, remain at this dialectical
level of terminology, then I argue that we, like Burke, will struggle to
productively address racial conflict. Temporary, uneasy compromise
will seem the only way to avoid the eruption of violence between blacks
and whites. Accord will be fleeting; divisiveness, inevitable.

There is another option, however, as we have seen: the development of an ultimate vocabulary for treating matters of race. As Burke's *Rhetoric* makes clear, an ultimate vocabulary of race would be quite different from any we have yet considered since it would not only account for the positive and dialectical terministic orders, but it would arrange, structure, or harmonize them, producing something new: an understanding of even dialectical oppositions as "successive positions or moments in a single process" (187). Although, within this text, Burke suggests Marxism as a way for minorities to transcend social conflict, he qualifies this argument—arguing that Marxism is a terminology whose "solution" is more a placebo than a cure. It is, he says, a dialectical terminology cloaked in the trappings of the ultimate. Yet, Burke offers no alternative within this text. Marxism appears as the best of a bad set of options. As a result, this discussion in the *Rhetoric* does not present the discovery of an ultimate vocabulary, but only Burke's terministic inability to reconcile the oppositions between white and black racial identities.

Ellison, I believe, was able to envision what Burke could not: the possibility of an ultimate vocabulary of race. He offered hints of this in his 1945 letter to Burke, arguing that Burke's proposal to separate racial from universal was inadequate: "To throw away the concern with racial . . . emphasis would for me be like cutting away the stairs leading from my situation in the world to that universalism of which you speak."[56] Although Burke was only able to interpret Ellison's words dialectically, here we see Ellison implying a new approach to racial identity—one that does not treat race as an insoluble binary conflict, or as separate from the concerns of human existence as a whole.

With these words, Ellison suggested an approach to race and racial identities that resembled less a heated parliamentary wrangle than a harmonious, ultimate transcendence; the difference between the two, according to Burke, is analogous to that separating a Cartesian from a mystic.[57] Unlike the dialectical Cartesian, the mystic exemplifies the ultimate order, he writes, since "at moments when a mystic vocabulary is most accurate, we should not expect to find a flat antithesis between 'body' and 'spirit.' Rather, we should expect 'body' . . . to be treated as a *way into* 'spirit'" (189; original emphasis).

In like fashion, Ellison attempted to transcend the antithesis between the generically human and the racial. Ellison, unlike Burke, realized that black and white identities are antagonistic only from within a limited symbolic framework. I believe that, in this letter, Ellison thus began to sketch a more Burkean position on race than Burke himself was able to achieve—a position that he continued to explore, in fiction and nonfiction, over the next five decades. Consequently, using Ellison's work as a guide, I believe that we have another option than that offered by Burke: a more complex, *ultimate* vocabulary, which would treat race as *central to the question of human existence*, not as a parliamentary cacophony without hope of true cooperation.

With such a vocabulary, we would be disposed to treat racial identities as more than antithetical positions; further, we would be more equipped to recognize the ways in which these identities reflect the resources, temptations, and implications of our all-too-human symbolic condition. In this sense, Ellison's attempts to trace the production and fortification of racial identity and racial discord in American thought can be seen to reflect a different order of thought than that represented by Burke's writings. Ellison, unlike Burke, was more successful in understanding the complex workings of race because he sought an ultimate vocabulary for the treatment of racial identity. Burke, by contrast, stopped at the dialectical level, hence was never able to transcend, much less see beyond, the dialectical stalemate of "black vs. white."

At the same time, Burke's blindness was not solely an individual condition; it stemmed not from conflict with Ellison, but from his own place in the American social hierarchy—and the discourse about race that he internalized in the 1930s and 1940s. Once invested in a discourse of racial binarism, Burke was unable to address Ellison's arguments except through the polarity of Ellison's blackness and his whiteness. As a result, he was unable to envision a solution to racial conflict that did not reduce the complexity of race. Further, since Burke was disposed to see an unbridgeable gap between himself and Ellison, the "'mystery' of courtship" became an indelible part of their interaction.

Caught up in this mystery, Burke was unable to clearly see the similarities *or* the differences between his views and Ellison's; he was unable to recognize the ways in which Ellison's own thought was both an adoption and an extension of his own work. As in the epigraph of this chapter, we can see Burke as plagued by a limited (and limiting) racial discourse, one haunting his perception of the American social order; Ellison, recognizing the impact of racial psychology on white Americans, hoped for Burke's help in dispelling it. Though Burke could not provide this assistance himself, his writings offered the basis for Ellison's literary and critical examinations of the psychology of racial identity and racialized discourse.

Ellison clearly felt that Burke's work had a great deal to offer his own studies of the rhetoric of race. Taking Ellison's position seriously, this chapter constitutes a call to return to Burke's work in light of Ellison's project, and Ellison's in terms of Burke's. If we do, I believe that we will reveal more than the underlying Burkean themes in Ellison's work. Their friendship coincided with the earliest manifestations of racial binarism; their relationship, and their writings, thus represent an opportunity to reflect critically upon the discursive conditions now taken for granted in our treatments and assumptions of race.

It is to this end that the next, and final, chapter of this book is dedicated. By combining Burke's ultimate order with Ellison's writings on race and identity, I believe that we can identify the symbolic roots of racial binarism—and thereby create the possibility of speaking differently about race. Attuned to the connections as well as the divergences between Burke and Ellison, I hope that we might thereby move closer to a rhetorical appreciation, theorizing, and discounting of the American "racial divide."

5 /   From Turmoil to Peace:
An Ultimate Vocabulary of Race

> *Call it fallacious if you want. That need not concern us here. We are discussing the rhetorical advantages of an ultimate vocabulary as contrasted with a vocabulary left on the level of parliamentary conflict. We are but pointing to a notable formal advantage, got by the union of drama and reason, a wholesome rhetorical procedure in itself, at a time when typical "parliamentary" works . . . would ask us rather to unite drama with unreason.*
>
> —KENNETH BURKE, *A RHETORIC OF MOTIVES*

The previous chapter introduced Burke's critique of binaristic thinking in *A Rhetoric of Motives*, and his tripartite distinction between positive, dialectical, and ultimate terms. Recognizing the incomplete nature of positive and dialectical terminologies, Burke's text instead advocates a terminology that moves beyond them, one providing the "principle of principles" enabling the creative transcendence of entrenched opposition.[1] As we have seen, caught up in the language of "black vs. white," Burke was unable to apply this same conceptual scheme to his own thinking about race. However, I believe that Ellison—thanks to his careful study of Burke's corpus—envisioned what his friend could not, a nondialectical approach to the analysis of race.

Drawing upon Burkean concepts to track the symbolic dimensions of race, Ellison sought a different order of terms than that enshrined within the American "racial divide." Ellison's interest in this alternative path can be seen as early as the November 1945 letter to Burke discussed in chapters 2 and 4. In a passage critiquing the separation between the racial and universal, Ellison writes: "In the dialectical sense the two are one. And I would say that it is not a concern with race that has harmed American Negroes, but that they were not concerned with it enough."[2] This implicit criticism of Burke qualifies Ellison's expressions of admiration earlier in the letter; a Burkean philosophy of rhetoric might bring one to the "dropping-off place" for the contemplation of race, but Burke was not, Ellison suggests, able to see (let alone hear) around the corner of his white identity. Blinded by his whiteness, Burke failed to recognize that the analysis of race is inseparable from concern with human existence.

In fact, as Ellison later recalled in a piece included in his *Collected Essays*, one of his primary objectives in writing *Invisible Man* was to demonstrate the interconnection of the universal and racial: "My task was one of revealing the human universals hidden within the plight of one who was both black and American, and not only as a means of conveying my personal vision of possibility, but as a ways of dealing with the sheer rhetorical challenge involved in communicating across our barriers of race and religion, class, color and region—barriers which consist of the many strategies of division that were designed, and still function, to prevent what would otherwise have been a more or less natural recognition of the reality of black and white fraternity."[3] As in his 1945 letter to Burke, Ellison indicates that the overcoming of difference requires attention to the seemingly divisive subject of race. His novel, though, was not simply an illustration of this philosophical argument. *Invisible Man*, according to Ellison, was also intended to underscore the consequences of the American evasion of race: "I believed that unless we continually explored the network of complex relationships which bind us together, we would continue being the victims of various inadequate conceptions of ourselves, both as individuals and as citizens of a nation of diverse peoples" (523).

This passage reflects the urgency that drove Ellison to persevere, over the course of several years, in the completion of his (as Burke later described it) "epoch-making" book. Read in light of Burke's tripartite scheme, Ellison's novelistic unification of black and white also indicates his rejection of a dialectical vocabulary of race. By treating race as more than a sharply drawn line in the sand, Ellison focuses our attention upon the shared humanity buried beneath social dichotomies, and thereby hints at his adoption of an ultimate vocabulary—or something approaching it—in the novel.

Since an ultimate vocabulary produces not opposition but reconciliation through transcendence, Burke notes that the mystic's "clash of images by oxymoron" best approximates the ultimate resolution of dialectical strife.[4] When placed alongside this description of the ultimate order, Ellison's imagery in *Invisible Man* is charged with new significance; we see the Burkean implications of his invocation of the whiteness of blackness and blackness of whiteness, the silence of sound, and the black pigment ensuring the "pure" whiteness of Liberty Paints. The novel relies upon paradox and oxymoron to portray the possibilities lying beyond dialectical opposition—using the only terms proper to the expression of such an alternative.[5]

The posthumous publication of *Juneteenth* and *Three Days before the Shooting*... has revealed Ellison's continued fascination with these themes, with a host of new characters, encounters, and imagery embodying the hidden unity of whiteness and blackness.[6] However, I contend that Ellison's contribution to the development of an ultimate vocabulary of race cannot be limited to his award-winning novel, or its long-delayed, unfinished, successor. Though this is often overlooked, Ellison spent forty years, off and on, writing nonfiction—and I believe that these works represent an underappreciated, rhetorically grounded approach to the theorizing of race in America. Drawing explicitly and implicitly upon Burkean concepts, his essays demonstrate that social order is not given so much as produced, symbolically constituted—but, contra Burke, that the subject of race is not an outgrowth of such matters, but at its heart.[7]

"Cultural Pluralism" and the American Language

Ellison's fiction has received much more acclaim, but from the 1940s through the 1980s he crafted an impressive array of speeches and essays—pieces that offer a unique analysis of the nature and function of the American "racial divide." These nonfictional works, though they span several decades and a broad range of topics, share one foundational assumption: that the greatest American misconception about race is the belief in racial purity, the essential difference between white and black identities and culture. Ellison's essays reject this belief as a troubling denial of the cultural pluralism that lies at the heart of American life. Indeed, Ellison terms this all-too-common faith in racial purity a "fantasy" (579).

This fantasy, Ellison adds, appears in many guises; it is as evident in blacks' belief that they have been excluded from mainstream culture as it is in whites' recurring dream of a "lily-white America" (689, 578–80). He is understandably outspoken in his criticism of the white supremacist, whom he calls "a hypocrite who boasts of a pure identity while standing with his humanity exposed to the world" (109). Ellison is no less harsh in his judgment of the supremacist's black counterpart; "one of our most 'angry' Negro writers," he notes, "rants and raves against society, but he's actually one of the safest Negroes on the scene. Because he challenges nothing, he can only shout 'taint' to some abstract white 'tis,' counter-ing lies with lies. The human condition? He thinks that white folks have ruled Negroes out of it" (727).[8]

Regardless of who gives voice to this fantasy, Ellison remarks, "When you find some assertion of purity, you are dealing with historical, if not cultural ignorance" (443). Ignorance is the applicable term, Ellison in-sists, since blacks have been integral to American society since its found-ing—and even before, given the importance of slavery in the British colonies.[9] Ellison summarizes his point quite simply: "Without the pres-ence of blacks, our political history would have been otherwise" (580). Few would deny that the social status of blacks has constituted one of the defining issues of American politics, from the contentious crafting of the newly independent nation to the election of Barack Obama; to El-lison, our long-standing arguments over race represent telling evidence of black Americans' profound impact upon our national history.

Yet, this is only a portion of Ellison's argument for cultural pluralism. He points out that the above-mentioned public debates often raged with-out blacks' participation while, behind the scenes, black Americans ex-erted a profound impact upon the cultural life of the nation. As Ellison's essays remind us, "for all the harsh reality of the social and economic injustices visited upon them, these injustices have failed to keep Negroes clear of the cultural mainstream; Negro Americans are, in fact, one of its major tributaries" (580).

On the surface dominated by whites, American culture has been pro-duced by and through the efforts of all its inhabitants, slave and free, citizen and noncitizen. Just as generations of wealthy white families used black women to nurse, comfort, and raise their children, white entertain-ers and artists leaned heavily upon black folklore, music, and traditions for their inspiration and materials. This appropriation was as deliberate as it was thorough: "Whites took over any elements of Afro-American culture that seemed useful: the imagery of folklore, ways of speaking, endurance of what appeared to be hopeless hardship, and singing and dancing" (511). As an example of this process, Twain could not have written *Huckleberry Finn*, Ellison emphasizes, without the existence of black Americans.[10]

As a result, he contends that any attempt to talk about whiteness or white culture as distinct from blackness or black culture is doomed to failure. Ellison describes first having this realization in school, when "it occurred to me that what some of my 'teachers' were calling 'white literature' was not really *white* at all" (527). Our history contains "such deceptive metamorphoses and blending of identities, values, and life-styles that most American whites are culturally part Negro American without even realizing it" (580). According to Ellison, one of the clearest indications of this characteristically American intermixture is as vital as it is familiar: our language.

Ellison delves beneath the cliché that the Americans and British are separated by a common language. "We forget," he says, "conveniently sometimes, that the language which we speak is not English, although it is based on English" (762). Ellison claims that the separation of our native tongue from British English has as much to do with those speaking the language as with anything that we might speak about; ours is not a product of one tradition, but many. As an example, he writes that "there was no word in the English language to describe those long, flat stretches of land which had few trees and a great abundance of grass, so we took the word *prairie* from the French" (453). Yet, of the many dialects contributing to the creation of an "American" English language—including the British, Dutch, French, German, and Native American—Ellison identifies the "Negro American idiom" as perhaps the most important.[11]

Despite the second-class status accorded blacks, "the American language owes something of its directness, flexibility, music, imagery, mythology, and folklore to the Negro presence" (430). Ellison maintains that the easiest way to discover the cultural presence and impact of blacks is to simply listen to an American speak. "Whether it is admitted or not," he argues, "much of the sound of that language is derived from the timbre of the African voice and the listening habits of the African ear. So there is a *de'z* and *do'z* of slave speech sounding beneath our most polished Harvard accents, and if there is such a thing as a Yale accent, there is a Negro wail in it—doubtless introduced there by Old Yalie John C. Calhoun, who probably got it from his mammy" (581).

Ellison attributes this linguistic intermingling of black and white Americans to the conditions surrounding its birth; American English, he explains, is a language of revolutionaries. As a "vernacular revolt against the signs, symbols, manners and authority of the mother country," our language reflects the decision to break with the traditions and mores of the British (581). Imbued with this revolutionary spirit, the American language drew its raw materials not from England, but from the peoples and folkways contained within this new context. Blacks' speech and traditions were central to this process, Ellison contends, since this rebellious language embraced all that "proper English" excluded, regardless of source. Even as some fought to retain Europe's status as the arbiter of taste, "the vernacular stream of our culture was creating itself out of whatever elements it found useful, including the Americanized culture of the slaves" (610).[12] As a result, Ellison concludes, "the language of the United States is partly black people's creation" (446).

Improvising an Identity

Ellison's emphasis upon the insubordinate, pluralistic nature of American English leads him to stress the importance of the "vernacular." He extends the term to include more than linguistic elements; according to Ellison, our entire culture—and not simply our language—is marked by the vernacular. As he defines it, the vernacular refers to "a dynamic *process* in which the most refined styles from the past are continually merged with the play-it-by-eye-and-by-ear improvisations which we invent in our efforts to control the environment and entertain ourselves" (608; original emphasis). In this passage, Ellison describes the vernacular as active, not static—and, more importantly, as the vibrant improvisational process that *produces* American culture.

The colonists' decision to break from England, Ellison explains, produced a Delphic imperative: create thyself. The American Revolution represented the rejection of more than a political system; it was a rejection of the solidified class and caste lines that defined England, and the Old World as a whole. These newly minted Americans needed to forge a culture as well as a government, to create an entirely new tradition from the elements at hand. Here, for Ellison, lies the true significance of the vernacular; this dynamic, performative process melding adaptation and appropriation of available materials became our primary "way of establishing and discovering our national identity" (609).[13] No other nation's identity was so consciously founded upon the shifting sands of improvisation, Ellison argues, because "in no other country was change such a given factor of existence; in no other country were the class lines so fluid and change so swift and continuous *and intentional*" (701; original emphasis).[14]

These unique cultural conditions, arising from the rejection of the solidified structures of Europe, had additional implications at the level of the individual. By initiating a sharp break between American and European traditions, the revolt against England produced a radical kind of freedom for those populating the new country—the freedom of each person to make the future different than the past, and thereby to become someone else. Thus, American identity is more a matter of change than permanence since "the cultural circumstances here described offer the intellectually adventurous individual what might be termed a broad 'social mobility of intellect and taste'—plus an incalculable scale of possibilities for self-creation" (494). Ellison calls this our quintessential "belief in a second chance that is to be achieved by being born again—and not simply in the afterlife, but here and now, on earth" (630).

Even as this newfound freedom created possibilities for rebirth, it introduced a necessity into the American context: the *obligation* of each inhabitant to fashion her character and place within society. This demand, though, could not be satisfied by a single performance of identity. On the contrary, given the lack of firm and fixed roles, and the intensity and speed of cultural change, no one performance of self could ever be complete, or even sufficient. Incessant change and absence of caste, Ellison contends, instead mandated the continuous recreation of identity. Freedom sentenced each American to an unending series of self-asserting, improvisational acts.

The distinctive qualities of this performative process produce a unique kind of identity. The American self is one that Ellison describes as quite unlike that produced by the strictures of the Old World. He argues that the act of improvisation inserts a duality into every American identity; it necessitates a gap between birth and rebirth, performing self and self performed. To be an American, he writes, is to always be other than one appears. In more colloquial terms, this means that "there is a bit of the phony built into every American" (546).[15] This air of falseness, of duplicity, leads Ellison to compare the American creation of self to the donning of a mask. We bring our desired, "second," self to life by experimenting, improvising from another set of possibilities, and assessing the result—metaphorically speaking, trying on a new self. He points out that this process is as old as the nation itself: "Americans began their revolt from the English fatherland when they dumped the tea into the Boston Harbor masked as Indians, and the mobility of the society created in this limitless space has encouraged the use of the mask for good and evil ever since" (108).

There is an echo of this Tea Party in all American performances of self, according to Ellison, since these similarly involve the re-creation of identity through the assumption of a mask. Lest we take this too literally, he cautions that the everyday form of masking is "more than the adoption of a disguise. Rather it is a playing upon possibility, a strategy through which the individual projects a self-elected identity and makes of himself a 'work of art'" (629). Ellison consequently summarizes American life as a dynamic process whereby its inhabitants "play-it-by-eye-and-by-ear," but where these playful acts of masking are geared toward two quite serious ends: the artistic assertion (and reassertion) of status and place, and the continuous re-creation of American identity.

Constitutional Inequality and the Origins of Race

Ellison's emphasis upon the performance of identity might be seen as a privileging of individual over society, division over unity. However, he contends that the centrifugal forces exerted by continuous improvisation—and by the influx of new actors, lured by the promise of America—are balanced by an equally strong centripetal force: the "sacred covenant" of our Constitution. According to Ellison, the Constitution binds together all those engaged in improvisation by sanctioning their ongoing performances of self (465). In short, he believes that our communal, inventive masking makes, without unmaking, American identity because the vernacular process is anchored in the texts that birthed the nation and secured our political unity.

Ellison describes the nation's "sacred documents"—including the Declaration of Independence and Bill of Rights, in addition to the Constitution—as the vital "grounds" for our daily actions, the "script by which we seek to act out the drama of democracy, and the stage upon which we enact our roles" (773).[16] These documents are usually discussed in purely political terms, as the mechanisms by which our governmental processes were established and clarified. Ellison reads them instead (in Burkean fashion) as vital, founding symbolic acts, as a collection of interrelated principles that set forth the possibilities for selfhood in the American context.[17]

These principles were supposed to ensure that the democratic promise of our Revolution would be realized through unfettered collective self-creation, that we would have "a society in which a great landmass allowed peoples to move about, to change their identities if they would, to advance themselves, to achieve results based on their own talents and techniques" (757). Yet, tragically, the American "edenic" moment was undermined by the decision to reserve this freedom for a portion of the country's inhabitants, while denying it to others (774–75). The acceptance of slavery and, later, segregation meant that "instead of the single democratic ethic for every man, there now existed two: one, the idealized ethic of the Constitution and the Declaration of Independence, reserved for white men, and the other, the pragmatic ethic designed for Negroes and other minorities, which took the form of discrimination" (90).

This agreement to apportion freedom, he contends, signaled the Founding Fathers' failure to fully eliminate the hierarchies of the Old World. With this deviation from the "sacred script" of the Declaration of Independence, "a conflict arose between the terms in which revolutionary action had been taken and those in which it would be fulfilled" (774).[18] The declaration of equality for all was cruelly countered by the servitude of some, creating a fissure between principle and enactment, sacred script and actual practice—thereby inserting "a new principle or motive in the drama of American democracy . . . race" (776).[19]

Ellison argues that the Founders' failure, their "fall from democratic innocence," caused race to assume its now-familiar and complex role within American society (775). At one and the same stroke, they created a promising new nation and a conflict that would threaten its core principles—and, in the late nineteenth century, its existence. Unintentionally, though, their actions also accorded blacks a prominent place in American culture. This is why Ellison famously insists that "we view the whole of American life as a drama acted out upon the body of a Negro giant, who, lying trussed up like Gulliver, forms the stage and the scene upon which and within which the action unfolds" (85).[20]

For Ellison, then, blacks symbolize the "flaw" at the heart of American democracy, "similar to the crack that appeared in the Liberty Bell" (775). Dedicating the country to the promise of equality, its founders enshrined within it a race-based hierarchy that negated this promise. Thus, from the first moment of the nation's history, the social standing of black Americans has served as a yardstick measuring our progress toward the realization of the principles in our "sacred documents." Ironically, the decision to exclude blacks from American society placed them at its center, as "keeper of the nation's sense of democratic achievement, and the human scale by which would be measured its painfully slow advance toward true equality" (778).[21]

According to Ellison, this rift between principle and enactment also ensured that race was deeply woven into the warp and woof of American identity. In one sense, the relegation of blacks to second-class status bound Americans to their racial identities in material, observable fashion. Whether codified in law or common practice, blackness (or its lack) served as a central determinant of an individual's place in society, one not considered subject to improvisational transformation.[22] However, at an even more fundamental level, blacks have decisively shaped the nature and contours of American life. Ellison contends that this is because whites' efforts to separate themselves from black Americans have backfired spectacularly: "As a symbol of guilt and redemption, the Negro entered the deepest recesses of the American psyche and became crucially involved in its consciousness, subconsciousness and conscience" (778).

Culturally, Ellison argues, the furtive (but ever-present) awareness of the contradiction between democratic principles and race-based discrimination produces a staggering amount of guilt for white Americans. This, he writes, is the explanation for the racial stereotypes and myths that continue to pervade American entertainment. There is no need for guilt, these familiar forms whisper, since blacks are naturally inferior; their second-class status was preordained, not created by human beings. Ellison nicely summarizes this point: "Whatever else the Negro stereotype might be as a social instrumentality, it is also a key figure in a magic rite by which the white American seeks to resolve the dilemma arising between his democratic beliefs and certain antidemocratic practices, between his acceptance of the sacred democratic belief that all men are created equal and his treatment of every tenth man as though he were not" (84).[23]

Drawing explicitly on Burkean themes, Ellison points out that these stereotypes transform black Americans into living scapegoats for the alleviation of whites' socially produced guilt. Through the symbolic magic of stereotype and ritual, Ellison argues, black Americans are converted into "sacrificial victims for the benefit of the rest" (777). The rebellion against England, according to Ellison, required the vilification of the previous social order, and the deification of democracy; simultaneously, the earliest inhabitants of the new nation sought to expunge their own undesirable qualities as they transformed themselves, from subjects into citizens. The desire, at both levels, to cast out the devil that lay within led to the search for a ready scapegoat—and thus whites took advantage of the opportunity presented by the country's black population.

Targeted for the purification of white identity, black Americans, Ellison writes, were "shackled to almost everything [whites] would repress from conscience and consciousness" (102). Here, Ellison claims, lies the explanation for the long-standing association between blacks and such "uncivilized" and "undemocratic" characteristics as violence, animality, indolence, slavishness, instinct, and unrestrained sexuality.[24] Through the dissemination and repetition of stereotypes and myths, white Americans attribute all of their undesirable traits to blacks, who then become "perfect victims for sacrifice . . . placed beyond any possibility of democratic redemption not because of any overt act of social guilt, but simply by virtue of their position in the social hierarchy" (778).[25] Since whites use this scapegoat process to achieve a measure of psychological relief, on Ellison's analysis stereotypes represent not a simple matter of ignorance, but a complex form of ritual. They operate at a cultural level, to soothe fears about blacks' place in society, and relieve whites' socially induced guilt.

At the same time, Ellison contends that racial stereotypes serve another function, that "the tenacity of the stereotype springs exactly from the fact that its function is no less personal than political" (84). He believes these stereotypes play a vital role in American selfhood: they are the means by which whites skirt the obligation to continuously fashion their identities. Rather than embracing the vernacular process, and accepting the status earned by their actions, many whites find this prospect "far less inviting than clinging to the conviction that they, by the mere fact of race, color, and tradition alone, [are] superior to the black masses below them" (640).

According to the logic of the American racial hierarchy, whites, like blacks, are accorded an identity by virtue of their race. Because stereotypes eliminate the need for self-creation—reinforcing this hierarchy by reasserting the inferiority of blacks—they play an indispensable role in white consciousness. At an individual level, images of black inferiority ease the pressures surrounding the vernacular process; their presence, Ellison claims, is a vital means by which white identity is protected. By invoking racial stereotypes, whites manufacture stability, assurance that their status in society is secure. Contrary to popular belief, then, "the object of the stereotype is not so much to crush the Negro as to console the white man" (97).[26]

However, given the necessarily performative character of American identity, white equanimity can only be maintained by the continued reaffirmation of black inadequacy. This, Ellison argues, explains the attempt by whites to personify, and thus reassert, stereotypes through the "national art" of minstrelsy. The American tradition of minstrelsy is, then, an outgrowth of the desire for security. The performer (white or black) donning the ritual mask of the minstrel brings the stereotype to life, compels it to speak, dance, and sing, and thus "substantiates the audience's belief in the 'blackness' of things black" (104). Yet, even the reassuring minstrel figure cannot fully dispel white anxiety, since "out of the counterfeiting of the black American's identity . . . arises a profound doubt in the white man's mind as to the authenticity of his own image of himself" (107).

The realization, however fleeting, of the improvised nature of selfhood removes the existential security provided by the ritual: "When the white man steps behind the mask of the trickster his freedom is circumscribed by the fear that he is not simply miming a personification of his disorder and chaos, but that he will become in fact that which he intends only to symbolize" (107). When the pressure bearing upon white selfhood grows too great, Ellison concludes, violence erupts. Afterward, shaking their heads, Americans ruefully invoke the "racial divide" and, tragically, evade confronting the underlying impetus for these acts of violence—thus ensuring that there will be no real solution to "the problem of the color line."

More Than Dialectical, but Not Yet Ultimate

This careful, historically driven analysis arms Ellison with unique insight into the place of race within American culture. When examined closely, his essays contend, it is clear that our "racial divide" is neither natural nor absolute. Blacks, though systematically excluded from the benefits and opportunities of democracy, have contributed mightily to the production of American culture—and have developed unique traditions, values, and styles despite oppression, threat, and violence. Similarly, whites' faith in racial purity is belied by their long-standing reliance upon blackness and all that it represents, the qualities ritually excluded from possibility, from dominant culture. Racial stereotypes justify blacks' second-class status and shore up white identity, but, as Ellison's essays point out, these efforts inadvertently place blacks at the heart of American culture, conscience, and consciousness. To grasp this interpenetration of white and black Americans, he continues, is to realize something vital about our national life: "The distance between Americans, Negroes and whites, is not so much spatial as psychological" (83–84).

At an individual level, Ellison argues that the American contradiction between principle and practice is responsible for the tension, instability, mistrust, and fear marking interaction between whites and blacks. Ellison points out that the ritual dehumanization of black Americans has had a tremendous impact on the nature of black selfhood, as seen, for example, in his analysis of Richard Wright's biography.[27] Yet, whites have also been shaped by the substitution of stereotypes for complex images of humanity; the reliance on stereotypes has produced a fractured white identity, a self both guaranteed and destabilized by the presence of blackness.

Taken as a whole, this complex dynamic, a product of our nation's birth, remains our legacy—even after the 2008 presidential campaign. Without a change in our discourse about race, no election can dispel the power of our "racial divide." Only by confronting the "fantasy" of racial purity, exploring our complex cultural pluralism, Ellison writes, can we begin the hard work of American democracy, with its demanding "puzzle of the one-and-the-many" (207). As Ellison concludes: "All blacks are part white, and all whites part black. If we can deal with that dilemma—and it is a dilemma—then we can begin to deal with the problem of defining the American experience as we create it" (442).

Ellison's essays offer something quite unique in their examination of the place of race, and of black Americans specifically, in the trajectory of American history. This uniqueness derives less from their subject matter, though, than from their approach to it. The essays pose questions about the ritual dimensions of race, including the psychological function of visual and verbal stereotypes of black Americans. They ask why racial divisions, and their reinforcement, are necessary to the maintenance of American social order—and American identity. Similarly, they interrogate the symbolic machinations that reinforce belief in the American "racial divide."

In addressing these, and other, related, questions, Ellison's essays do not advocate the elimination of distinction, thereby equating the universal with uniformity. Nor do they propose an oppositional social order, a wholesale rejection of the white-dominated American social order. Given the political trends and upheavals of the 1950s, 1960s, and 1970s, this position did not endear Ellison to others, black or white, who espoused more oppositional—dialectical—vocabularies.[28] However, I believe that this position, when restated in Burkean terms, reflects Ellison's desire to achieve a higher order of analysis.

Through his nonfiction, I believe that Ellison took steps toward an ultimate vocabulary, by providing a complex analysis of the nature and function of the American "racial divide." Yet, I also believe that he did not, in the end, fully transcend the second, dialectical order of terminology identified by Burke. By pushing Ellison's insights further—toward the symbolic conditions motivating the production of racial binarism—I contend that we can move closer to the ultimate account of race begun within Ellison's essays. First, however, we must finish preparing the ground for this Burkean-Ellisonian vocabulary, by contrasting it to the two orders that it must transcend.

Visible Differences: Race and the Positive Order

As described in chapter 4, Burke's explication of his tripartite scheme in *A Rhetoric of Motives* begins not with the top of the hierarchy, but with the bottom: the positive order.[29] In part, this choice reflects Burke's argument that these three orders are nested, that each level of the hierarchy is contained within the one that transcends it; as a result, ultimate transcendence is impossible without the disciplined movement through the first two stages of the hierarchy. This choice also reflects common assumptions about the nature of language. Most often, as Burke acknowledges, words are understood to be vehicles for designating the things of the world.

Recognizing both the popularity and the practical value of this view of language, Burke inscribes it within the first level of his terministic hierarchy; he defines the positive order as the set of terms that corresponds to the contents of sensory experience. Burke even borrows a Kantian framework to explain this relationship between word and thing: "The 'sensibility' receives a bundle of 'intuitions,' intimations of size, shape, texture, color, and the like; and as the 'understanding' clamps a unifying term, a 'concept,' upon the lot, we can say, 'This is a house.'"[30] Though Burke does not wholly adopt Kant's perspective as his own, it provides him with a handy analogy since the positive order involves the direct application of a term to a particular, empirically given, portion of the world.

Burke is careful to point out that the referential power of the positive order is limited to the nonsymbolic realm; positive terms refer to events and processes that are independent of (and logically prior to) human symbolicity.[31] Given this strong link between the positive order and perceptual immediacy, Burke notes that "a positive term is most unambiguously itself when it names a visible and tangible thing which can be located in time and place."[32] Positive terms, then, isolate and identify portions of the empirical world—with the existence and fixity of each object determining, even guaranteeing, the meaning of each word.

On first glance, the subject of race would seem an especially good match for this terministic order. Race is commonly thought to be a matter of perceptual immediacy, of nature—that to talk about race is to refer to the perceivable physiological characteristics that distinguish one human population from another. Just as in Burke's Kantian analogy, on this everyday view, race involves the application of linguistic labels to clusters of perceptual data. To use a racial term is not to imply a judgment, but to indicate the color of someone's skin, or the shape of someone's eyes—objective data, in other words, which are not subject to interpretation.[33] Similarly, to identify someone as a member of the "white race" or "black race" is merely to classify them, to identify their group membership from a set of empirically observable and stable characteristics, such as skin color, physiognomy, and bone structure.

The emphasis upon racial classification further resonates with Burke's description of the positive order. As we have seen, positive terms fall within the same "order," in the sense of "category" or "realm." However, there is a second sense in which positive terms constitute an "order"; order, Burke suggests, is as much a verb as a noun. In other words, the positive order represents both a specific kind of term, *and* a particular way of arranging these terms. Expanding upon this point, Burke claims that not only do positive terms "name par excellence the things of experience, the *hic et nunc*," but also that "they are defined *per genus et differentiam*, as with the vocabulary of biological classification."[34] According to Burke, then, terms are categorized as positive because they name the contents of perception—but positive terms are also ordered taxonomically.

Similarly, for the past three centuries, discourse about race has involved more than a simple list of terms; it has also involved the arrangement of these terms into racial taxonomies.[35] Despite the differences between Dillingham's forty-five,[36] Blumenbach's five,[37] and the U.S. government's fifteen[38] different racial categories, these schemes evince a common desire to provide an accurate, exhaustive delineation of the "natural kinds" of humanity. This is not to say that *particular* taxonomies have avoided serious challenge.[39] However, the cataloging of human differences itself remains an accepted part of popular, political, and scholarly treatments of race. Yet, I would argue that the disagreement, instability, and uncertainty surrounding these taxonomies are symptomatic of a larger problem: when examined more closely, race involves more than a simple reference to the nonsymbolic realm.

Separating Symbolic from Nonsymbolic: "Race" vs. "Ethnicity"

Burke is careful to praise the "positivist ideal of language" as "athletic and exacting."[40] He elaborates, pointing out that "not only is the positive order of vocabulary 'allowable'; we should be reluctant to leave this order. Every question should be reduced to such terms, insofar as the nature of its subject-matter permits."[41] The problem, according to Burke, is that with many subjects the relationship between language and world is more complex than it appears—that, in such cases, our experience is as much a product of the symbolic as the nonsymbolic. Burke describes this as "an area where nonverbal things, in their capacity as 'meanings,' also take on the nature of words, and thus require the extension of dialectic into the realm of the physical. Or, otherwise put, we come to the place where the dialectical realm of ideas is seen to permeate the positive realm of concepts."[42] Topics involving a mixture of idea and concept, he tells us, cannot be adequately addressed using a positive vocabulary.

The examples that Burke draws upon are architectural, the "meanings" concretized in the upward sweep of church spires and skyscrapers. Though these neatly illustrate his point, Burke might just as easily have cited the subject of race. As described in chapter 1, American racial discourse has long displayed a tendency to combine social characteristics with natural ones—that is, a tendency to associate physical features with nonphysical traits such as intelligence, criminal tendency, political views, and capacity for self-governance.[43] In the 1930s and 1940s, scholars like Franz Boas, Ruth Benedict, and Ashley Montagu targeted these unwarranted associations in their critiques of racialist thinking.[44] In Burkean terms, these scholars warned against the sinister confusion of the empirical and the ideational, the nonsymbolic and the symbolic, the positive and the dialectical. According to Boas, Benedict, and Montagu, "scientists" of race saw biology at work in every social difference, and ignored evidence to the contrary—thereby smuggling normative judgments into their "positive" descriptions and taxonomies of the human species.

Inspired by these critiques of racialist thought, in the mid-twentieth century like-minded scientists, scholars, activists, and governmental officials attempted to definitively disentangle the natural and social dimensions of group identity. One notable product of this intellectual movement was the 1950 "Statement on Race," created under the auspices of the United Nations Educational, Scientific, and Cultural Organization (UNESCO).[45] This document, widely circulated through the press, explicitly attempted to separate the symbolic from the nonsymbolic in the classification of human beings: "The biological fact of race and the myth of 'race' should be distinguished. For all practical social purposes 'race' is not so much a biological phenomenon as a social myth."[46]

The key recommendation offered by the "Statement" was a logical outgrowth of this position: "National, religious, geographic, linguistic and cultural groups do not necessarily coincide with racial groups: and the cultural traits of such groups have no demonstrated genetic connexion with racial traits. Because serious errors of this kind are habitually committed when the term 'race' is used in popular parlance, it would be better when speaking of human races to drop the term 'race' altogether and speak of ethnic groups."[47] This proposal was initially derided as unrealistic by many commentators, but, in subsequent decades, scholars, politicians, and members of the public loosely adopted the recommended distinction between "race" and "culture" or "ethnicity."[48] This terministic distinction—still alive within contemporary discussions of race—was felt to more accurately distinguish symbolic from nonsymbolic, biology from society, in matters of identity.

Yet, although this distinction appears to celebrate the symbolic dimensions of identity, it does not actually represent the transcendence of a positive terminology of race. According to this revised set of terms, "race" designates those aspects of human difference not dependent upon symbolicity, while "culture" and "ethnicity" designate symbolically or socially produced differences in group identity. In other words, this distinction simply splits the vocabulary of race in two, with one set of terms corresponding to the empirical, nonsymbolic differences between human beings. The use of this distinction does not, as a consequence, signal the relinquishing of a positive terminology of race. On the contrary, it signals a willingness to accept the *truth*, just not the *significance*, of racial difference. This distinction tries to eliminate the everyday use of racial terms, while tacitly accepting these terms' positive referents.

The race/ethnicity pairing redirects our attention—toward the differences in identity that are due to culture—but does not represent a true alternative to the positive terminology of race. Not surprisingly, this modification of American racial discourse has similarly failed to realize the hopes expressed in the UNESCO "Statement on Race." It has not eliminated the "social myth" of race, nor has it prevented problematic associations between physical features and nonphysical traits. On the contrary, many critics argue that the slippery nature of these two terms has instead contributed to the creation of new errors and misunderstandings in our conception of race.

The defects of the race/ethnicity pairing have become glaringly apparent in one important context: the U.S. Census.[49] In 1997, after a much-publicized review of federal standards, the government's official list of

racial categories was revised—a process that led to the inclusion of biracial and multiracial identity within the 2000 Census.[50] News coverage of
this change, though, threatened to eclipse another story generated by the
results: the government's pronouncement that Latino/as had incorrectly
completed the form.[51] Their "error" had less to do with the mechanics
of the process than with the assumptions embedded within the Census
form. Simply put, the government claimed that millions of Latino/as had
failed to accurately distinguish their race from their ethnicity.

This mistake was made possible by the 2000 Census's inclusion of one
question about race, and one about respondents' "Hispanic origins."[52]
The form thereby proposed a clear and fundamental separation between
culture/language/social identity and race—aspects of identity that are
social, and aspects that are natural. Disregarding this distinction, and
the government's instructions, millions of Latino/as indicated that their
race and ethnicity were identical. Failing to recognize themselves in the
Census's racial categories, they checked "other" for their race, and wrote
in "Hispanic," "Latino," "Mexican," or the like.[53] According to the federal standards, this is incorrect: "The government . . . says none of those
is a race. Hispanic or Latino is a culture, a language, a social identity.
Mexican (or some other country name) is a nationality."[54] As evidenced
by news reports such as this, the government's complaint stemmed from
the separation of race from culture, language, and social identity (i.e.,
ethnicity), and a belief that Latino/as do not represent a "natural kind,"
unlike whites, blacks, or Asians.[55]

The objections raised to these assumptions by advocacy groups led
to a revision of the form for the 2010 U.S. Census, and a clarification
of the status of Latino/as within the tally. The new version of the form
added a definitional statement: "For this census, Hispanic origins are
not races."[56] Yet, even this decree failed to fully dispel the ambiguity
surrounding Latino/a racial identity—since the government's solution
remained rooted in the troublesome distinction between race and ethnicity. On the amended 2010 Census form, a question targeted to those
of "Hispanic, Latino, or Spanish origin" appeared just below the definition described above. This question, as on the previous three censuses,
provided Latino/as an opportunity to specify their ethnic heritage. They
were also asked, on the subsequent question, to report their race. As a
result, Latino/as were uniquely accorded a double identity: an ethnic origin, which involved their identity as "Hispanic, Latino, or Spanish," and
a race, which did not.[57]

Although the inclusion of a definitional statement on the 2010 Census form made it less likely that respondents would "misidentify" their race as "Hispanic, Latino, or Spanish," it highlighted the government's acceptance of a curious set of distinctions. For example, according to the categories enshrined in the 2010 Census, "Mexican" and "Cuban" are defined as ethnicities, but not races, while "Japanese" and "Filipino" are defined as races, but not ethnicities.[58] Left unexplained is how the latter two terms, unlike the former two, indicate something independent of human symbolicity—how, that is, "Japanese" represents a "natural kind," while "Mexican" does not.

This odd categorical contrast represents more than a minor embarrassment for the U.S. Census Bureau; it represents the instability of the discursive framework relied upon in the construction of the form. To address the problems arising from the Census, in other words, requires more than a slight alteration of the government's form; it requires alteration of the racial discourse that the Census draws upon and reinforces. The first wave of assaults on the dominant American conception of race resulted in the separation of "race" from "ethnicity"—a distinction that was intended to end the association of biological features and social differences. However, as the U.S. Census clearly demonstrates, this distinction multiplies, not reduces, the ambiguity surrounding race.

The complications created by the official tally of Latino/as are indicative of the central problem with the race/ethnicity pairing: the problem of correctly distinguishing natural groupings from cultural groupings. The only way to distinguish race from ethnicity is to assume that the former term (unlike the latter) designates something empirical, that it corresponds to real, self-evident, portions of the nonsymbolic realm. This attempt to police the boundary separating social from natural difference does not so much critique the positive order as quietly cling to it. For this reason, many contemporary scholars—recognizing that race is a subject where "nonverbal things, in their capacity as 'meanings,' also take on the nature of words"[59]—have advocated the merging of this pair of terms. They have tried to effect a shift in our discourse of race, from a positive vocabulary to an explicitly dialectical one.

The "Social Construction" of Difference: Race and the Dialectical Order

Over the last three decades, scholars from across the academy have rejected the race/ethnicity pairing, denying the existence of *any* positive referent for the term "race." A substantial body of scholarship has grown around this position, scholarship typically summarized as the argument for the "social construction of race."[60] Put simply, constructionists contend that the origin, objects, and effects of racial discourse derive purely from social (and not natural) processes. Although their conclusions often reflect dramatically different disciplines and methodologies, in Burkean terms what unites these scholars is their agreement upon one central point: race is a subject that cannot be adequately addressed by the positive order of terms.

Scholars from the natural and social sciences are among the most prominent constructionists in the academy, given their willingness to tackle the evidence supporting the positivist view of race. These scholars have developed systematic programs of study interrogating the assumption that race is, in fact, "a basic terminology of perception grounded on sensation, memory, and 'imagination' (in the general, nonpsychological, nonpoetic meaning of the word)."[61] Results of their studies have cast considerable doubt on this proposition, and on the related attempts to distinguish race from ethnicity.[62]

Studies of childhood development, for example, have established the learned nature of racial perception—and reconstructed the processes that socialize children into the distinctions that later appear self-evident.[63] Psychological studies of race and cognition have similarly concluded that "the presence of kind labels may organize and drive perception, gracefully explaining why children who know racial terms do not sort individuals into racial categories on the basis of the perceptual features used by adults."[64] Findings such as these suggest that there is no way to separate symbolic processes from the determination of difference—even if that difference appears to be naturally occurring. There is no way, in other words, to cleanly distinguish the perceptual markers of race from the social cues typically associated with ethnicity.[65]

Moreover, researchers within the natural sciences have accumulated significant evidence refuting the biological basis of American racial categories.[66] Population geneticists, for example, have determined that there is little relationship between physiognomy and genetic ancestry. This means that, despite popular assumptions to the contrary, appearance offers little clue to the genetic makeup of an individual—that, to cite but one example, "skin tone is so ephemeral and so sensitive to a few genes, that it is nearly useless as an indicator of either Afro-European ancestry or Afro-European genetic admixture (which are themselves different things)."[67]

Further, researchers have found no correlation between racial categories and patterns of genetic difference. There is so little relationship, in fact, that "most physical variation, about 94%, lies within so-called racial groups. Conventional geographic 'racial' groupings differ from one another only in about 6% of their genes. This means that there is greater variation within 'racial' groups than between them."[68] Research in genetics thus indicates that racial categories fail to map onto any empirical, nonsymbolic differences between humans—that genetic patterns make a mockery of our "natural kinds."[69] "Because of the extensive evidence for genetic interchange through population movements and recurrent gene flow going back at least hundreds of thousands of years ago," most geneticists conclude that "there is only one evolutionary lineage of humanity and there are no subspecies or races under either the traditional or phylogenetic definitions."[70]

Other scholarly accounts, by contrast, focus less on matters of proof than of process. Studies of this latter type contend that race is both politically charged and culturally relative—a product of social needs, not natural law.[71] Thus, supplementing the science-driven research described above, constructionists from the humanities utilize philosophical, legal, and historical analysis to reveal the contingency and artificiality of our racial vocabulary. This portion of the constructionist literature constitutes a different, but formidable, type of assault on American racial discourse: an explicit demonstration of its dialectical character.

Chapters 2 and 4 have already described Burke's second, dialectical, order, the realm of "words for *principles* and *essence*," not perceptual data.[72] Dialectical terms "refer to *ideas* rather than to *things*. Hence they are more concerned with *action* and *attitude* rather than with *perception* (they fall under the head of *ethics* and *form* rather than *knowledge* and *information*)."[73] Just as Burke draws these comparisons to help explain the dialectical order, many constructionist accounts begin with a similarly stark contrast: "Racial categories are often seen as 'natural' or as having some inherent biological component. But some have understood for decades that categories of race in the United States have little to do with natural history and a great deal to do with social and political history.... Racial categories are produced and reproduced ideologically and culturally: they are constructed."[74]

This quote summarizes a basic tenet of the constructionist position: race is inseparable from the symbolic negotiation of power and position, more a product of social and political processes than of nature. Yet, accounts such as these contribute something more valuable than a simple contrast between the biological and social; they also provide a delineation of the constitution, evolution, and consequences of our accepted racial categories. Further, by emphasizing race as an idea, as an attitude, and not an extant object or body of knowledge, these analyses effect a definitional shift: "The effort must be made to understand race as an unstable and 'decentered' complex of social meanings constantly being transformed by political struggle. With this in mind, let us propose a definition: *race is a concept which signifies and symbolizes social conflicts and interests by referring to different types of human bodies.*"[75] This expanded definition, representative of constructionist accounts, implies that race should be treated less as a narrow positive term than as a broader dialectical one, less as a Kantian concept, that is, than as a Burkean *title*.

Race as "Ideology": The Dialectical Dilemmas of Constructionism

In contrast to positive terms, which involve a referential relationship between word and world, Burke describes dialectical terms as titles.[76] Just as the title of a book encapsulates a wealth of details about characters, settings, and plot, dialectical terms "sum up a vast complexity of conditions which might conceivably be reduced to a near-infinity of positive details."[77] This same relationship between title and contents is suggested by constructionist texts, which depict race as an assembly of interrelated processes, institutions, and objects—or, as in the above-quoted passage, "a complex of social meanings . . . referring to different types of bodies." According to this formulation, race can implicate, but not objectively represent, any portion of the nonsymbolic world. Like Burke's examples of "Elizabethanism" and "capitalism," race functions as a dialectical title, uniting a complex set of materials, symbolic and nonsymbolic, under its head.[78]

As redefined by constructionist scholars, then, the dialectical principle of race summarizes or entitles a multifaceted situation (Burke's "vast complexity of conditions") whose elements are biological, environmental, geographical, affective, cultural, economic, political, governmental, and linguistic. Though scholars disagree over the precise formulation of this dialectical relationship, they agree on its general outlines. Smedley, for example, calls race not a word but a "worldview," "a way of imposing order and understanding on complex realities in which one group asserted dominance over others."[79] Others, like Gross, define race as "a powerful ideology, which came into being and changed forms at particular moments in history as the product of social, economic, and psychological conditions."[80] Still others, emphasizing race as perspectival, use the language of "framing" to describe the complex entitlement characteristic of race. Feagin thus names the dominant American discourse of race the "white racial frame," which is "a centuries-old worldview [that] has constantly involved a *racial construction of reality* by white and other Americans, an emotion-laden construction process that shapes everyday relationships and institutions in fundamental and racialized ways."[81] Despite the slight differences in emphasis between "frame," "ideology," and "worldview," these formulations position race as a complex title, not as a simple term—as "shorthand" for an entire structure of mutually reinforcing terminologies, practices, and institutions.

However, the dialectical order is not simply the realm of titles, but also the realm of heated conflict *between* titles. This reflects the dual nature of Burke's "orders": as with the positive order, the dialectical is both a type of term and a mode of arrangement. The second characteristic of the dialectical order, then, is the establishment of a contentious parliament, the organization of "a conflict among spokesmen for competing ideas or principles, . . . a situation wherein there is no one clear choice" between them.[82]

In part, this parliamentary conflict is generated from *within* dialectical vocabularies—since gathered under any summarizing title is an interrelated set of subtitles. Reflecting the nature of dialectical ordering, these subtitles are constituted as antagonists; they relate to each other as combatants sharing only a common battlefield.[83] Thus, conflict emerges within a dialectical vocabulary because the process of entitlement is simultaneously the creation of competition, not cooperation, between the elements that it summarizes.

Chapters 1 and 4 have detailed the ways in which the American vocabulary of race—like Burke's own—embodies this parliamentary quality of the dialectical order. Although our accepted racial categories have shifted over time, their hierarchical, competitive relationship has not; American racial discourse arranges its categories into a contentious cacophony, a congress of warring racial "spokesmen." As one constructionist summarizes this point, "Central to racial thinking is not only the notion that the categories of white, black, brown, yellow, and red mark meaningful distinctions among human beings but also that they reflect inferiority and superiority."[84]

During the 1930s and 1940s, as described in chapter 1, this parliamentary struggle was distilled to the purest, most polarized form of parliamentary conflict—the binary opposition between the subtitles of "white" and "black." It is this tenacious, paralyzing version of dialectical discord that the "social construction of race" attempts to address, by highlighting the relative, and reductive, nature of this dialectical division between the races. Some constructionist efforts thus critically examine the antagonism between blacks and whites,[85] while others highlight the exclusionary nature of this divide, celebrating the groups marginalized by this artificial binary.[86] Regardless of the particular strategy selected, these studies attack the American reluctance to abandon the positive order, and our tendency to readily accept race as a natural division between black and white. In Burkean terms, by making the dialectical nature of American racial discourse explicit, these constructionist accounts hope to expose its utter artificiality, and more effectively combat it.

However, according to Burke, there is another type of parliamentary conflict characteristic of the dialectical order: the competition between different ways of entitling the same "near-infinity of positive details." As Burke explains, the elements drawn together or entitled by a dialectical principle are not, strictly speaking, tied to that particular principle. On the contrary, these elements can be recombined, and retitled, under a different heading; such retitling, however, typically generates enmity between these alternative titles. It is this inclination toward titular antagonism, Burke writes, that explains why "terms of this sort are often called 'polar.'"[87]

This second type of parliamentary conflict suggests a critical limitation of the arguments for the "social construction of race." The exposure of the dialectical nature of American racial discourse represents a significant achievement; such scholarship highlights the quixotic nature of our efforts to match symbolic categories to the uncooperative nonsymbolic realm, whether through the Census form or the reduction of race to a combative binary. Yet, because it simply asserts the contingent nature of race, the constructionist position can only offer an alternate entitlement of the same set of particulars—an opposing structure of terms to use in summarizing the American social scene. Unless such a vocabulary shifts ground and moves toward an ultimate order, Burke would point out, it merely generates another polarity—in this case, racial binarism versus social construction. Under such conditions, as with the binary of black vs. white, "there is no one clear choice."[88]

In this respect, the constructionist view of race resembles a project critiqued by Burke in the *Rhetoric*: the "relationism" of Karl Mannheim's *Ideology and Utopia*. Burke summarizes his view of Mannheim in the working notes from this section of text: an "ultimate ordering gives a way in, way through, and ultimate direction—as vs. the this-against-that kind of terminology."[89] For Burke, projects like those advocated by Mannheim fall into the latter category. They represent the continuation of a fruitless parliamentary debate, not its resolution, because they fail to move beyond terministic stalemate.

Mannheim's contention is that "a human terminology of motives is necessarily partial; accordingly, whatever its claims to universal validity, its 'principles' favor the interests of some group more than others."[90] Mannheim's "sociology of knowledge" utilizes this insight to "neutralize" vocabularies, exposing the biased relationship between any vocabulary (or "ideology") and its motivational ground—the myriad details comprising a past or current social order. Burke remarks that this systematic discounting of ideology *seems* to provide the arranging order of an ultimate vocabulary, the transcending of partisanship through elimination of bias. However, he cautions, Mannheim's project fails to achieve such transcendence; Burke thus labels it a "pro-ultimate" vocabulary.[91]

The problem, Burke writes, is that Mannheim's project cannot avoid its own critique. Since it, too, can be discounted as an "ideology" by an opposing vocabulary, it cannot provide the guidance needed to organize discordant dialectical voices. Mannheim's vocabulary remains mired in the dialectical "this-against-that"; it adds a new voice to the parliamentary wrangle of the dialectical realm, rather than offering a hierarchizing arrangement of it. By discounting every vocabulary, including his own, Mannheim fails to provide the "way in, way through, and ultimate direction" of an ultimate vocabulary.

I believe that Burke's argument against Mannheim equally applies to the scholarship advocating the "social construction of race." Constructionist accounts echo Mannheim's emphasis upon the partiality of "ideologies" in their attempts to demystify race, to expose the prejudice hidden behind its apparent objectivity. They examine the ways in which, though apparently neutral, the idea of race is mobilized to secure symbolic and material advantages for particular groups within American society—largely, though not exclusively, white Americans. Just as Mannheim's attack on "ideologies" is susceptible to its own critique, the constructionist argument is no less partial, and no less dialectical, than the discourse that it critiques.

To celebrate the constitutive power of language, and thereby redescribe race as an "ideology," "worldview," or "frame," is to open oneself up to the same charge. Because it attacks the representational power of language, the constructionist argument, when challenged, is on no surer ground than the discourse it rejects; it cannot point to any foundation that would guarantee the accuracy of its critique. This is, I argue, the problem with the constructionist position: it points out the dialectical qualities of American racial discourse, but does not thereby transcend the dialectical realm. Like Mannheim, it adds to, but does not resolve, the parliamentary debates over race.

Witness, as evidence of this point, the reactionary assaults on the "ideology" of social construction. Although the blogosphere abounds with examples,[92] assaults also appear in more scholarly texts: "The proposal to scrap the concept of race altogether is currently only one extreme in a range of views. It is certainly not shared by all anthropologists and is by no means the majority opinion of the public at large. It appears to be a conclusion reached more on the basis of political and philosophical creeds than on scientific arguments."[93] In dialectical fashion, works such as this level point-by-point rebuttals of the constructionist view. In response to the scientific debunking of race, race defenders assert the priority of empirical evidence. They contend that constructionists are blind to the obvious reality of and evidence for race—that constructionists' desire to see a "color-blind" world clouds their vision, and distorts their findings. In response to the charge of white privilege, defenders offer a countercharge: the constructionist argument is no less partisan since it reflects an antiwhite and pro-minority bias. Operating in this fashion, echoing each of the critiques leveled against them, race defenders have been successful in repelling the constructionist assault on race.[94]

Because its vocabulary remains at the dialectical level, the constructionist argument is highly susceptible to these countercharges; its retitling of American society can be readily neutralized by the reassertion of the principle of race. Faced with entrenched opposition, constructionists are drawn into an unresolvable, demoralizing, binaristic conflict—the same type of conflict that their vocabulary hoped to dispel. They reassert their evidence, extend their analyses, and seek new evidence of white privilege; none of these tactics can end the conflict with race defenders since none of these addresses the underlying problem. The defect that Burke identifies within Mannheim's vocabulary is the same one that mars the constructionist position: in its inability to seek a higher order of terminology, the "social construction of race" represents less the transcendence of dialectical discord than its continuation.

Like those advocating a constructionist position, Ellison sought an alternative to the American "racial divide," our characteristically dialectical vocabulary of race. Through his nonfiction, Ellison took careful aim at racial binarism, dismantling it through careful analysis. His argument for the "cultural pluralism" at the heart of American democracy remains a powerful attack on those who remain wedded to the either/or of the "racial divide." At the same time—unlike constructionist accounts—Ellison's writings offer more than an oppositional stance toward the principle of race. Instead, reflecting his Burkean roots, they display his desire to place this principle within a new, overarching terminology; this terminology would productively transcend dialectical polarities of all kinds, not add one more voice to the parliamentary debate. Although I believe that Ellison's approach stops short of the ultimate vocabulary described by Burke, it represents an initial step toward this end. To take the next step, to combine Ellison's vision with Burke's, we must turn, one final time, to consideration of Burke's ultimate terministic order.

From Turmoil to Peace: Race and the Ultimate Order

At several points throughout this book, I offer descriptions of Burke's ultimate order, though these efforts have consisted more of negative than of positive definition; rather than stating what the ultimate order *is*, I have simply contrasted it to the dialectical order. In part, this is because Burke, too, often relies upon definition by differentiation in his explanation of the final order. According to Burke, the two orders sharply differ in their mode of terministic arrangement: while "the 'dialectical' order would leave the competing voices in a jangling relation with one another . . . the 'ultimate' order would place these competing voices themselves in a *hierarchy*, or *sequence*, or *evaluative series*, so that, in some way, we went by a fixed and reasoned progression from one of these to another, the members of the entire group being arranged *developmentally* with relation to one another."[95]

Yet, if we look closely at Burke's text, we see that his descriptions of the ultimate order extend beyond this comparison to the dialectical. Like Burke's other two orders, an ultimate vocabulary arranges terms in characteristic ways; such a vocabulary works to resolve entrenched parliamentary disputes. Like the other two orders, however, the ultimate also represents a category or type of terminology. Although, to this point, I have focused upon the ultimate order's mode of terministic arrangement, a complete account of Burke's final order requires an explication of its characteristic kind of term.

Understandably, according to Burke, an ultimate vocabulary cannot be composed of dialectical titles, the voices whose contentious debates epitomize the dialectical order. On the contrary, the transcendence of these polarities requires the transcendence of the terminologies that produced them. It is this failure to abandon the realm of ideas that dooms scholars like Mannheim, or (I would add) those advocating the social constructionist position; a vocabulary built upon principles or ideas "cannot figure ultimate motives, and but brings us to the edge of them."[96] Burke further explores this point in "Ideology and Myth," the essay that, as mentioned in chapters 2 and 4, "set off a few bells in [Ellison's] head": "There is the way of Mannheim's 'sociology of knowledge,' which would still think in political and social terms. . . . Or there could be another way: by using terms that were not strictly social or political at all, but moved to another plane. This would be the step from 'ideology' to 'myth.'"[97] Here, Burke claims, is the key to the transcending arrangement of the ultimate order: an ultimate vocabulary is composed not of ideas, but of *myth*.

As Burke defines it, a myth is not an idea but an *image*, a term that "takes us from the order of reason to the order of imagination."[98] This contrast explains why Burke describes ultimate terms as mythic; myth represents the nonideational vocabulary necessary for the transcendence of the dialectical order. Dialectical vocabularies, as we have seen, consist of titles, ideas, or principles that summarize a wealth of positive details. Instead of offering another dialectical entitlement, another collection of ideas, an ultimate vocabulary moves to "another plane." Since it is not a principle, title, or idea, a mythic image cannot be captured or opposed by the abbreviating framework of another dialectical title—thereby allowing it to escape the paralyzing polarity of the dialectical realm.

More specifically, by moving beyond the ideational, myth pushes *through* dialectical disputes, toward their originating ground. He explains: "Here is where *ideological* purpose should move on to, or back to, a grounding in *mythic* purpose. Another way of saying it is that political or social motives cannot be ultimate, since they must in turn be grounded in motives outside or beyond the political or social."[99] Myth presents the motives that lie "outside or beyond" the social; it reconciles the competing social or political motives of the dialectical realm by symbolizing their common source.[100]

Myth transforms dialectical conflict through its *unifying, imagistic terminology of origins*. Rather than adding another title to the dialectical order's parliamentary jangle, myth instead depicts the underlying unity of these opposing voices—portraying "the nonpolitical ground of the political, not as antithetical to it, but as the 'prepolitical' source out of which it is to be derived."[101] Burke thus describes myth not as fiction, but as the imagistic presentation of archetypes or "firsts," visions of the "mythic ancestry" of principles, the "ideal mythic type" at the root of principles.[102] Since it symbolizes the common origins of otherwise-opposing vocabularies, myth creates "a possible alternative, whereby a somewhat formless parliamentary wrangle can, by an 'ultimate' vocabulary, be creatively endowed with design."[103] By shifting this parliamentary jangle to "another plane," myth arranges these discordant voices into "successive positions or moments in a single process."[104] Through myth, then, we move from the turmoil of the dialectical to the peace of the ultimate.

In some respects, Ellison's critical essays reflect this description of the ultimate order; his writings refuse to set black and white Americans at odds, and instead treat them as partners in a single process, the tragic, troubled constitution of our country and our culture. Ellison's perspective, derived from Burke's work, thus tries to transcend our endless, demoralizing struggles over the American "racial divide." However, I believe that Ellison's vocabulary, though it displays the proper intent, is not "ultimate" enough to meet the criteria set forth in Burke's *Rhetoric*.

As we have seen, according to Ellison the roots of the "racial divide" lie within American history. Yet, this diagnosis, when scrutinized more closely, stops short of an ultimate statement of motives. This is evidenced by Ellison's choice of 1776 as the pivotal moment in the construction of our "racial divide." He identifies race as a dialectical principle, one emerging alongside the Revolution as a mechanism for coping with the freedom of the new national context. This rather arbitrary designation leaves Ellison's account incomplete; after all, modern hierarchies of race first emerged in the seventeenth century, and the African slave trade was well established by the Revolutionary era. In other words, his account may begin prior to the inclusion of race in the Constitution, but it begins well *after* the colonists' acceptance of the reality of racial differences. By focusing upon America's birth, Ellison fails to recognize the more primary question of the "outside or beyond" of our social order—the archetypal *origins* of the racial discourse at work prior to our Declaration of Independence.

Since its ultimate designs are not matched by an equally ultimate terminology, Ellison's vocabulary, like the constructionist's, remains vulnerable to counter-statement.[105] Rather than moving to the "nonpolitical

ground of the political," Ellison seems to rest his account of race on social and political grounds: the decision by the Founders to accept the divisions and hierarchies of race when crafting the new nation. As a result,
Ellison remains solidly within the divisive, dialectical realm of ideas—no
better off than Mannheim or the social constructionist. Ellison's essays
thus appear little more than an alternate entitling of American society,
one that may (or may not) persuasively summarize the particulars of our
history.

There are tantalizing hints in Ellison's essays of a different kind of account, though, one that would more closely resemble a Burkean ultimate
vocabulary. In an early essay, Ellison observes that "the most insidious
and least understood form of segregation is that of the word. . . . For if
the word has the potency to revive and make us free, it has also the power
to blind, imprison and destroy" (81). A later essay picks up this theme, in
an explicitly Burkean meditation: "It is through language that man has
separated himself from his natural biologic condition as an animal, but it
is through the symbolic capabilities of language that we seek simultaneously to maintain and evade our commitments as social beings" (772).

In these quotes, Ellison identifies the role played by language in the
creation of our racial "drama." Deeply influenced by Burke's work, Ellison links race to human symbolicity, but he does not develop these
meditations into the ultimate vocabulary advocated by Burke; simultaneously, Burke celebrates the constitutive power of the symbolic, but
he is blind to its implications for the analysis of race. Combining these
insights from Burke and Ellison, I argue, therefore yields a new, and
urgently needed, ultimate vocabulary of race—a mythic statement of
the motives prior to the "racial divide," the archetypal motives derived
from human symbolicity itself. Such an account, I believe, also answers
Burke's call for "the 'ideal myth' of today: a vision that transcend[s] the
political, yet that ha[s] political attitudes interwoven with it."[106]

A Burkean-Ellisonian ultimate vocabulary does not bypass race
in its concern for the universals of human existence, but directs our
attention toward the roots of racial conflict. Its foundation in mythic,
and not dialectical, terms equips us to work toward the transcending of our ongoing, demoralizing racial binaries. Within American
popular culture, such a vision of racial peace is almost invariably expressed as a "healing"—a term which posits the possibility of bridging
or easing the deep divide separating black and white Americans.[107]
Yet, a Burkean-Ellisonian "'ideal myth' of today" would envision a
quite different kind of peace: "If we are going to have peace at all, it

must be a peace without pacification, that is, a peace without war, a peace *before* war."[108]

Burke's "peace *before* war" suggests that a language of racial "healing" or "bridging" is insufficiently ultimate because it posits a preexisting division that requires healing or bridging. To "heal" or "bridge" racial differences is to accept their existence, objectivity, and reality; though evocative, such language cannot end the dialectical stalemate of "black vs. white." Given Burke's description of the ultimate terministic order, our "ideal myth" of race should begin not with the entrenched polarity of this "racial divide," but *before* it—with an imagistic portrayal of its origins, its formal conditions of existence, the motives that lie beyond or beneath it. In other words, this myth directs us not toward the healing of races already made distinct, but *toward that which makes these divisions possible, intractable, and seemingly necessary.*

A Burkean-Ellisonian Ultimate Vocabulary of Race

As described earlier in this chapter, the key terms that drive Ellison's analysis of the American "racial divide" involve our national history, our rebellion against European standards and caste. The interlocking concepts of Revolutionary language, the vernacular, and the "sacred covenant" of the Constitution provide Ellison a flexible, powerful vocabulary for the critique of racial binarism. When read alongside Burke, however, these terms appear to reflect less the particularities of American life than the generic qualities of the symbolic realm.

This is where Ellison's account, with its ideational, dialectical vocabulary, is deepened through encounter with Burke. With Burke's assistance, we can shift the terms of the discussion, from the rational terms of the dialectical to the imagistic "beyond" of the mythic:

> So, the myth of society's return to the child, or the child's return to the womb, or the womb's return to the sea, can all but point towards a myth still farther back, the myth of a power prior to all parturition. Then divided things were not yet proud in the private property of their divisiveness. Division was still but "enlightenment." The notion of the Son as bringer of light seems in its essence to suggest that the division of the part from the whole is enlightening, a principle that might be stated dialectically thus: Partition provides terms; thereby it allows the parts to comment upon one another. But this "loving" relation allows also for the "fall" into

terms antagonistic in their partiality, until dialectically resolved by reduction to "higher" terms.[109]

Properly understood, this passage from Burke represents the "ideal myth" of race missing from (but implicated by) Ellison's nonfiction. It suggests not only that, as Ellison says, "we seek simultaneously to maintain and evade our commitments as social beings" *through* symbolicity—but also that we do this *because of* symbolicity. A vocabulary melding Burkean and Ellisonian insights thus redefines race as a primary means by which we grapple with our thoroughly and radically symbolic existence.

According to Ellison, the American language is revolutionary in nature, a rejection of Europe and the European cultural milieu. However, Ellison's historical analysis, properly understood, contains an insight more ultimate than dialectical in nature. When reread through the terms of Burke's myth, the political origins of this linguistic revolution appear grounded in motives far more fundamental—motives originating from symbolicity itself. In other words, the political revolution embodied in the American language is but an analogue of the revolutionary inauguration of the symbolic realm.

The narrative embodied within Burke's myth posits a primary unity, one that is shattered by the irruption of human symbolicity. Prior to the emergence of individual identities, the myth suggests, was a fundamental unity between symbolic and nonsymbolic, individual and group, part and whole—it is only through symbolic rebellion that distance emerges between them. In a later work, Burke condenses this myth into two simple lines: "In the beginning there was universal Nothing. Then Nothing said No to itself and thereby begat Something, Which called itself Yes."[110]

This "Creation Myth" wryly suggests that the introduction of words *about* the nonsymbolic requires (and thereby introduces) a distinction between the two, a symbolic refusal of unity that separates self from other, speaker from spoken-about. With this rebellious emergence of language, the part becomes able to talk about the whole, other parts, and their interrelation. Meaning, or "enlightenment," is the result of this process; it materializes with the gap between symbolic and nonsymbolic.[111] Symbols, according to Burke, confer the power of transcendence over the "state of nature."[112] In other words, they unleash a new power in the world, for they allow human beings to both go beyond the nonsymbolic realm and comment upon it—the division through terms, as the myth suggests, which is enlightening. Our symbolic prowess thereby introduces a radical break in experience that enables us to constitute a meaningful world.

Here, too, we find the roots of the vernacular process celebrated by Ellison. He uses the term to describe the American process of forging a culture from materials new and old, but this political improvisation rests upon, even mirrors, the more originary process described above. The emergence of symbolicity is a revolt both creative and enlightening since the introduction of terms makes it possible for them, in Burke's words, "to comment on one another." This playful, world-making commentary is what makes possible the "play-it-by-eye-and-by-ear improvisations" that Ellison identifies in American life (608). As a result, the vernacular in Ellison points beyond itself, thanks to Burke's myth, and toward the necessarily constitutive power of symbol-use; to emphasize the creative, improvisational dimensions of social life is not to point to an *American* quality, but to an attendant quality of our symbolicity.

This "enlightening" power of the symbolic, however, carries within it the seeds of anxiety; to be born human, Burke implies, is to emerge without the protection of instincts, to open onto a world devoid of inherent meaning. Although he does not include it within the myth quoted above, at key moments in his diagnosis of human existence, Burke points to the precariousness of this symbolic condition—the *anxiety* produced by our necessarily symbolic existence. In his "Definition of Man," for example, Burke notes: "The 'symbol-using animal,' yes, obviously. But can we bring ourselves to realize . . . just what that formula implies, just how overwhelmingly much of what we mean by 'reality' has been built up for us through nothing but our symbol systems? . . . To meditate on this fact until one sees its full implications is much like peering over the edge of things into an ultimate abyss."[113] This same language appears thirty years earlier, in the last line of *Permanence and Change*: "In this staggering disproportion between man and no-man, there is no place for purely human boasts of grandeur, or for forgetting that men build their cultures by huddling together, nervously loquacious, at the edge of an abyss."[114] Though these statements span thirty years, both equate existence with clinging desperately to discourse, symbolically diverting attention from our plight—that is, to be human is to be threatened with the collapse of reality, the shattering glimpse into a bottomless abyss of meaninglessness.

Our loquaciousness is nervous precisely because it is our lone defense against the overpowering totality of our environment; from the confusion of the nonsymbolic realm, we symbolically constitute a world, but these efforts are constantly threatened. The "abyss" is the anxiety-filled realization that we, with our symbolic prowess, are responsible for the meanings that we find and respond to in our environment. Ellison recognized as much in his insistence upon the role of race in the reconciliation of "order and chaos, illusion and reality, nonentity and identity" (106).

It is, in other words, anxiety in the face of Burke's abyss that is assuaged through the categories of race. To doubt the inevitability of the meanings that surround us is to simultaneously face their contingency—the fact that they could be otherwise. This realization shakes the foundations of our existence, and calls into question the reality of all that we take for granted. To avoid recognizing our responsibility for the symbolic constitution of our social world—to avoid looking into the abyss—we attempt instead to ground our social meanings upon natural fact, upon the solidity of bodies.

In other words, unlike the constitutional "grounds" examined in Ellison's essays, the pressures of symbolicity require not the creation of texts but the reassertion of natural fact. This, I believe, is the archetypal (mythic) motive behind our stubbornly held racial divisions; by asserting the facticity of race, we avoid confrontation with our radically symbolic existence, our responsibility for the meanings that surround us. Thanks to the symbolic constitution of racial differences, the artificiality of our symbolically produced categories can be hidden behind "natural" differences in shape of head, curve of eye, shade of skin, width of nose, and length of bone. We point to the objectivity of this data to justify our acts of categorization, since attributing racial distinctions to the nonsymbolic world eases our awareness of their contingency. Moreover, once we have thoroughly adopted these distinctions, they become operative in perception—enabling us to see, hear, smell, touch, and taste the differences they purport to name.[115] By converting our terministic distinctions into simple observations, we force nature to bear the responsibility for our social and symbolic acts.

To posit such an account of the origins of race is to address the subject not dialectically, through an alternate entitling of American society, but through the identification of a mythic image—an imagistic statement of the archetypal or ancestral motive behind our "racial divide." To adopt this mythic account of race is also to echo Burke's analysis of Hitler's "Battle" discussed in chapter 1; like Hitler's anti-Semitism, although race is charged with political and economic significance, it cannot be reduced to such terms. Race is not merely the cynical project of a ruling elite; there is a spontaneous, even visceral, dimension to race, one that reflects the vicissitudes of human symbolic existence, not the simple desire for money and power.

In his accounts of American social life, Ellison directs our attention toward this ritualistic dimension of race—the connection between race and individual identity within our national context. Through a constellation of racialized and racializing terms, we convert gradations of difference into qualitative distinctions, categories with firm edges; these constructed divisions produce courtly embarrassment and rampant rumor,[116] but also the clear and distinct boundaries of everyday life. The trouble is, as Burke and Ellison would point out, that these efforts are never final. Our categories keep coming unfixed from their "natural" anchors in the nonsymbolic realm, something that requires drastic action if we are to avoid recognition of our complicity in the creation of meaning—and, more radically, the crumbling of our categories and confrontation with the yawning abyss.

Here again we see the connection between the Burkean myth of origins and Ellison's analysis of the American "racial divide." Burke's "ideal myth" suggests that the roots of race lie in the human symbolic act of division and distinction; out of these distinctions, we humans have remade our environments and ourselves, introduced freedom into a nonverbal realm of necessity. Out of these distinctions arise the building blocks of culture, which are assembled and reassembled according to the improvisational logic that Ellison identifies as the vernacular. Out of these distinctions, though, arises anxiety—and, both Burke and Ellison suggest, out of anxiety arise hatred and violence. Symbolically generated pressures tempt us to naturalize our categories, shore up—assure—the fixity and inevitability of our constitutional foundations; the joke (laden with anxiety) is, as Ellison's essays tell us, that there is no whiteness without blackness, no foundation beneath the act, no firm identity behind the mask, no origin that is not a human symbolic product. Even our names, he says, have to be earned.

This realization, though, is not easy to stomach. Within the American experience, the responsibility generated by the founding act of symbolic constitution was too much for the founding (white) consciousness to bear; black Americans, whose inferiority was perpetually reiterated, perpetually compelled, served as the counterbalance to the unbearable freedom represented and enshrined by the constitutive acts of white men (and, at times, women). This is the tragedy at the heart of American culture, the dissonance that Ellison's essays still call us to address.

Yet, when transformed through the Burkean "ideal myth" of race, Ellison's ultimate vocabulary does not leave us with the demoralization of partisan cacophony, the sort of stalemate, or muddle, characteristic of Burke's dialectical thinking. When pushed to their ultimate foundations, Ellison's meditations on the relationship between symbolic constitution and race disclose the possibility of a different future. The trick, he tells us, is not to seek a way out of distinction, hierarchy, and order; the trick is to embrace the responsibility inherent to our social order— the moral nature of our symbolic constitutions, both big *C* and little *c*. To flee this responsibility is to cheat ourselves, and others, of our full humanity—and to thus do nothing to ameliorate the blindness and violence so characteristic of the history of race in this country.

Ellison proposes to us, in his essays—and in his "epoch-making," deeply Burkean novel—an alternative to the present. This alternative is no less arduous, requires no less discipline or self-awareness. Indeed, in Burkean fashion he tells us that it requires "consciousness, consciousness, *consciousness*" (425; original emphasis). It requires vigilant attention to the ontological conditions of our existence—that is, our archetypal existence as Burkean "bodies that learn language"—and the corresponding accountability that we all-too-readily flee.

Although Burke and Ellison were not, themselves, able to reach such an accord, I believe that the ideas generated by these two men productively combine to form this ultimate rhetorical vocabulary. This vocabulary recognizes that it is *because* of language that we are driven to seek refuge in nature, in the solidity of bodies—and that, subsequently, "through the symbolic capabilities of language . . . we seek simultaneously to maintain and evade our commitments as social beings" (772). Though such a vocabulary would not aim at the "healing" of our racial divide, it might yet produce a transcending kind of harmony.

If there is a fitting end to the project—intellectual and personal—begun by Burke and Ellison in 1942, it lies in such an ultimate vocabulary of race, a way of speaking about race that would yield Burke's "peace without pacification, that is, a peace without war, a peace *before* war."[117] Rather than look away, choosing shadows over reality, specters over real human beings, a Burkean-Ellisonian vocabulary of race calls us to accept responsibility for our symbolic existence, and, in the process, for our acts within the scene of the American social drama. As Burke reminds us, "there is much that no vocabulary can do in these matters. Where there are so many intense conflicts of an extraverbal sort, no merely verbal manipulations can remove them. But verbal manipulations may offer a more orderly approach to them, permitting them to be contemplated with less agitation. And where this is the case, verbal manipulations are the very opposite of the 'evasive.'"[118] Like Burke, I would readily admit that the future is not guaranteed with the adoption of an ultimate vocabulary, but it is most certainly guaranteed *without* one; the solution to the "problem of the color line" might be more than terministic, but its foundations lie in an adequate choice of terms. Ellison's essays, combined with Burke's terministic hierarchy, urge us to this arduous but necessary task; they rouse us—whether we have been sleepwalking or hibernating—to adopt an appropriately ultimate vocabulary, and, in so doing, to act.

NOTES

Introduction

1. There is never an easy way to handle the question of inclusive language, especially with someone, like Burke, who used the masculine to indicate the universal. In the interest of accuracy and readability, I have chosen not to alter any quotes throughout this book, though my own usage reflects my belief in the consequential nature of gendered language.

2. Burke, *Counter-Statement*, vii.

3. Hyman, *Armed Vision*, 347.

4. Barrett et al., "New Criticism," 88; Yagoda, "Kenneth Burke," 66; Selzer, *Kenneth Burke in Greenwich Village*, 16–17.

5. Wess, *Kenneth Burke*, 1–2.

6. Yagoda, "Kenneth Burke," 66.

7. Selzer, *Kenneth Burke in Greenwich Village*, 17.

8. For Burke's relation to modernism, see Selzer, *Kenneth Burke in Greenwich Village*; to war, Weiser, "Burke and War"; to science and technology, Rueckert, *Kenneth Burke and the Drama of Human Relations*; and Wess, *Kenneth Burke*. For his relation to Marxism, see George and Selzer, *Kenneth Burke in the 1930s*; Bygrave, *Kenneth Burke*; and Lentricchia, *Criticism and Social Change*. For his relation to ecology, see Blankenship, "Kenneth Burke on Ecology"; Seigel, "One Little Fellow Named Ecology"; Roorda, "KB in Green"; and Wess, "Ecocriticism and Kenneth Burke."

9. Rampersad, *Ralph Ellison*, 3.

10. Ralph Ellison to Kenneth Burke, 23 November 1945, Kenneth Burke Papers.

11. Kenneth Burke to Ralph Ellison, 16 December 1945, Ralph Ellison Papers, box I:38, folder 8.

12. Burke, *Rhetoric of Motives*, 208.

13. Ellison, *Collected Essays*, 109.

14. Ibid., 83–84.

15. This is not to say that the two did not venture from American soil but rather that neither Burke nor Ellison joined the American artists and intellectuals living in exile—a community that included, among others, Burke's friend Malcolm Cowley and Ellison's friend Richard Wright.

16. Ellison moved a few times, but was a devoted resident of New York (Rampersad, *Ralph Ellison*). Although Burke lived in his farmhouse in the wilds of Andover, New Jersey, he was a frequent visitor to the city; he also frequently entertained guests from the city—including, as illustrated in chapters 2 and 3, the Ellisons. Since Burke's rural retreat even afforded a view of Manhattan, as Selzer aptly notes, "Andover was no hermitage" (*Kenneth Burke in Greenwich Village*, 59).

17. Of course, paraphrasing Burke, the story of race in America is more complicated than that. An adequate approach to the subject must address the insufficiency of this binary to address the multiplicity of American racial identities, as well as the binaristic constitution of race that emerged in the early twentieth century. However, given the power and ubiquity of the binaristic conception of race, use of Ellison's preferred term the "racial divide" is most apt for approaching the Burke-Ellison relationship (e.g., Guterl, *Color of Race in America*).

1 / Birth of an Ancestor

1. Ellison is the source of this narrative (e.g., Ellison, *Collected Essays*, 471). Although it is corroborated by some of his biographers (Burke and Davis, *Ralph Ellison*, 215–17; L. Jackson, *Ralph Ellison*, 319–21), Rampersad argues that the novel's famous opening was written over months, if not years—and that the story of this mysterious voice simply represents Ellison's preferred "myth of origins" (*Ralph Ellison*, 194–95). Rampersad suggests that Ellison may have been working on as many as three different novels from 1944 to 1945—including an early draft of *Invisible Man* (*Ralph Ellison*, 193–94). From my perspective, we need not pass final judgment concerning the origins of Ellison's novel; what is certain, for present purposes, is that *Invisible Man*, in both mythical and factual dimensions, is central to the intellectual and personal relationship that he developed with Kenneth Burke.

2. I do not wish to overlook the fictional works that have appeared since Ellison's death. Ellison's literary executor, John Callahan, first delved into Ellison's unpublished writings and carved out a novel, entitled *Juneteenth*. More recently, Callahan and Bradley again mined Ellison's papers, and extracted a new volume: *Three Days before the Shooting . . .* However, I have chosen not to address these works in the present book; since these writings did not appear during Ellison's lifetime, they played little role in his relationship with Burke. For more on Ellison's unfinished second novel, see Bradley, *Ralph Ellison in Progress*; and Rampersad, *Ralph Ellison*.

3. Despite the hopeful attitudes taken by some (e.g., Seaton, "Ellison the Essayist," 497; and Wright, *Shadowing Ralph Ellison*), the reduction of Ellison's career to his fiction is common; even Rampersad's recent biography of Ellison suffers somewhat from this narrowed focus. Much of Rampersad's narrative focuses on Ellison's failure to produce a second novel—a focus that precludes detailed attention to Ellison's essays, especially his late collection *Going to the Territory*. This is symptomatic of an all-too-common attitude taken toward Ellison's criticism.

4. Not only are Burke's writings relatively quiet on matters of race (as I discuss in chapter 2), but the same is true of the secondary literature. Some scholars have connected Burke to race (e.g., Bobbitt, *Rhetoric of Redemption*; Carlson, "'You Know It When You See It'"; Crable, "Race and *A Rhetoric of Motives*"; Crable, "Symbolizing Motion"; Klumpp, "Burkean Social Hierarchy"; and Lynch, "Race and Radical Renamings"). In many respects, however, Burkean scholarship focuses more on issues of class than of race (or of gender).

5. As I discuss in chapter 3, Ellison's omission of Burke from his list of ancestors became a central point of contention; however, Ellison, for better or worse, used the distinction to reject what he considered to be others' reductive categorization of him as a "black writer." For more on this issue, and its connection to Ellison's reputation among other black writers and activists, see L. Jackson, "Ralph Ellison's Invented Life."

6. Ellison, *Collected Essays*, 185–87.

7. Ellison received the grant of $1,800 in April 1945 from the foundation (Rampersad, *Ralph Ellison*, 187; L. Jackson, *Ralph Ellison*, 318). Given Rosenwald's relationship to Booker T. Washington (and Tuskegee), Rosenwald likely served as one of the inspirations for *Invisible Man*'s character Norton. For more on Rosenwald's philanthropic support of black Americans' education, see Sealander, *Private Wealth and Public Life*, 67–72.

8. Ralph Ellison to Kenneth Burke, 23 November 1945, Kenneth Burke Papers. The implications of *Invisible Man* being a work dedicated to Burke are explored in chapter 3.

9. Ibid.

10. Jacobson, *Whiteness of a Different Color*, 11. See also Gossett, *Race*; Guterl, *Color of Race in America*; and Smedley, *Race in North America*.

11. To be sure, "white" and "black" were significant identity positions prior to the 1930s or 1940s—and antiblack racism (slavery, Jim Crow, and lynching) certainly existed prior to this time. However, despite the tendency to read our assumptions into the discourse of the past, "white" was not a unified, monolithic identity at the beginning of the twentieth century. This point is further elaborated in chapters 4 and 5 as part of a Burkean-Ellisonian perspective on race in America.

12. The epithet is from Bodnar, Simon, and Weber, *Lives of Their Own*, 13; the authors point out that the city was known for its polluted environs as early as 1830. As for Burke, biographical materials on him are, in a word, scarce. It often seems as though he was born and then transmogrified into a high school student—with only a couple of obligatory anecdotes in between. However, for the basic facts of Burke's birth, see Selzer, *Kenneth Burke in Greenwich Village*, 10.

13. Bodnar, Simon, and Weber, *Lives of Their Own*, 13–18; Lubove, *Pittsburgh*; Oestreicher, "Working-Class Formation, Development, and Consciousness in Pittsburgh," 129–39.

14. Jacobson, *Barbarian Virtues*, 51–55, 75–85.

15. Woodward, *Strange Career of Jim Crow*, 71–72. As Woodward points out, though these laws were distinctly southern products, the North played a role in creating and legitimating them.

16. Ibid., 97–102. Schweik offers a compelling account of the simultaneous rise of Jim Crow and of the "Ugly Laws" aimed at the disabled—underscoring the association of blackness and "disease" in American discourse of this period (*Ugly Laws*, 184–204).

For more on Jim Crow, see Chafe, Gavins, and Korstad, *Remembering Jim Crow*; Packard, *American Nightmare*; and Williamson, *Crucible of Race*, 249–58.

17. Arnesen, *Black Protest and the Great Migration*; Gottlieb, *Making Their Own Way*; Lemann, *Promised Land*; C. Marks, "Social and Economic Life of Southern Blacks during the Migration"; Scruggs, *Sweet Home*.

18. Faires, "Immigrants and Industry," 9–10. See also Bodnar, Simon, and Weber, *Lives of Their Own*, 19–21; Gottlieb, "Migration and Jobs," 272–74; Gottlieb, *Making Their Own Way*, 1. Unfortunately, the connection between Pittsburgh's growth and heavy industry meant that economic stagnation occurred much earlier than elsewhere in the nation—with detrimental effects on the city's black community (Glasco, "Black Experience," 70).

19. Glasco, "Black Experience," 74. Testimony to this early connection between black Americans and Pittsburgh can be seen in August Wilson's series of plays *The Pittsburgh Cycle*.

20. Bodnar, Simon, and Weber, *Lives of Their Own*, 30; Epstein, *Negro Migrant in Pittsburgh*, 7. Others offer the more conservative time frame of 1890–1910 for this doubling of the black population (see Gottlieb, *Making Their Own Way*, 32).

21. Daniels, *Coming to America*, 185–89, 213–20. Following Daniels, I have avoided contrasting the "old" immigration, consisting of people from northern and western Europe, to the "new" immigration, consisting of people from southern and eastern Europe. Such a viewpoint ignores, for example, the Asian immigration that occurred during this period, as Japanese and other Asian nationals exploited the narrow focus of the Chinese Exclusion Act of 1882 (Jacobson, *Barbarian Virtues*, 81). Yet discussion of Burke's Pittsburgh necessitates discussion of the increase in immigration from southern and eastern European countries between 1880 and 1910 (Guterl, *Color of Race in America*, 14–23; Jacobson, *Barbarian Virtues*, 60–69; Jacobson, *Whiteness of a Different Color*, 39–44; Roediger, *How Race Survived U.S. History*, 136–38).

22. Bodnar, Simon, and Weber, *Lives of Their Own*, 20. Accounts of turn-of-the-twentieth-century immigrant populations in Pittsburgh focus their primary attention on Italians and Poles; it should be noted, however, that Poland was not a distinct and autonomous country until the end of World War I. Thus, figures on Polish immigration from this time period draw upon secondary data (e.g., immigrants' self-reports of "mother tongue") rather than country of origin. Until 1919, most (but not all) of the immigrants categorized as "Polish" arrived from Russia, Austria-Hungary, and Germany (Daniels, *Coming to America*, 215).

23. Bodnar, Simon, and Weber, *Lives of Their Own*, 60–67; Epstein, *Negro Migrant in Pittsburgh*, 30–33; Faires, "Immigrants and Industry," 11; Glasco, "Black Experience," 73–79; Jacobson, *Barbarian Virtues*, 63–69; Weber, "Community-Building and Occupational Mobility in Pittsburgh," 365–67.

24. Glasco, "Black Experience," 73. As Glasco points out, however, this was not without its drawbacks for the black community: the integration of the school system prevented black teachers from finding employment in Pittsburgh.

25. According to one study, by 1930, "Italians could be found in 91 percent of the city's census tracts, while blacks and Poles resided in three-fourths of the tracts" (Bodnar, Simon, and Weber, *Lives of Their Own*, 202). See also ibid., 70–72; Glasco, "Black Experience," 79–80; Glasco, *WPA History of the Negro in Pittsburgh*, 24–29; and Gottlieb, *Making Their Own Way*, 66–69.

26. Bodnar, Simon, and Weber, *Lives of Their Own,* 70.

27. Glasco, *WPA History of the Negro in Pittsburgh,* 219; Gossett, *Race,* 292–309; Guterl, *Color of Race in America,* 19; Jacobson, *Barbarian Virtues,* 69–73; Roediger, *How Race Survived U.S. History,* 136–42.

28. Abu-Lughod, *Race, Space, and Riots,* 11; Jacobson, *Whiteness of a Different Color,* 56–57, 68–69.

29. Jacobson, *Whiteness of a Different Color.* See also Gossett, *Race*; Guterl, *Color of Race in America*; Jacobson, *Barbarian Virtues*; Smedley, *Race in North America.*

30. Burke, *Complete White Oxen,* xvii.

31. Jay, *Selected Correspondence of Kenneth Burke and Malcolm Cowley,* 81n. The passages in the correspondence cited by Jay (and listed in the index as "Burke, Kenneth, racial slurs of") typically, but not always, involve reference to Burke's friend Matthew Josephson (e.g., 79, 98, 121). Although Jay does not call attention to them, elsewhere in the text Burke's correspondence with Cowley refers to such stereotypical figures as the "Jewess" (23, 83) and the threat posed by the importation of "three million Chinks" (38)—and even muses on the contrast between the "Anglo-Saxon" and "Slavic" "view[s] of life" (23). Letters between Burke and Cowley not included in Jay's volume confirm that these were not anomalous statements; Burke's early correspondence was often filled with such remarks. In this respect (if none other), it would seem that Burke was following in the footsteps of his father, who, after leaving Pittsburgh, became "a member of a strictly anti-Jewish golf club" (Kenneth Burke to Malcolm Cowley, 12 November 1921, Kenneth Burke Papers). For present purposes, we should simply conclude that all of these statements reflect the ubiquitous hierarchies of race that Burke and his fellow Pittsburghers internalized.

32. Rountree, "Richard Kostelanetz Interviews Kenneth Burke," 2.

33. Warren, "Kenneth Burke," 226.

34. Quoted in Bak, *Malcolm Cowley,* 37–38.

35. Rountree, "Richard Kostelanetz Interviews Kenneth Burke," 2. See also Baker, "Biography in Progress," 379; and Burke and Cowley, "Kenneth Burke and Malcolm Cowley," 182, 192.

36. Bodnar, Simon, and Weber, *Lives of Their Own,* 172–73. It is likely that the established nature of these communities initially drew Burke's grandparents to the area.

37. Epstein, *Negro Migrant in Pittsburgh,* 9; Faires, "Immigrants and Industry," 11; Glasco, *WPA History of the Negro in Pittsburgh,* 256; Gottlieb, *Making Their Own Way,* 66–67; Weber, "Community-Building and Occupational Mobility in Pittsburgh," 362, 364.

38. Burke, *Complete White Oxen,* xvii. Brushton and Homewood were middle-class communities in the early 1900s (see, e.g., Bodnar, Simon, and Weber, *Lives of Their Own,* 172–73, 176–77; Glasco, *WPA History of the Negro in Pittsburgh,* 256; and Lubove, *Twentieth-Century Pittsburgh,* 165). Though the two neighborhoods are often linked in histories of Pittsburgh, Burke's quote indicates that Homewood was the "preferred" address of the two. Squirrel Hill, during Burke's childhood, transformed from a collection of large family estates to a wealthy suburb consisting of "hundreds of large homes for steel company middle management" (Squirrel Hill Historical Society, "Squirrel Hill History," http://squirrelhillhistory.org/index.php?sqh_history; see also Bodnar, Simon, and Weber, *Lives of Their Own,* 21–25). Issues of class and race intersected in this hierarchy of neighborhoods; the Homewood-Brushton area, for

example, "was divided by the Mainline of the Pennsylvania Railroad," with the "predominantly white [population] south of the tracks, and Negro to the north" (Lubove, *Twentieth-Century Pittsburgh*, 165)—while Squirrel Hill was predominantly Jewish.

39. Bodnar, Simon, and Weber, *Lives of Their Own*, 172.

40. Glasco, *WPA History of the Negro in Pittsburgh*, 256.

41. Rountree, "Richard Kostelanetz Interviews Kenneth Burke," 2.

42. Yagoda, "Kenneth Burke," 67.

43. Burke felt this to be a clear diminution of status, in some respects. He resorted to the use of his grandmother's address in order to attend a "better school" in East Liberty than he would have attended in Brushton (Baker, "Biography in Progress," 380; Burke and Cowley, "Kenneth Burke and Malcolm Cowley," 181–82).

44. Rountree, "Richard Kostelanetz Interviews Kenneth Burke," 2. See also Baker, "Biography in Progress," 379–80.

45. Woodcock, "Interview with Kenneth Burke," 12.

46. Anthony Burke, telephone conversation with author, 22 March 2009.

47. Rountree, "Richard Kostelanetz Interviews Kenneth Burke," 2.

48. Anthony Burke, telephone conversation with author, 22 March 2009. According to Anthony Burke, James did, in fact, invent something useful: the plastic strip that allowed for an "easy-open" cigarette pack. However, he was told by his patent lawyer that the device was worthless—the same lawyer who soon patented the invention, cheating James (so the story went) out of millions. Another invention, though less practical, was more successful: after leaving Pittsburgh, James successfully patented a "sanitary egg-opener" and may have sold as many as one thousand of the items (Kenneth Burke to Malcolm Cowley, 12 November 1921, Kenneth Burke Papers).

49. Yagoda, "Kenneth Burke," 67.

50. The importance that Burke placed on the fall seems clear, since discussion of it crops up occasionally in his published works, in fictional and nonfictional forms (Burke, *Permanence and Change*, xlviii; Burke, *Complete White Oxen*, 255–56).

51. Rountree, "Kenneth Burke," 20.

52. Quoted in Simons, "Introduction," 23. See also Baker, "Biography in Progress," 379.

53. Rountree, "Kenneth Burke," 20. See also Baker, "Biography in Progress," 379.

54. Burke and Cowley, "Kenneth Burke and Malcolm Cowley," 182.

55. Bak, *Malcolm Cowley*, 26–27, 29–32; Burke and Cowley, "Kenneth Burke and Malcolm Cowley," 182.

56. The story of their first meeting has a couple of variations; since Burke was four at the time, and Cowley was three, neither man retained firsthand memory of the event. As Cowley was told the story, his family had called upon the Burke family, whereupon "I walked around your parlor touching things, and you walked after me saying, Don't touch. Mustn't" (Jay, *Selected Correspondence of Kenneth Burke and Malcolm Cowley*, 201). See also Burke and Cowley, "Kenneth Burke and Malcolm Cowley," 181–82; and Cowley, *Second Flowering*, 244–45.

57. Cowley, *Exile's Return*, 15–16. See also Burke and Cowley, "Kenneth Burke and Malcolm Cowley," 182; Parker and Herendeen, "KB & MC," 90.

58. Pittsburgh Peabody High School, "Our History," www.pps.k12.pa.us/147020102711241696o/blank/browse.asp?A=383&BMDRN=2000&BCOB=0&C=61453.

59. Cowley, *Exile's Return*, 15. See also Bak, *Malcolm Cowley*, 27–32. Bak repeats Cowley's descriptions of Peabody, though interestingly, he expands upon them, stating that "the attending pupils were socially and racially mixed and Cowley consorted with youngsters from various backgrounds" (27). Although Cowley's description of the school includes mention of "a handsome Italian who later became a big-time mobster" and "a tall, serious and stupid Negro boy," Bak either overstates the case or implicitly notes the racism directed toward Pittsburgh's new immigrants (Cowley, *Exile's Return*, 15). Since available records indicate that in 1935—twenty years *after* Burke and Cowley's graduation—Peabody only had five black students in its graduating class, Peabody's racial demographics likely skewed toward the Irish, Polish, Hungarian, Italian, and German populations that would later become assimilated into the "white" race (Glasco, *WPA History of the Negro in Pittsburgh*, 245).

60. Rountree, "Richard Kostelanetz Interviews Kenneth Burke," 3. See also Rountree, "Kenneth Burke," 20.

61. Selzer, *Kenneth Burke in Greenwich Village*, 35. For Burke and Cowley, the magazine opened their eyes to the emerging modernist literary culture, primarily through the contributions of the influential columnist and critic James Gibbons Huneker. For more on the magazine, see Curtiss, *Smart Set*.

62. Warren, "Kenneth Burke," 227. See also Burke and Cowley, "Kenneth Burke and Malcolm Cowley," 198–99; Parker and Herendeen, "KB & MC," 96; and Yagoda, "Kenneth Burke," 67.

63. Selzer, *Kenneth Burke in Greenwich Village*, 3–19.

64. Woodcock, "Interview with Kenneth Burke," 705. See also Bak, *Malcolm Cowley*, 35–36.

65. Parker and Herendeen, "KB & MC," 94. This antitechnological element of Burke's thought, generated (he later claimed) by the horrors of the "steel city," would remain a constant, even as his overall perspective shifted from the aesthetic, and toward the symbolic and rhetorical.

66. Ellison, *Collected Essays*, 602.

67. Here I follow Jackson and Rampersad in listing Ellison's birth date as 1913, although he would later insist it was 1914 (L. Jackson, *Ralph Ellison*, 1; Rampersad, *Ralph Ellison*, 5–6). In sharp contrast to Burke, Ellison's life has been the subject of several biographers' attention. Though the remainder of this chapter touches upon the most relevant points for the story of Burke and Ellison, the interested reader should consult the much more comprehensive and detailed biographies cited above.

68. Though Ellison insisted that Oklahoma "had no tradition of slavery" (Graham and Singh, *Conversations with Ralph Ellison*, 255), conditions were far from ideal: "After Emancipation, the treatment of the freedmen varied from tribe to tribe. At their worst, the Choctaws and Chickasaws were reluctant even to admit the end of slavery" (Hirsch, *Riot and Remembrance*, 32). See also Brophy, *Reconstructing the Dreamland*, 2; and Chafe, Gavins, and Korstad, *Remembering Jim Crow*, 74–76.

69. Burke and Davis, *Ralph Ellison*, 9–10.

70. Ellison, *Collected Essays*, 601. See also Burke and Davis, *Ralph Ellison*, 10–11; Hirsch, *Riot and Remembrance*, 33–34; and Scales and Goble, *Oklahoma Politics*, 3–5.

71. Ellison, *Collected Essays*, 50.

72. According to (hysterical) accounts in white newspapers, McCabe planned to attract one hundred thousand new black settlers into the Territory (see Burke and

Davis, *Ralph Ellison*, 10–11; Ellsworth, *Death in a Promised Land*, 19; Graham and Singh, *Conversations with Ralph Ellison*, 254–58; Hirsch, *Riot and Remembrance*, 32–37; L. Jackson, *Ralph Ellison*, 11; and Rampersad, *Ralph Ellison*, 4–6).

73. Hirsch, *Riot and Remembrance*, 36; see also Johnson, *Development of State Legislation Concerning the Free Negro*, 167.

74. The law limited voting to those who could vote on 1 January 1866—or their descendents—and only excepted immigrants. Essentially, if a man's grandfather had been eligible to vote, *he* was eligible to vote (and I mean "he"; women did not receive the vote until 1918) (see Brophy, *Reconstructing the Dreamland*, 2; Burke and Davis, *Ralph Ellison*, 10–13; Ellsworth, *Death in a Promised Land*, 19; Hirsch, *Riot and Remembrance*, 33–38; L. Jackson, *Ralph Ellison*, 15; and Scales and Goble, *Oklahoma Politics*, 19).

75. The law required all previously ineligible voters to register with officials within a few days—or relinquish their right to vote (see Brophy, *Reconstructing the Dreamland*, 15; Burke and Davis, *Ralph Ellison*, 13–14; Ellsworth, *Death in a Promised Land*, 18–19; and Scales and Goble, *Oklahoma Politics*, 83–85).

76. Rampersad, *Ralph Ellison*, 10–11.

77. Burke and Davis, *Ralph Ellison*, 20–21; L. Jackson, *Ralph Ellison*, 14–17; Rampersad, *Ralph Ellison*, 10–11.

78. Ellison, *Collected Essays*, 42. See also Burke and Davis, *Ralph Ellison*, 22–23; Ellison, *Collected Essays*, 787; L. Jackson, *Ralph Ellison*, 19–22; and Rampersad, *Ralph Ellison*, 11–12.

79. Burke and Davis, *Ralph Ellison*, 22; L. Jackson, *Ralph Ellison*, 19–20; Rampersad, *Ralph Ellison*, 11.

80. L. Jackson, *Ralph Ellison*, 21.

81. Burke and Davis, *Ralph Ellison*, 24; L. Jackson, *Ralph Ellison*, 36–45; Rampersad, *Ralph Ellison*, 13, 18–19.

82. L. Jackson, *Ralph Ellison*, 44.

83. Rampersad, *Ralph Ellison*, 13, 17

84. Ellison, *Collected Essays*, 821.

85. Burke and Davis, *Ralph Ellison*, 25; Ellison, *Collected Essays*, 821–22; L. Jackson, *Ralph Ellison*, 29–30; Rampersad, *Ralph Ellison*, 13–14.

86. Burke and Davis, *Ralph Ellison*, 26. According to Lawrence Jackson, "the entire lower half of the state had earned the nickname 'Little Dixie' on account of its thoroughgoing institution of jim crow practices" (*Ralph Ellison*, 33–34).

87. Ellison, *Collected Essays*, 824. It was also a lesson in the comedy attending racial tragedy since the white man's angry words were converted into a family punch line: "'Well, I think you'll have to go now, both you and your chillun too!'" (ibid).

88. Allen, *Only Yesterday*, 47–50; Arnesen, *Black Protest and the Great Migration*, 33; Gossett, *Race*, 339–40; Hirsch, *Riot and Remembrance*, 162–67; Jacobson, *Whiteness of a Different Color*, 118; Scales and Goble, *Oklahoma Politics*, 108–11.

89. According to one estimate, nearly three thousand lynchings occurred in the United States from 1890 to 1930 alone (Hirsch, *Riot and Remembrance*, 51). Based upon his historical survey of newspaper accounts, Ginzberg estimates the number of lynchings between 1859 and 1962 at nearly five thousand (*100 Years of Lynchings*, 253).

90. Congressman L. C. Dyer regularly introduced antilynching bills during the 1920s, but opposition prevented their passage (Sitkoff, *New Deal for Blacks*, 22–25). For

more on the fight to outlaw lynching, see Terborg-Penn, "African-American Women's Networks in the Anti-Lynching Crusade"; and Zangrando, *NAACP Crusade against Lynching.*

91. Arnesen, *Black Protest and the Great Migration,* 33.

92. The unprecedented number of black soldiers in the military produced an increase in race-based violence between members of the military—and between soldiers and civilians. Racial tension was not eased with the war's end, since the rapid demobilization of the military left little time for American companies to adjust to a postwar economy. As ex-soldiers of all races tried to return to the workforce, many found that their jobs had been taken by women or by black migrants. When an economic downturn followed the war's end, the competition over jobs intensified, as did the competition over affordable housing. Although such competition was rarely resolved in favor of black Americans, these factors added to the volatility surrounding race during this period. For more on this topic, see Astor, *Right to Fight.*

93. Abu-Lughod, *Race, Space, and Riots,* 56. See also Arnesen, *Black Protest and the Great Migration,* 33; Astor, *Right to Fight,* 122–26; Hirsch, *Riot and Remembrance,* 58; and Voogd, *Race Riots and Resistance,* 20–21.

94. Graham and Singh, *Conversations with Ralph Ellison,* 255.

95. Ibid.

96. Guterl, *Color of Race in America,* 123–24.

97. Abu-Lughod, *Race, Space, and Riots,* 17; Arnesen, *Black Protest and the Great Migration,* 33; Guterl, *Color of Race in America,* 48–51; Voogd, *Race Riots and Resistance,* 4–5.

98. Hirsch, *Riot and Remembrance,* 6.

99. Ellison, *Collected Essays,* 451. During the Tulsa riot, "as many as 25,000 whites systematically looted the black community for three days. By the time their fury was spent, the mob had gutted two square miles of black-owned property" (Scales and Goble, *Oklahoma Politics,* 106–7). See also Brophy, *Reconstructing the Dreamland;* Ellsworth, *Death in a Promised Land;* and Hirsch, *Riot and Remembrance.*

100. Johnson, *Development of State Legislation Concerning the Free Negro,* 167.

101. Jacobson, *Whiteness of a Different Color,* 155–61. There are differences between the racial binarism of Oklahoma and that of other western states. Whereas Oklahoma's constitution set forth a broad definition of "white," opposing it to those of "African descent," the western "frontier" mentality pitted whites against all "others"—uniting under the category of "other" such disparate groups as black Americans, Mexicans, Native Americans, and Chinese.

102. Illustrating the complexity of race in American history, Lewis Ellison was one of the black American soldiers ordered to shoulder the "white man's burden" and subdue the rebellious Filipino army (L. Jackson, *Ralph Ellison,* 5–10; Rampersad, *Ralph Ellison,* 9). For more on the racial dynamics of this conflict, see Jacobson, *Barbarian Virtues,* 250–52.

103. Jacobson, *Barbarian Virtues,* 61. "Old Stock" Americans were "composed largely of Dutch, English, and French 'stock'" (Guterl, *Color of Race in America,* 42).

104. Jacobson, *Whiteness of a Different Color,* 78.

105. According to Blumenbach, the major "divisions of mankind" are Caucasian, Ethiopian, Mongolian, Malay, and American. For more on the Dillingham

Commission and its use of (and deviation from) Blumenbach, see Guterl, *Color of Race in America,* 31; and Jacobson, *Whiteness of a Different Color,* 78–80.

106. Grant was responsible for the popularization of Nordicism, but his work drew heavily upon William Z. Ripley's 1899 division of Europe into Teutonic, Alpine, and Mediterranean races (J. Jackson, *Science for Segregation,* 21–23; Gossett, *Race,* 354).

107. Allen, *Only Yesterday,* 33–55; Gossett, *Race,* 360–64; Guterl, *Color of Race in America,* 43; Jacobson, *Whiteness of a Different Color,* 80–85.

108. The act established immigration quotas "based on 2 percent of each group's population according to the 1890 census" (Jacobson, *Whiteness of a Different Color,* 83). After "the passage of this so-called National Origins Act in 1924, immigration from Southern and Eastern Europe, Asia, and the West Indies nearly ceased" (Guterl, *Color of Race in America,* 47). The results were so dramatic that emigration of non-"Nordics" soon exceeded immigration (Allen, *Since Yesterday,* 212).

109. Jacobson, *Whiteness of a Different Color,* 87.

110. Ibid., 78.

111. *Dangerous Drugs* was the title of the book that Burke ghostwrote for Colonel Arthur Woods. For more on the Bureau of Social Hygiene and its influence on Burke's early thought, see Hawhee, "Burke on Drugs" or Jack, "'Piety of Degradation.'" The bureau was explicitly founded upon the ideas of the famous eugenicist Charles Davenport, though his influence had diminished by the time that Burke was hired by Woods. Apart from an equation of opium and the "Mohammedan" (Woods, *Dangerous Drugs,* 9) and a warning about the effects of cocaine on "inferior or abnormal minds and nervous systems" (ibid., 27–28), Burke's ghostwritten book contains little to connect it, in even the slightest way, with the eugenics movement. By contrast, the strong link between the bureau and eugenics is evident from examination of letters exchanged by key figures in the bureau (including its founder, John D. Rockefeller Jr.) and in the eugenics movement. For example, Katharine Bement Davis, the bureau's general secretary, corresponded (on bureau stationery) with Davenport, seeking information from the Eugenics Record Office useful to those, like her, who were "interested in the movement and would like to understand the scope and resources of the [Eugenics Record Office's] work" (19 November 1925, Charles Davenport Papers, American Philosophical Society, Philadelphia). For more on the link between the bureau and the science of eugenics, see Institute for the Study of Academic Racism, "Sources in the Study of Eugenics #2: The Bureau of Social Hygiene," www.ferris.edu/HTMLS/othersrv/isar /archives2/sources/bsh.htm. For an interesting account of the history and mission of the bureau (albeit one that focuses exclusively upon sex, not upon race), see Sealander, *Private Wealth and Public Life,* 160–88.

112. Jack, "'Piety of Degradation,'" 446, 448.

113. Hoffman, Allen, and Ulrich, *Little Magazine,* 97.

114. Bak, *Malcolm Cowley,* 46; Rountree, "Richard Kostelanetz Interviews Kenneth Burke," 3; Selzer, *Kenneth Burke in Greenwich Village,* 10–11; Woodcock, "An Interview with Kenneth Burke," 704.

115. Burke and Cowley, "Kenneth Burke and Malcolm Cowley," 185–86; Cowley, *Exile's Return,* 23–27; Josephson, *Life among the Surrealists,* 36–37; Rountree, "Richard Kostelanetz Interviews Kenneth Burke," 3–4; Selzer, *Kenneth Burke in Greenwich Village,* 20–21; Warren, "Kenneth Burke," 227–28; Woodcock, "An Interview with Kenneth Burke," 704; Yagoda, "Kenneth Burke," 67.

116. Woodcock, "An Interview with Kenneth Burke," 704.

117. Jay, *Selected Correspondence of Kenneth Burke and Malcolm Cowley*, 56.

118. Josephson, *Life among the Surrealists*, 41.

119. Woodcock, "An Interview with Kenneth Burke," 706. Based on Burke's re-cycling of stationery for private correspondence, he likely worked for the B. Seaboldt Corporation: "Designers and Manufacturers of Special Gauges and Machine Tools."

120. Hoffman, Allen, and Ulrich, *Little Magazine*, 49; Selzer, *Kenneth Burke in Greenwich Village*, 185–88.

121. Selzer, *Kenneth Burke in Greenwich Village*, 14–15, 42–43; Warren, "Kenneth Burke," 228–29.

122. Bak, *Malcolm Cowley*, 123.

123. Selzer, *Kenneth Burke in Greenwich Village*, 59.

124. Bak, *Malcolm Cowley*, 115–18, 164; Jay, *Selected Correspondence of Kenneth Burke and Malcolm Cowley*, 66–67, 74–75, 81–83, 88–92; Josephson, *Life among the Surrealists*, 66–72; Selzer, *Kenneth Burke in Greenwich Village*, 188–91.

125. Burke's father, James, was not keen on the idea until Kenneth's doctor, notic-ing "a poor set of glands in [Kenneth's] neck," recommended country living as health-ier for the young man than city living—at which point James became an advocate for his son's pastoral lifestyle (Kenneth Burke to Malcolm Cowley, 14 January 1921, Kenneth Burke Papers).

126. Burke later recalled his first visit to Andover: "Oh, it was a horrible place—the place had only two rooms, and they were papered with newspaper, and between the two rooms was a dead chicken bleeding on the floor" (Burke and Cowley, "Kenneth Burke and Malcolm Cowley," 190–91). See also Bak, *Malcolm Cowley*, 214, 343; Cow-ley, *Exile's Return*, 226–27, 291; Josephson, *Life among the Surrealists*, 300–301, 305; Rountree, "Richard Kostelanetz Interviews Kenneth Burke," 5–6, 10; Selzer, *Kenneth Burke in Greenwich Village*, 59–60; Woodcock, "An Interview with Kenneth Burke," 706; Yagoda, "Kenneth Burke," 67.

127. Joost, *Scofield Thayer and The Dial*, 267. The *Dial* had originally been devoted to leftist politics. Financial pressures led to a change in editorial policy, driven by the vision of its financial backers, Scofield Thayer and Sibley Watson. Under their leader-ship, the magazine became instead a leading proponent of the modernist aesthetic (see Hoffman, Allen, and Ulrich, *Little Magazine*, 196–203; Joost, *Scofield Thayer and The Dial*, 3–27; and Selzer, *Kenneth Burke in Greenwich Village*, 115–18).

128. Munson, *Awakening Twenties*, 104.

129. Woodcock, "An Interview with Kenneth Burke," 707. The other was the offer of a teaching position at Bennington College.

130. Burke and Cowley, "Kenneth Burke and Malcolm Cowley," 191, 199; Roun-tree, "Richard Kostelanetz Interviews Kenneth Burke," 6; Warren, "Kenneth Burke," 229–30. For more on Burke's complicated career at the *Dial*, see Selzer, *Kenneth Burke in Greenwich Village*, 119–24, 132–36. For more on the Dial Award and Burke's selec-tion, see Hoffman, Allen, and Ulrich, *Little Magazine*, 202; Joost, *Scofield Thayer and The Dial*, 71–72; and Selzer, *Kenneth Burke in Greenwich Village*, 136.

131. Jack, "'Piety of Degradation,'" 448. Through an exceedingly complex set of events, Burke divorced Lily after falling in love with her younger sister, Elizabeth (Lib-bie). Afterward, the two families were able to coexist in close proximity, and Burke remained devoted to Libbie until her untimely death in 1968.

132. Woodcock, "An Interview with Kenneth Burke," 707. Hawhee argues that the importance of this work for Woods was even greater than Burke realized since it deepened his understanding of and emphasis upon the body (see Hawhee, "Burke on Drugs").

133. Jack, "'Piety of Degradation,'" 446, 448; Selzer, *Kenneth Burke in Greenwich Village*, 134–35, 168–69; Woodcock, "An Interview with Kenneth Burke," 707–8.

134. Selzer, *Kenneth Burke in Greenwich Village*, 118; see also 18, 154–59.

135. Kenneth Burke to Malcolm Cowley, 6 March 1923, Kenneth Burke Papers.

136. Kenneth Burke to Malcolm Cowley, 12 July 1923, Kenneth Burke Papers.

137. The closest that Burke came to rejecting this aspect of the bureau was his critique of the "moralist" view of crime and addiction in *Permanence and Change* (Jack, "'Piety of Degradation,'" 454–55). In Burke's correspondence, though he does not critique the eugenic aspects of the bureau, he suggests that working for Woods was not altogether satisfactory; discussing a new opportunity, he wrote Cowley that "the job will not pay much, but it will pay enough—and above all, it is a job for which I can respect myself, as I could never respect myself while hired to keep morphinists from getting their morphine, or to treat crime as an absolute" (Kenneth Burke to Malcolm Cowley, 4 June 1932, Kenneth Burke Papers).

138. Selzer, *Kenneth Burke in Greenwich Village*, 154–59.

139. Cowley, *Second Flowering*, 240.

140. There were those in the "Youngest Generation" who were not "Nordic." This was rare enough to prove notable, however—as evidenced by comments on Matthew Josephson's Judaism in letters between Burke and Cowley (e.g., Jay, *Selected Correspondence of Kenneth Burke and Malcolm Cowley*, 79, 98, 121).

141. Cowley, *Exile's Return*, 60. The inclusion of "female equality" might seem surprising, since Cowley suggests that the "Youngest Generation" was primarily populated by men. However, the Greenwich Village circles included a number of notable female artists (Selzer, *Kenneth Burke in Greenwich Village*, 9). Moreover, as with Cowley's first wife, Peggy, "female equality" was often *demanded* by a male Villager's female partner—in a way that racial equality was not (Bak, *Malcolm Cowley*, 132–34).

142. Burke, like most Americans, could not have avoided news of Garvey's exploits, or the thousands who attended his rallies. Further, as discussed in chapter 2, Burke was familiar enough with Garvey to describe Ellison as an "intellectual Garveyite" (Kenneth Burke to Stanley Edgar Hyman, 4 December 1945, Kenneth Burke Papers). For more on Garvey and his Universal Negro Improvement Association (UNIA), see Guterl, *Color of Race in America*, 131–44; Lewis, *When Harlem Was in Vogue*, 34–45.

143. Munson, *Awakening Twenties*, 5. This quote echoes the description offered in Allen's canonical text, *Only Yesterday* (see the portrait of the implicitly Nordic "Mr. and Mrs. Smith" on pages 1–10). Compare both of these to David Levering Lewis's account of the 1920s—which juxtaposes the February 1919 celebratory march by the all-black 369th Infantry Regiment with the terrible violence unleashed on black communities by the year's end (Lewis, *When Harlem Was in Vogue*, 3–24).

144. Selzer, *Kenneth Burke in Greenwich Village*, 9. As Selzer's account makes clear, this disregard for the Harlem Renaissance is even more remarkable since Jean Toomer, author of *Cane*, was a member of Burke's circles throughout the 1920s. On the other hand, given Toomer's ambivalent attitude toward his biracial identity, the

Villagers' disregard of race may have been a factor attracting Toomer to them (Guterl, *Color of Race in America*, 154–83). Indeed, nothing in Burke's correspondence with or about Toomer (apart from a reference to Toomer's "negro blood" in a 17 December 1923 letter to Lily archived in the Kenneth Burke Papers) even mentions matters of race. For more on the Burke-Toomer relationship, see Scruggs's "Jean Toomer and Kenneth Burke and the Persistence of the Past," though Scruggs focuses more on their correspondence than their extensive contact. For more on the Harlem Renaissance, see Huggins, *Harlem Renaissance*; Lewis, *When Harlem Was in Vogue*; or Locke's controversial anthology *The New Negro*.

145. Cowley, *Exile's Return*, 236; original emphasis.

146. Burke and Davis, *Ralph Ellison*, 56–57; Ellison, *Collected Essays*, 198–99; Graham and Singh, *Conversations with Ralph Ellison*, 257; L. Jackson, *Ralph Ellison*, 42–43, 48–49; Rampersad, *Ralph Ellison*, 29–30.

147. L. Jackson, *Ralph Ellison*, 39. See also Ellison, *Collected Essays*, 198–99.

148. L. Jackson, *Ralph Ellison*, 39; Rampersad, *Ralph Ellison*, 29.

149. For a discussion of jazz in Oklahoma City, see Burke and Davis, *Ralph Ellison*, 79–95—or Ellison's essays on the subject from *Shadow and Act* (Ellison, *Collected Essays*, 227–77).

150. Burke and Davis, *Ralph Ellison*, 44–46; Graham and Singh, *Conversations with Ralph Ellison*, 303–4; L. Jackson, *Ralph Ellison*, 57–65.

151. Burke and Davis, *Ralph Ellison*, 50; L. Jackson, *Ralph Ellison*, 68–69.

152. L. Jackson, *Ralph Ellison*, 68–69, 75–77.

153. Graham and Singh, *Conversations with Ralph Ellison*, 88; L. Jackson, *Ralph Ellison*, 83–88; Rampersad, *Ralph Ellison*, 44–47.

154. Burke and Davis, *Ralph Ellison*, 106–112; Graham and Singh, *Conversations with Ralph Ellison*, 248–49; L. Jackson, *Ralph Ellison*, 88–91; Rampersad, *Ralph Ellison*, 47–49.

155. For the classic account of the "Scottsboro Boys" case, see Carter, *Scottsboro*. For the trial's place within Ellison's trip, see Burke and Davis, *Ralph Ellison*, 113–14; Ellison, *Collected Essays*, 769–70; Graham and Singh, *Conversations with Ralph Ellison*, 248; L. Jackson, *Ralph Ellison*, 92–93; Rampersad, *Ralph Ellison*, 49, 51. For accounts of the contentious relationship between the Communists and the NAACP regarding the case, see Murray, "NAACP Versus the Communist Party," 267–81; and Naison, *Communists in Harlem during the Depression*, 57–94.

156. Burke and Davis, *Ralph Ellison*, 112–116; Ellison, *Collected Essays*, 769; L. Jackson, *Ralph Ellison*, 91–94; Rampersad, *Ralph Ellison*, 49–51.

157. L. Jackson, *Ralph Ellison*, 94. Ellison remained notably silent about the injuries—though it is likely that they occurred during his encounter with the detectives.

158. Rampersad, *Ralph Ellison*, 54–55.

159. L. Jackson, *Ralph Ellison*, 98–100, 103–4; Rampersad, *Ralph Ellison*, 54–55.

160. Rampersad, *Ralph Ellison*, 59; see also Burke and Davis, *Ralph Ellison*, 123; L. Jackson, *Ralph Ellison*, 100.

161. Rampersad, *Ralph Ellison*, 59; see also L. Jackson, *Ralph Ellison*, 105–7.

162. Jackson, *Ralph Ellison*, 117–19. See also, for example, Ellison, *Collected Essays*, 181–82, 631–37.

163. L. Jackson, *Ralph Ellison*, 109, 150–51; Rampersad, *Ralph Ellison*, 56–60, 63–66, 78–79.

164. L. Jackson, *Ralph Ellison*, 109, 115, 130–35, 148–51; Rampersad, *Ralph Ellison*, 67–69, 72, 76–78.

165. Burke and Davis, *Ralph Ellison*, 132, 135–37; L. Jackson, *Ralph Ellison*, 116–17, 120–23; Rampersad, *Ralph Ellison*, 60–61, 64–69.

166. Rampersad, *Ralph Ellison*, 67–69.

167. Burke and Davis, *Ralph Ellison*, 142; Ellison, *Collected Essays*, 712; Graham and Singh, *Conversations with Ralph Ellison*, 292; L. Jackson, *Ralph Ellison*, 136–37.

168. As Lawrence Jackson points out, Ellison's dedication of *Shadow and Act* to Sprague indicates how important this relationship was to Ellison's development as a writer (*Ralph Ellison*, 104).

169. Burke and Davis, *Ralph Ellison*, 148–49; L. Jackson, *Ralph Ellison*, 104–5, 138–39, 148–53; Rampersad, *Ralph Ellison*, 75–77.

170. Ellison, *Collected Essays*, 203.

171. Graham and Singh, *Conversations with Ralph Ellison*, 90.

172. Burke and Davis, *Ralph Ellison*, 148–49; Graham and Singh, *Conversations with Ralph Ellison*, 90–91; Ellison, *Collected Essays*, 202–3; L. Jackson, *Ralph Ellison*, 151–54; Rampersad, *Ralph Ellison*, 76–77.

173. L. Jackson, *Ralph Ellison*, 154.

174. Ibid., 118–19, 123–26, 135, 155, 158; Rampersad, *Ralph Ellison*, 77–79.

175. Ellison, *Collected Essays*, 203.

176. As Rampersad makes clear, Ellison appears to have had enough money to finance his last year at Tuskegee (*Ralph Ellison*, 80). For more on this momentous decision, see Burke and Davis, *Ralph Ellison*, 152–53; Graham and Singh, *Conversations with Ralph Ellison*, 90; Ellison, *Collected Essays*, 203–4; L. Jackson, *Ralph Ellison*, 157–60; Rampersad, *Ralph Ellison*, 79–80.

177. Ellison, *Collected Essays*, 615.

178. Rampersad, *Ralph Ellison*, 282.

179. Ellison, *Collected Essays*, 615.

180. Guterl, *Color of Race in America*, 122.

181. Ibid., 50.

182. Abu-Lughod, *Race, Space, and Riots*, 136–37; Sitkoff, *New Deal for Blacks*, 35–36.

183. As Guterl argues, New York played a decisive role in the propagation of this new understanding of race. Since the city was "the new media and financial capital of the world," the ideas and images that were salient to New Yorkers dominated the nation's art, advertising, business, and journalism—and thus had a disproportionate impact on the American conception of race (*Color of Race in America*, 11).

184. Jacobson, *Whiteness of a Different Color*, 95.

185. Guterl, *Color of Race in America*, 50.

186. Jacobson, *Whiteness of a Different Color*, 95. See also Guterl, *Color of Race in America*, 49–50; and McGreevy, *Parish Boundaries*, 78.

187. Jacobson, *Roots Too*, 1–10. The term "Caucasian" is more than a synonym for "white" identity since "it brought the full authority of modern science to bear on white identity. . . . The idea of a 'Caucasian race' represents whiteness ratcheted up to a new epistemological realm of certainty" (*Whiteness of a Different Color*, 94). Although I agree with Jacobson, for present purposes I want to emphasize the shift in popular understandings of race—from many races to two.

188. Jacobson, *Whiteness of a Different Color,* 98. See also Guterl, *Color of Race in America,* 3–7.

189. Allen, *Since Yesterday,* 26. Cowley offers a vivid portrait of the Depression in *Dream of the Golden Mountains* (22–30).

190. Sitkoff, *New Deal for Blacks,* 34. See also Abu-Lughod, *Race, Space, and Riots,* 139–41.

191. Ibid., 52. For the complex relationship between FDR and the black community, see Fishel, "Negro in the New Deal Era," 7–28.

192. Naison, *Communists in Harlem during the Depression,* 31.

193. George and Selzer, *Kenneth Burke in the 1930s,* 7.

194. Sitkoff, *New Deal for Blacks,* 35–39.

195. Ibid., 143.

196. Ibid., 141.

197. Naison, *Communists in Harlem during the Depression,* xvii. This strategic decision to concentrate efforts on Harlem reflected another practical reality: "Half the Party's total national membership was in New York" (Denning, *Cultural Front,* 16).

198. Naison, *Communists in Harlem during the Depression,* 57. See also Sitkoff, *New Deal for Blacks,* 145–49.

199. Naison, *Communists in Harlem during the Depression,* 31–39, 41–52, 58–61, 108–9; Sitkoff, *New Deal for Blacks,* 141–45.

200. Aaron, *Writers on the Left,* 356–57; Aaron et al., "Thirty Years Later," 497–99; George and Selzer, *Kenneth Burke in the 1930s,* 20–21; Naison, *Communists in Harlem during the Depression,* 169–88; Sitkoff, *New Deal for Blacks,* 149.

201. Denning, *Cultural Front,* 4. For this reason, the Popular Front should not be construed as a puppet or front for the Communist Party—but instead as "a broad and tenuous left-wing alliance of fractions of the subaltern classes" (ibid., 6).

202. Naison, *Communists in Harlem during the Depression,* 127. See also Sitkoff, *New Deal for Blacks,* 149.

203. The riot began on 19 March 1935, when a black teenager was accused of shoplifting in a white-owned store; when rumors spread that he had been beaten, and ultimately killed, by police, an angry crowd formed—which, by the end of a day-long protest, engaged in window smashing and looting. The Communists were a voice for order during the chaos, and worked to prevent racial violence. Later, they highlighted the discrimination that had led Harlem residents to take to the streets (see Abu-Lughod, *Race, Space, and Riots,* 139–49; and Naison, *Communists in Harlem during the Depression,* 140–50).

204. The Communist Party was responsible for drafting the call, but it was "signed" by artists outside the party, including Burke (George and Selzer, *Kenneth Burke in the 1930s,* 13). See also Aaron, *Writers on the Left,* 213–14, 223–30, 280–83; Aaron et al., "Thirty Years Later," 495–97; Cowley, *Dream of the Golden Mountains,* 269–73; Folsom, *Days of Anger, Days of Hope,* 90–95; George and Selzer, *Kenneth Burke in the 1930s,* 20–25.

205. Aaron et al., "Thirty Years Later," 496; Cowley, *Dream of the Golden Mountains,* 273.

206. Denning, *Cultural Front,* 59. Hughes, another modernist-turned-Communist, "was unable to attend but sent a paper that was read at the opening session" (George and Selzer, *Kenneth Burke in the 1930s,* 16). For more on the Communist

"conversion" experienced by modernists like Cowley and Hughes, see Aaron, *Writers on the Left*, 149–60; 334–42; Allen, *Since Yesterday*, 260–62; Cowley, *Dream of the Golden Mountains*, 31–62.

207. George and Selzer, *Kenneth Burke in the 1930s*, 16.

208. Cowley, *Dream of the Golden Mountains*, 274.

209. This episode was traumatic for Burke; he described it as a public trial and stoning—though it appears that, as George and Selzer conclude, the situation is better understood as "Burke's overly personal response to an overly charged situation brought about not by his speech but by the situation of radicals and semi-radicals at the meeting" (*Kenneth Burke in the 1930s*, 28). See also Aaron, *Writers on the Left*, 287–92; Aaron et al., "Thirty Years Later," 506–8; Cowley, *Dream of the Golden Mountains*, 275–79; Denning, *Cultural Front*, 55–56; George and Selzer, *Kenneth Burke in the 1930s*, 16–29; Lentricchia, *Criticism and Social Change*, 21–38; Rountree, "Richard Kostelanetz Interviews Kenneth Burke," 21–22; Woodcock, "Interview with Kenneth Burke," 708.

210. Antiblack racism also derailed Wright's travel arrangements for the Congress (Aaron, *Writers on the Left*, 281–82; Felgar, *Richard Wright*, 33–34; Folsom, *Days of Anger, Days of Hope*, 93–95; Gayle, *Richard Wright*, 78–82; George and Selzer, *Kenneth Burke in the 1930s*, 22–23; Wright, *American Hunger*, 94–98).

211. Cowley, *Dream of the Golden Mountains*, 279; George and Selzer, *Kenneth Burke in the 1930s*, 27.

212. Gayle, *Richard Wright*, 79–80, 82.

213. Rampersad, *Ralph Ellison*, 96.

214. In an incident that Ellison artistically reimagined in *Invisible Man*, one letter was hardly a recommendation; as a result, he "decided to destroy all but one, from his Tuskegee art instructor, Eva Hamlin" (Rampersad, *Ralph Ellison*, 82).

215. Ibid., 82. See also Burke and Davis, *Ralph Ellison*, 158; Ellison, *Collected Essays*, 441, 660–61; Graham and Singh, *Conversations with Ralph Ellison*, 292–93; L. Jackson, *Ralph Ellison*, 163–64; Rampersad, *Life of Langston Hughes*, 329.

216. L. Jackson, *Ralph Ellison*, 164.

217. Ibid., 164–68; Rampersad, *Ralph Ellison*, 83–86.

218. Rampersad, *Ralph Ellison*, 89–90.

219. Burke and Davis, *Ralph Ellison*, 158; Ellison, *Collected Essays*, 205; Graham and Singh, *Conversations with Ralph Ellison*, 292; L. Jackson, *Ralph Ellison*, 164, 168–175; Rampersad, *Ralph Ellison*, 83, 90–93.

220. Rampersad, *Ralph Ellison*, 93.

221. Burke and Davis, *Ralph Ellison*, 158–59; Ellison, *Collected Essays*, 661; Graham and Singh, *Conversations with Ralph Ellison*, 292–93; L. Jackson, *Ralph Ellison*, 178–79; Rampersad, *Ralph Ellison*, 96–97.

222. Ellison, *Collected Essays*, 659.

223. Ibid., 660. Ellison rarely credited Hughes with introducing him to Wright's poetry, but Lawrence Jackson's account suggests otherwise (e.g., *Ralph Ellison*, 175 n. 38).

224. Ellison, *Collected Essays*, 661 (Ellison incorrectly gives the date as July 1937); Gayle, *Richard Wright*, 98–99; L. Jackson, *Ralph Ellison*, 178–79; Rampersad, *Ralph Ellison*, 96–97.

225. Wright claimed that the final straw was an altercation during the 1937 May

Day parade (*American Hunger*, 130–35). For more on Wright's time in Chicago, see Ellison, *Collected Essays*, 662; Felgar, *Richard Wright*, 34–35; Gayle, *Richard Wright*, 66–96; L. Jackson, *Ralph Ellison*, 178; Rampersad, *Ralph Ellison*, 96; and Wright, *American Hunger*, 60–135.

226. Ellison, *Collected Essays*, 662; Felgar, *Richard Wright*, 35; Gayle, *Richard Wright*, 100.

227. Fabre, *Unfinished Quest of Richard Wright*, 145–46; L. Jackson, "Birth of the Critic," 322–24; L. Jackson, *Ralph Ellison*, 179–83; Rampersad, *Ralph Ellison*, 96–98. For more on the Second American Writers' Congress, see, for example, Aaron, *Writers on the Left*, 359–61; and Folsom, *Days of Anger, Days of Hope*, 6–10.

228. Rowley, *Richard Wright*, 129.

229. Ellison, *Collected Essays*, 662.

230. Rampersad, *Ralph Ellison*, 98.

231. Though the review was published, the story appeared in print posthumously (Ellison, *Flying Home*); Wright reserved it for the second, never-completed, issue of *New Challenge*. Wright's professional jealousy may have been responsible for the story's demise (Rampersad, *Ralph Ellison*, 100). For more on Ellison's first works, see Burke and Davis, *Ralph Ellison*, 161–62; Deutsch, "Ellison's Early Fiction"; Ellison, *Collected Essays*, 663–64; Fabre, *Unfinished Quest of Richard Wright*, 145–46; Graham and Singh, *Conversations with Ralph Ellison*, 293; L. Jackson, *Ralph Ellison*, 187–90; Rampersad, *Ralph Ellison*, 99–100; and Rowley, *Richard Wright*, 131.

232. Graham and Singh, *Conversations with Ralph Ellison*, 293.

233. L. Jackson, *Ralph Ellison*, 190. See also Rampersad, *Ralph Ellison*, 101–2.

234. Burke and Davis, *Ralph Ellison*, 169–74; L. Jackson, *Ralph Ellison*, 191–97; Rampersad, *Ralph Ellison*, 101–7.

235. Graham and Singh, *Conversations with Ralph Ellison*, 294; Rampersad, *Ralph Ellison*, 109.

236. The salary proved helpful in September, when he married a radical entertainer named Rose Poindexter. Although the marriage was short-lived—her parents disapproved of the marriage—Ellison remained with the Project for four years (see Burke and Davis, *Ralph Ellison*, 175–82; L. Jackson, *Ralph Ellison*, 199–203, 212, 215–16; and Rampersad, *Ralph Ellison*, 109–16).

237. L. Jackson, *Ralph Ellison*, 211–14; Rampersad, *Ralph Ellison*, 118–21.

238. Graham and Singh, *Conversations with Ralph Ellison*, 124.

239. Ibid.

240. Rampersad, *Ralph Ellison*, 121. For an opposing view, see Foley, "Ralph Ellison as Proletarian Journalist."

241. Ellison, *Collected Essays*, 666.

242. George and Selzer, *Kenneth Burke in the 1930s*, 199–203; Pauley, "Criticism in Context." See also L. Jackson, *Ralph Ellison*, 180–82; Rampersad, *Ralph Ellison*, 96–97—though, since Ellison (wrongly) insisted that the lecture was in 1937, his biographers trace the episode to the Second American Writers' Congress.

243. Burke delivered an abridged version of his paper at the Congress; complete versions of the essay later appeared in *Southern Review* and *The Philosophy of Literary Form* (George and Selzer, *Kenneth Burke in the 1930s*, 200–203; Pauley, "Criticism in Context"). In this chapter, I cite the published version of the essay since my focus is

Burke's overall intention—to unite Marx and Freud in the analysis of a rhetor's symbolic edifice.

244. Barkan, *Retreat of Scientific Racism,* 279–85, 332–40; Jacobson, *Whiteness of a Different Color,* 99–101.

245. Burke, *Complete White Oxen,* xvii.

246. Efforts to minimize differences between the "Jewish" and "Aryan" races essentially widened the gap between whites and blacks. In effect, as Jacobson argues, Hitler's opponents cast doubt on his "false" racial distinctions by reinforcing "real" ones (*Whiteness of a Different Color,* 102–9).

247. Burke, "Rhetoric of Hitler's 'Battle,'" 207 n, 3, 204 (see also 216–17), 214; original emphasis.

248. Ibid., 214, 211; original emphasis.

249. Ibid., 205.

250. Ibid., 218, 219.

251. Rampersad, *Ralph Ellison,* 97.

252. Ralph Ellison to Kenneth Burke, 23 November 1945, Kenneth Burke Papers.

253. Graham and Singh, *Conversations with Ralph Ellison,* 364.

2 / Antagonistic Cooperation

1. Ibid., 364.

2. Jay, *Selected Correspondence of Kenneth Burke and Malcolm Cowley,* 351. The quotation is from Cowley, reporting Ellison's statement to Burke, who had not attended the event.

3. Ellison, *Collected Essays,* 60.

4. Burke, "Ralph Ellison's Trueblooded *Bildungsroman,*" 359. This essay is discussed further in chapter 3. For now, note simply that "Nortonism" refers to a character in *Invisible Man*—the rich, northern, white philanthropist whose donations to Invisible Man's school hide an insidious form of racism.

5. Ibid. The description is Burke's; the place of race in this "nonracial 'we'" is explored more fully in chapter 4.

6. Burke, *Grammar of Motives,* xvii.

7. For more on the initial, two-part design of the *Rhetoric* project, see Crable, "Distance as Ultimate Motive." Secondary articles and books on Burke's rhetorical theory began appearing in the 1950s—most famously, in the work of Marie Hochmuth Nichols—and continue to appear today. For books on the relevance of Burke in the twenty-first century, see Biesecker, *Addressing Postmodernity;* Brock, *Kenneth Burke and the 21st Century;* Crusius, *Kenneth Burke and the Conversation after Philosophy;* and Hawhee, *Moving Bodies.*

8. Burke mentions racial violence and the "Negro spiritual" in his early work *Permanence and Change* (15–16, 37). Additionally, Burke's review of "Run, Little Chillun!" is included in *The Philosophy of Literary Form* (361–68). Otherwise, the subject crops up only occasionally in his published work, as in the late essays "Rhetorical Situation" (268, 271), and "Comments" (181–82). Compare this, though, to the many discussions within the *Rhetoric* (32, 34, 104, 115, 117, 126, 193–95, 259, 282, 284–85, 300, 312–13). For present purposes, this discussion of Burke's published work is sufficient; however, as is discussed in chapter 4, there are also interesting allusions to race within Burke's unpublished correspondence.

9. Ellison's correspondence makes clear both his familiarity with the text and his

difficulty in securing a personal copy. See, for example, Ralph Ellison to Stanley Edgar Hyman, hand-dated "[ca. 1942–43]," Stanley Edgar Hyman Papers.

10. As several commentators have pointed out, *Counter-Statement* is a text at war with itself. Its earliest chapters, primarily written in the early 1920s, focus on the aesthetic, to the neglect of social factors. By the end of the book, this view of art is "corrected" and receives as a corollary a political-economic "program." For more on this fractured text, see Frank, *Kenneth Burke*, 44–71; Rueckert, *Kenneth Burke and the Drama of Human Relations*, 8–33; Selzer, *Kenneth Burke in Greenwich Village*, 137–64; Wess, *Kenneth Burke*, 39–54.

11. Between *Counter-Statement* (1931) and *Permanence and Change* (1935), Burke attempted, and abandoned, two book projects. Since his one completed manuscript, *Auscultation, Creation, and Revision*, was published in 1993, Ellison would have been unaware of it in the early 1940s (see Burke, "Auscultation, Creation, and Revision"; Crusius, "Kenneth Burke's *Auscultation*"; and George and Selzer, *Kenneth Burke in the 1930s*, 58–87).

12. Ellison's personal library includes first editions of both books, inscribed "Ralph Ellison, 42." The books are filled with notations, underlines, and marginal comments, made by multiple implements—including pencil, red pencil, black ink, and green ink. These extensive markings demonstrate the seriousness with which Ellison studied them. Further, since his library includes later editions of the books—bearing similar signs of study—it seems likely that the majority of these notations occurred in the early 1940s.

13. The second edition of the text, released during the heyday of McCarthyism, was revised—with all mentions of communism expurgated. Burke's argument for the "poetic orientation," though, still represented a strong critique of ideology. For more on this text and its history, see Crable, "Ideology as 'Metabiology'"; George and Selzer, *Kenneth Burke in the 1930s*, 88–140; Schiappa and Keehner, "Lost Passages of Kenneth Burke's *Permanence and Change*"; and Wess, *Kenneth Burke*, 55–83.

14. Burke, *Attitudes toward History*, 102, 171; original emphasis. For more on Burke's text, see Selzer, *Kenneth Burke in the 1930s*, 141–80; and Wess, *Kenneth Burke*, 84–107.

15. For a complementary account of Ellison's "comic corrective," see Wright, *Shadowing Ralph Ellison*, 78–129.

16. Rampersad, *Ralph Ellison*, 156.

17. Graham and Singh, *Conversations with Ralph Ellison*, 364.

18. Ralph Ellison to Kenneth Burke, 23 November 1945, Kenneth Burke Papers. Originally, the last word was "o," not "do." Ellison's letters—both early and late in life—contain frequent misspellings, though it seems clear that he recognized the weakness. Writing Burke in the early 1980s, he ended with an amusing postscript: "I wrote the above on a word-processor but my spelling hasn't improved a damned bit!" (Ralph Ellison to Kenneth Burke, 20 June 1983, Kenneth Burke Papers). I have chosen to silently correct minor errors of spelling in Ellison's—and others'—correspondence.

19. L. Jackson, *Ralph Ellison*, 221–22, 235–36, 255.

20. Ibid., 217–20, 230–33.

21. Denning, *Cultural Front*, 23, 24.

22. L. Jackson, "Birth of the Critic," 327, 330–33; L. Jackson, *Ralph Ellison*, 253–59, 265; Rampersad, *Ralph Ellison*, 140–42.

23. L. Jackson, "Birth of the Critic," 333–36; L. Jackson, *Ralph Ellison*, 263–71; Rampersad, *Ralph Ellison*, 152–63. For Herndon's impact on Ellison's career, see Griffiths, "Ralph Ellison, Richard Wright, and the Case of Angelo Herndon."

24. L. Jackson, "Birth of the Critic," 334.

25. Ibid., 329; L. Jackson, *Ralph Ellison*, 256–57; Rampersad, *Ralph Ellison*, 141, 146. *Direction* was allied with the League of American Writers. By 1941 (when Ellison's essay was published), Burke was a member of the editorial board and its "chief fiction editor" (George and Selzer, *Kenneth Burke in the 1930s*, 199). It is possible that the two corresponded regarding the essay, but, since it was not a work of fiction, unlikely.

26. This quote, and the ensuing description of the initiation of their relationship, is drawn from an untitled series of pages labeled "File Stanley Hyman" in the Ralph Ellison Papers, box I:188, folder 10; though undated, they represent Ellison's efforts to craft a memorial for Hyman after his untimely death in 1970. See also Ralph Ellison to Stanley Edgar Hyman, 22 June 1942, Stanley Edgar Hyman Papers; and Rampersad, *Ralph Ellison*, 156.

27. Oppenheimer offers a slightly different version of the friendship's origin: "One day [Hyman] wandered by the offices of The Negro Quarterly, looking for a new market for his critical reviews. He and the young managing editor hit it off at once" (*Private Demons*, 103). Since Ellison and Hyman seem to have exchanged letters before meeting, Oppenheimer's story seems less likely than Ellison's recollected version.

28. Ralph Ellison to Stanley Edgar Hyman, 22 June 1942, Stanley Edgar Hyman Papers.

29. Stanley Edgar Hyman to Ralph Ellison, 24 June 1942, Ralph Ellison Papers, box I:58, folder 14. "Mister Toussan" had appeared in *New Masses* in late 1941 (Rampersad, *Ralph Ellison*, 146). Hyman retained his "Ellison, Ralph" folder for the rest of his life. As he wrote Ellison in 1966: "Can you tell me where I can get a copy of your 1964 pamphlet with Karl Shapiro? Is it in print? If not, can you help me get one or get one for me? My Ellison collection is incomplete until I get one" (Stanley Edgar Hyman to Ralph Ellison, 4 May 1966, Ralph Ellison Papers, box I:51, folder 15).

30. Stanley Edgar Hyman to Ralph Ellison, 19 July 1942, Ralph Ellison Papers, box I:51, folder 14.

31. Ralph Ellison to Stanley Edgar Hyman, hand-dated "ca. 1942–'43," Stanley Edgar Hyman Papers. Given the date of the letter to which this is a reply, it was likely written in July 1942.

32. This quote is drawn from the untitled, undated pages labeled "File Stanley Hyman" in the Ralph Ellison Papers, box I:188, folder 10.

33. Stanley Edgar Hyman to Kenneth Burke, 16 December 1942, Kenneth Burke Papers. According to Oppenheimer, the rapid pace of the Hyman-Ellison relationship was typical: "Shirley and Stanley were the center and chief focal point for a large network of friends. Stanley was always bringing home somebody new, pulling him or her into the fold" (*Private Demons*, 103).

34. Stanley Edgar Hyman to Kenneth Burke, 16 December 1942, Kenneth Burke Papers. After meeting in 1939, Hyman and Burke had exchanged a few letters and met once at Andover in 1940 (George and Selzer, *Kenneth Burke in the 1930s*, 204, 259 n. 8; Kenneth Burke to Stanley Edgar Hyman, 1 October 1940, Stanley Edgar Hyman Papers; Kenneth Burke to Stanley Edgar Hyman, 9 October 1940, Stanley Edgar Hyman Papers; Kenneth Burke to Stanley Edgar Hyman, 16 October 1940, Stanley

Edgar Hyman Papers). Apparently, while at Andover, Hyman met Slochower, who was Burke's neighbor. Ellison had met (and impressed) Slochower in March 1942 (see L. Jackson, *Ralph Ellison*, 270; and Stanley Edgar Hyman to Ralph Ellison, 19 July 1942, Ralph Ellison Papers, box I:51, folder 14). For more on Slochower and Burke, see Hyman, *Armed Vision*, 371–72.

35. Kenneth Burke to Stanley Edgar Hyman, 25 March 1943, Stanley Edgar Hyman Papers.

36. Ellison's book, dated April 1943, was simply inscribed, "To Ralph Ellison, greetings, Kenneth Burke." Burke apparently did not get Ellison's address since he sent both to Hyman, in care of his employer, the *New Yorker*. See, for example, Stanley Edgar Hyman to Kenneth Burke, 16 March 1943, Kenneth Burke Papers; Kenneth Burke to Stanley Edgar Hyman, 15 April 1943, Stanley Edgar Hyman Papers. Given the date of Burke's letter (and his previous letter, dated 25 March 1943), it is likely that Hyman's letter is a month off—and should be dated 16 April 1943.

37. Stanley Edgar Hyman to Kenneth Burke, 16 March 1943, Kenneth Burke Papers. Due to financial difficulties (and, it seems, Herndon's rather shady fund-raising activities), *Negro Quarterly* ceased publication following its Winter-Spring 1943 issue (see, for example, Rampersad, *Ralph Ellison*, 162–63).

38. Stanley Edgar Hyman to Kenneth Burke, 16 March 1943, Kenneth Burke Papers.

39. L. Jackson, *Ralph Ellison*, 281; Rampersad, *Ralph Ellison*, 167–68.

40. L. Jackson, *Ralph Ellison*, 288; Rampersad, *Ralph Ellison*, 164–66. See also Stanley Edgar Hyman to Kenneth Burke, 26 May 1943, Kenneth Burke Papers; Ralph Ellison to Stanley Edgar Hyman, 2 June 1943, Stanley Edgar Hyman Papers.

41. Ralph Ellison to Kenneth Burke, 28 May 1943, Kenneth Burke Papers.

42. Ibid. Ellison's mention of Coleridge may refer to Burke's review in the *New Republic* (George and Selzer, *Kenneth Burke in the 1930s*, 226)—though it could also refer to the opening chapter of *The Philosophy of Literary Form* (or an excerpt published in the *Southern Review*). In discussing Burke's "five terms," however, Ellison is likely referring to Burke's essay, "The Tactics of Motivation" (which appeared in Spring 1943) or to "The Five Master Terms, Their Place in a 'Dramatistic' Grammar of Motives" (which appeared under a June 1943 date). The Burkean pentad, the basic grammatical elements governing human symbol-use, includes act, agent, agency, scene, and purpose—as well as the ratios connecting these terms. For more on the pentad, see Burke, *Grammar of Motives*, xv–xxiii; 127–320.

43. Stanley Edgar Hyman to Kenneth Burke, 24 September 1943, Kenneth Burke Papers.

44. L. Jackson, *Ralph Ellison*, 282–83, 296; Rampersad, *Ralph Ellison*, 168.

45. Stanley Edgar Hyman to Kenneth Burke, 8 October 1943, Kenneth Burke Papers. See also Kenneth Burke to Stanley Edgar Hyman, 26 September 1943, Stanley Edgar Hyman Papers.

46. Stanley Edgar Hyman to Kenneth Burke, 12 November 1943, Kenneth Burke Papers. See also Kenneth Burke to Stanley Edgar Hyman, 6 November 1943, Stanley Edgar Hyman Papers; Kenneth Burke to Stanley Edgar Hyman, 11 November 1943, Stanley Edgar Hyman Papers.

47. Stanley Edgar Hyman to Kenneth Burke, 30 November 1943, Kenneth Burke Papers. See also Kenneth Burke to Stanley Edgar Hyman, 6 December 1943, Stanley

Edgar Hyman Papers. Hyman's letter refers to Isidor Schneider, who was active in the Communist Party and *New Masses*. Since Burke and Ellison rejected strict party orthodoxy, both men had significant differences of opinion with Schneider. For more on Ellison and Schneider, see L. Jackson, *Ralph Ellison*, 324; for more on Burke and Schneider, see George and Selzer, *Kenneth Burke in the 1930s*, 11; and Selzer, *Kenneth Burke in Greenwich Village*, 166.

48. Stanley Edgar Hyman to Kenneth Burke, 14 January 1944, Kenneth Burke Papers. Ellison was "certified for duty as a second cook and baker" and departed New York on 27 December (Rampersad, *Ralph Ellison*, 169).

49. L. Jackson, *Ralph Ellison*, 282–83, 296; Rampersad, *Ralph Ellison*, 171–73.

50. Stanley Edgar Hyman to Kenneth Burke, 17 January 1944, Kenneth Burke Papers; Stanley Edgar Hyman to Kenneth Burke, 15 May 1944, Kenneth Burke Papers; Stanley Edgar Hyman to Kenneth Burke, 13 February 1945, Kenneth Burke Papers.

51. Stanley Edgar Hyman to Kenneth Burke, 22 February 1944, Kenneth Burke Papers; Stanley Edgar Hyman to Kenneth Burke, 22 June 1944, Kenneth Burke Papers; Stanley Edgar Hyman to Kenneth Burke, 20 December 1944, Kenneth Burke Papers; Stanley Edgar Hyman to Kenneth Burke, 7 March 1945, Kenneth Burke Papers.

52. Kenneth Burke to Stanley Edgar Hyman, 29 January 1944, Stanley Edgar Hyman Papers; Kenneth Burke to Stanley Edgar Hyman, 23 March 1945, Stanley Edgar Hyman Papers. See also Jay, *Selected Correspondence of Kenneth Burke and Malcolm Cowley*, 264–66.

53. L. Jackson, *Ralph Ellison*, 296–99; Rampersad, *Ralph Ellison*, 171–84.

54. Ralph Ellison to Kenneth Burke, 23 November 1945, Kenneth Burke Papers; Ellison, *Collected Essays*, 521; Jackson, *Ralph Ellison*, 309, 311–12; Rampersad, *Ralph Ellison*, 180.

55. L. Jackson, *Ralph Ellison*, 299–300; Rampersad, *Ralph Ellison*, 179. The subject of this novel is unclear—it was not the same as the novel proposed for the Rosenwald—but may have involved the protagonist of "Flying Home" (L. Jackson, *Ralph Ellison*, 299).

56. L. Jackson, *Ralph Ellison*, 306–9; Rampersad, *Ralph Ellison*, 184–85.

57. Ellison, *Collected Essays*, 349. See also Ellison, *Collected Essays*, 471, 521–22; L. Jackson, *Ralph Ellison*, 311; Rampersad, *Ralph Ellison*, 186–87.

58. L. Jackson, *Ralph Ellison*, 318; Rampersad, *Ralph Ellison*, 187. Though Lawrence Jackson indicates the award came through in late August, I agree with Rampersad (based on correspondence) that it was awarded in late April or early May.

59. Stanley Edgar Hyman to Ralph Ellison, 30 May 1945, Ralph Ellison Papers, box I:51, folder 14.

60. L. Jackson, *Ralph Ellison*, 312–15; Rampersad, *Ralph Ellison*, 187–89.

61. Rampersad, *Ralph Ellison*, 178. The decision to cut the manuscript was political, and angered Wright. Though the expurgated material was later published under the title *American Hunger*, contemporary editions of *Black Boy* contain both halves of Wright's life story—thus realizing, decades later, Wright's original vision for the book. For more on the saga of *Black Boy*, see Felgar, *Richard Wright*; and Gayle, *Richard Wright*.

62. Wright, *Black Boy*, 37.

63. See, for example, L. Jackson, "Birth of the Critic."

64. Ellison, *Collected Essays*, 129.

65. Burke, *Attitudes toward History,* 3–4.

66. Ellison, *Collected Essays,* 133.

67. Burke, *Philosophy of Literary Form,* 1. Given its 1941 publication date, Ellison had most likely read *The Philosophy of Literary Form* by the time that he wrote "Richard Wright's Blues." Ellison's library contains a worn copy of the first edition of the text—and its notations suggest that, during one reading of the text, Wright and *Native Son* were at the forefront of Ellison's thoughts. However, since Ellison signed the text ("Ralph W. Ellison," in both ink and pencil) without dating it, I cannot be absolutely certain when it was acquired.

68. Burke, *Philosophy of Literary Form,* 6.

69. Ellison, *Collected Essays,* 137.

70. Ralph Ellison to Kenneth Burke, 28 May 1943, Kenneth Burke Papers.

71. Burke, *Grammar of Motives,* 9.

72. Ellison, *Collected Essays,* 133.

73. Ibid., 131.

74. Ibid., 143.

75. Ibid., 129.

76. Ibid., 143.

77. Ibid., 128.

78. Ibid., 131.

79. Rampersad, *Ralph Ellison,* 187–88.

80. L. Jackson, *Ralph Ellison,* 318–20; Rampersad, *Ralph Ellison,* 191–95.

81. Ralph Ellison to Stanley Edgar Hyman, 21 August 1945, Stanley Edgar Hyman Papers.

82. Stanley Edgar Hyman to Ralph Ellison, 22 August 1945, Ralph Ellison Papers, box I:51, folder 14. In his initial invitation, Hyman wrote: "I hope you will come. You can speak on anything you want, but I'd rather you spoke on literature than anything else. If you want to make a speech entitled The White Menace, though, I wouldn't complain" (Stanley Edgar Hyman to Ralph Ellison, 30 May 1945, Ralph Ellison Papers, box I:51, folder 14).

83. Ralph Ellison to Stanley Edgar Hyman, 16 September 1945, Stanley Edgar Hyman Papers.

84. Quoted in Oppenheimer, *Private Demons,* 117.

85. Stanley Edgar Hyman to Ralph Ellison, 19 October 1945, Ralph Ellison Papers, box I:51, folder 14.

86. Rampersad, *Ralph Ellison,* 199–201. See also Ralph Ellison to Stanley Edgar Hyman, 21 August 1945, Stanley Edgar Hyman Papers.

87. L. Jackson, *Ralph Ellison,* 314.

88. Libbie Burke to Shirley Jackson, hand-dated "December 1945," Shirley Jackson Papers. Libbie did not write Ellison herself, so Hyman subsequently reported her praise (Stanley Edgar Hyman to Ralph Ellison, 24 November 1945, Ralph Ellison Papers, box I:51, folder 14)—suggesting that Libbie's letter was likely written in November.

89. Stanley Edgar Hyman to Ralph Ellison, 27 October 1945, Ralph Ellison Papers, box I:51, folder 14. The fourth person mentioned was Leonard Brown, one of Hyman's teachers—and the man who had introduced Hyman to Burke. Hyman, with a little assistance from Burke, was attempting to have Brown hired at Bennington. His visit, ultimately unsuccessful, coincided with Ellison's lecture.

90. Stanley Edgar Hyman to Kenneth Burke, 27 October 1945, Kenneth Burke Papers.

91. Kenneth Burke to Stanley Edgar Hyman, 30 October 1945, Stanley Edgar Hyman Papers.

92. Ibid.; original emphasis.

93. L. Jackson, *Ralph Ellison*, 324–25; Rampersad, *Ralph Ellison*, 201–2.

94. Rampersad, *Ralph Ellison*, 202. Hyman later wrote Ellison that "just before the term ended we took a poll of the students on their reactions to evening meetings, and your nonsense ranked among the three highest, the other two being faculty. So you have been elected Most Likely to Succeed" (Stanley Edgar Hyman to Ralph Ellison, 25 July 1946, Ralph Ellison Papers, box I:51, folder 14).

95. Stanley Edgar Hyman to Ralph Ellison, 24 November 1945, Ralph Ellison Papers, box I:51, folder 14.

96. Ibid.

97. Ralph Ellison to Kenneth Burke, 23 November 1945, Kenneth Burke Papers.

98. Ibid. As noted in chapter 1, Ellison added that his novel in progress—the novel that would become *Invisible Man*—was conceived as a means of repaying his intellectual debt to Burke.

99. Ibid.

100. Ellison's letter focuses on Burke's note to Hyman, but Ellison's framing of the question, and some of the topics discussed, imply they had other conversations on these points. Jackson suggests the existence of such conversations—as when he reports that Ellison "told Kenneth Burke in November of 1943 that the important artistic achievement lay in demolishing the stereotypes and caricatures that white Americans used to keep the humanity of black Americans at bay" (*Ralph Ellison*, 326)—but I can find no other trace of these conversations.

101. Ralph Ellison to Kenneth Burke, 23 November 1945, Kenneth Burke Papers. Here Ellison refers to the "Southern Agrarian" Donald Davidson and his essay, "The White Spirituals and Their Historian," which characterizes the "Negro spiritual" as derived from the European-influenced "white spiritual"—thereby denying that black Americans had any influence on American music and culture. For more on Burke's relationship to the Agrarians, see George and Selzer, *Kenneth Burke in the 1930s*.

102. Ralph Ellison to Kenneth Burke, 23 November 1945, Kenneth Burke Papers. The implications of this point are explored more fully in chapters 4 and 5; for present purposes, I wish only to focus on this early back-and-forth between the two men.

103. Ibid.

104. Ibid.

105. Ibid.

106. Ibid. I return to Ellison's argument on allegiance and organization—and Burke's response to it—in chapter 4.

107. Ibid.

108. Ibid.

109. Kenneth Burke to Stanley Edgar Hyman, 4 December 1945, Stanley Edgar Hyman Papers.

110. Ralph Ellison to Stanley Edgar Hyman, 12 December 1945, Stanley Edgar Hyman Papers; Kenneth Burke to Stanley Edgar Hyman, 20 April 1946, Stanley Edgar

Hyman Papers; Stanley Edgar Hyman to Kenneth Burke, 24 April 1946, Kenneth Burke Papers.

111. Ralph Ellison to Stanley Edgar Hyman, 12 December 1945, Stanley Edgar Hyman Papers.

112. Stanley Edgar Hyman to Ralph Ellison, 6 January 1946, Ralph Ellison Papers, box I:51, folder 14.

113. Kenneth Burke to Stanley Edgar Hyman, 20 April 1946, Stanley Edgar Hyman Papers.

114. Stanley Edgar Hyman to Kenneth Burke, 24 April 1946, Kenneth Burke Papers.

115. Burke, "Rhetoric of the Negro," n.d., Kenneth Burke Papers. In a paragraph that Burke bracketed in pencil, Ellison's letter asserted that "Carver was inflated into the symbol of the achievement possible for Negroes who stayed in their place, bowed to the white folks, prayed to God and left politics alone.... When I see you I'd like to discuss this further. Carver was one of the most insidious hoaxes ever created by a ruling class to keep a people under control" (Ralph Ellison to Kenneth Burke, 23 November 1945, Kenneth Burke Papers).

116. Burke, "Rhetoric of the Negro," n.d., Kenneth Burke Papers.

117. Ibid.

118. Kenneth Burke to Malcolm Cowley, 7 December 1945, Kenneth Burke Papers.

119. Burke, "Rhetoric of the Negro," n.d., Kenneth Burke Papers.

120. Ibid. Burke's list includes "the Negro spiritual," "the comic Negro," "the Blues Negro," "Garveyite," "the Carver type," "the 'bad nigger,'" "the Marxist," "the uncertain servant," and "the part-Negro."

121. Since Burke did not describe this section, it is unclear whether it would have summarized Ellison's argument, or whether it would have challenged his interpretation of Wright's text.

122. Ibid. Although the notes are somewhat disjointed regarding this section, the interpretation offered here fits with Burke's other published statements about Wright (e.g., Burke, *Philosophy of Literary Form,* xxi–xxii; *Rhetoric of Motives,* 117).

123. Burke, "Rhetoric of the Negro," n.d., Kenneth Burke Papers.

124. Ibid.

125. Kenneth Burke to Ralph Ellison, 16 December 1945, Ralph Ellison Papers, box I:38, folder 8.

126. Ibid.

127. Ibid.

128. Ibid.

129. Ibid. As is explored in chapter 3, although both Burke and Ellison admire Dostoevsky, this disagreement over his characters reflects important differences in their approach to matters of race.

130. Ibid.

131. Ibid.

132. L. Jackson, *Ralph Ellison,* 335; Rampersad, *Ralph Ellison,* 207.

133. Ralph Ellison to Stanley Edgar Hyman, 20 June 1946, Stanley Edgar Hyman Papers.

134. Ibid. According to Rampersad, though, Ellison did not marry Fanny until late August 1946 (*Ralph Ellison,* 209).

135. Ralph Ellison to Stanley Edgar Hyman, 20 June 1946, Stanley Edgar Hyman Papers.

136. Stanley Edgar Hyman to Kenneth Burke, 18 July 1946, Kenneth Burke Papers; Kenneth Burke to Stanley Edgar Hyman, 21 July 1946, Stanley Edgar Hyman Papers; Stanley Edgar Hyman to Kenneth Burke, 25 July 1946, Kenneth Burke Papers.

137. Stanley Edgar Hyman to Kenneth Burke, 25 July 1946, Kenneth Burke Papers.

138. Kenneth Burke to Stanley Edgar Hyman, 29 July 1946, Stanley Edgar Hyman Papers.

139. Ralph Ellison to Kenneth Burke, 23 September 1946, Kenneth Burke Papers.

140. Rampersad, *Ralph Ellison,* 209. See also Ralph Ellison to Richard Wright, 24 August 1946, Richard Wright Papers.

141. Ellison's response to Burke's letter—and its implications for *Invisible Man*—are explored more fully in chapter 3.

142. Stanley Edgar Hyman to Ralph Ellison, 2 October 1946, Ralph Ellison Papers, box I:51, folder 14; Ralph Ellison to Kenneth Burke, 4 December 1946, Ralph Ellison Papers, box I:38, folder 8. The list of "Negro writing" was in response to a request made by a Bennington student.

143. Kenneth Burke to Stanley Edgar Hyman, 8 January 1947, Stanley Edgar Hyman Papers.

144. Libbie Burke to Fanny Ellison, 13 May 1947, Ralph Ellison Papers, box I:38, folder 8. See also Fanny Ellison to Libbie Burke, 29 April 1947, Ralph Ellison Papers, box I:38, folder 8.

145. Ralph Ellison to Stanley Edgar Hyman, 17 June 1947, Stanley Edgar Hyman Papers.

146. Ralph Ellison to Kenneth Burke, 25 August 1947, Kenneth Burke Papers.

147. Kenneth Burke to Stanley Edgar Hyman, 8 November 1947, Stanley Edgar Hyman Papers. See also Stanley Edgar Hyman to Kenneth Burke, 6 October 1947, Kenneth Burke Papers.

148. Kenneth Burke to Ralph Ellison, 14 January 1948, Ralph Ellison Papers, box I:38, folder 8. I return to this letter, and its significance for the Burke-Ellison relationship, in chapter 4.

149. The concept of "mystery" has become a standard part of the rhetorical lexicon; it indicates the presence of social difference, with its attendant awkwardness. Chapters 4 and 5 thus return to mystery, in relation to the "racial divide."

150. Kenneth Burke to Ralph Ellison, 14 January 1948, Ralph Ellison Papers, box I:38, folder 8.

151. Kenneth Burke to Stanley Edgar Hyman, 13 January 1948, Stanley Edgar Hyman Papers.

152. Burke, *Rhetoric of Motives,* 34, 104, 115, 126, 259, 284–85, 300, 312–13.

153. Less than two weeks after Burke's letter to Ellison, Burke indicated to Hyman that he had begun the section published as part 3 of the *Rhetoric*: "Order." Further, he told Hyman that "the section . . . should incorporate a revised version of my bleat on Ideology and Myth" (Kenneth Burke to Stanley Edgar Hyman, 26 January 1948, Stanley Edgar Hyman Papers).

154. Burke, *Rhetoric of Motives,* 183–84. The description offered here is provisional; the distinction between these three orders of terminology, and its relevance to Burke's conception of race, is developed in greater detail in chapters 4 and 5.

155. Ibid., 187, 192.

156. Ibid., 193.

157. Ibid.

158. Here my focus is strictly upon the argument contained within the *Rhetoric* and how it reflects Burke's dialogue with Ellison on matters of race. In chapter 4, I return to the *Rhetoric*, and critically examine Burke's appropriation of Ellison's essay.

159. Ellison, *Collected Essays*, 129.

160. Burke, *Rhetoric of Motives*, 192.

161. Ibid. The quote, though unattributed, is from "Richard Wright's Blues" (see Ellison, *Collected Essays*, 140). This quotation and Ellison's reaction to it are the subject of further analysis in chapter 4.

162. Burke, *Rhetoric of Motives*, 193.

163. Ibid., 282.

164. Ibid., 194; see also 117, 259.

165. Stanley Edgar Hyman to Kenneth Burke, 10 October 1950, Kenneth Burke Papers. "Red Taurus" was one of the *Rhetoric*'s nicknames within the Burke-Hyman correspondence.

166. Kenneth Burke to Stanley Edgar Hyman, 7 January 1957, Kenneth Burke Papers.

167. Gibson, "No to Nothing," 255.

168. Although Burke equated Ellison's arguments with Gibson's, Ellison would have disagreed. As he wrote to Albert Murray: "I'm sick to my guts of reading stuff like the piece by Richard Gibson in *Kenyon Review*. . . . If he thinks he's the black Gide why doesn't he write and prove it? Then the white folks would read it and shake their heads and say 'Why, by God, this here is really the pure Andre Richard Gibson Gide! Yes, sir, here's a carbon copy!'" (Murray and Callahan, *Trading Twelves*, 20).

169. Burke, "Ralph Ellison's Trueblooded *Bildungsroman*," 350.

3 / From Acceptance to Rejection

1. M. Burke, "Visitors." According to this memoir, provided by Burke's youngest son, Burke purchased a home audio-recording device in 1950—and used it to capture Ellison reading the "Battle Royal" scene at Andover, prior to its appearance in the novel. A letter from Burke in 1957 corroborates this memory (Kenneth Burke to George Knox, 16 July 1957, Kenneth Burke Papers). Since "Battle Royal" was published first in 1947, and again in 1948 (Rampersad, *Ralph Ellison*, 216–17), the reading most likely occurred during the Ellisons' visit in August 1951.

2. L. Jackson, *Ralph Ellison*, 435–37; Rampersad, *Ralph Ellison*, 258–63.

3. Ralph Ellison to Kenneth Burke, 23 November 1945, Kenneth Burke Papers.

4. Ellison, *Collected Essays*, 471–85.

5. Burke, "Ralph Ellison's Trueblooded *Bildungsroman*," 349, 359.

6. Ibid., 349.

7. Eddy, *Rites of Identity*, 18.

8. Pease, "Ralph Ellison and Kenneth Burke," 74.

9. Rampersad, *Ralph Ellison*, 217–18.

10. These revisions even involved the plot of the novel. For more on the writing of

this "letter," see: Kimberly Benston to Kenneth Burke, 15 July 1981, Kenneth Burke Papers; Kimberly Benston to Kenneth Burke, 28 February 1982, Kenneth Burke Papers; Ralph Ellison to Kenneth Burke, 7 November 1982, Kenneth Burke Papers; Kenneth Burke to Ralph Ellison, 26 December 1982, Kenneth Burke Papers; Kenneth Burke to Ralph Ellison, 20 May 1983, Kenneth Burke Papers; Ralph Ellison to Kenneth Burke, 20 June 1983, Kenneth Burke Papers; Kenneth Burke to Ralph Ellison, 16 August 1983, Ralph Ellison Papers, box I:38, folder 9; Kenneth Burke to Kimberly Benston, 24 September 1983, Ralph Ellison Papers, box I:38, folder 9.

11. Moreover, since their spouses played a key role in their relationship, my analysis also draws upon the correspondence of Libbie Burke, Fanny Ellison, and Shirley Jackson.

12. Ellison, *Collected Essays,* 218.

13. See, for example, Fabre, "From *Native Son* to *Invisible Man*," 208; Forrest, "Luminosity from the Lower Frequencies," 308; L. Jackson, *Ralph Ellison,* 353.

14. In a June 1947 letter to Hyman, Ellison invoked these terms—but in reference to Francis Steegmuller's work, not his own. Ellison reported attempting to intervene with Random House on Steegmuller's behalf: "They are quite interested. I only hope that I reported its contents correctly, having depended upon my memory of your description of it. I'm sure I got one thing straight: PURPOSE, PASSION, PERCEPTION—the nature of tragic rhythm. Which, God knows, is a neat enough packaging of a profound concept (commodity) to make a publisher smack his lips" (Ralph Ellison to Stanley Edgar Hyman, 17 June 1947, Stanley Edgar Hyman Papers). Since Steegmuller's *Maupassant* was published by Random House in 1949, Ellison's efforts were clearly successful. For more on Ellison and Steegmuller, see L. Jackson, *Ralph Ellison,* 383–84; and Rampersad, *Ralph Ellison,* 212–13.

15. Rampersad, *Ralph Ellison,* 205–6.

16. Rampersad argues that Ellison gleaned these ideas from the portion of the *Grammar* published in 1943 as "The Tactics of Motivation" (*Ralph Ellison,* 206); however, this essay contains only a brief passage on tragic action—and does not develop the Greek terms that appear to be the source of Ellison's formula (Burke, "Tactics of Motivation," 27). Since Ellison began studying the *Grammar* soon after its publication in 1945, it is more likely that Ellison's appropriation of these concepts dates from early 1946. Even so, they obviously played an early role in the development of Ellison's novel. Ellison's library contains a heavily worn copy of the first edition of the *Grammar,* which indicates that he spent a good deal of time studying the text—and not just published selections from it—during the initial stages of the writing of *Invisible Man.*

17. Burke, *Grammar of Motives,* 39.

18. Ibid., 39–40.

19. Ibid., 41.

20. Ibid., 39–40.

21. Ralph Ellison to Kenneth Burke, 23 November 1945, Kenneth Burke Papers.

22. Ibid.

23. Ibid. The quotation in Ellison's letter is taken from the *Grammar* (see Burke, *Grammar of Motives,* 308).

24. Burke, *Grammar of Motives,* 308.

25. Ralph Ellison to Kenneth Burke, 23 November 1945, Kenneth Burke Papers.

26. Ellison, *Collected Essays,* 162. The reference is to Bigger Thomas, *Native Son's* protagonist.

27. Ralph Ellison to Kenneth Burke, 23 November 1945, Kenneth Burke Papers.

28. Ibid.

29. Ibid.

30. Kenneth Burke to Ralph Ellison, 16 December 1945, Ralph Ellison Papers, box I:38, folder 8.

31. Ibid.

32. Lantz, *Dostoevsky Encyclopedia,* 60.

33. Dostoevsky, *Brothers Karamazov,* 26.

34. Paris, *Dostoevsky's Greatest Characters,* 190. Dostoevsky similarly describes him as "an early lover of humanity," who had "adopted the monastic life, . . . simply because at that time it struck him, so to say, as the ideal escape for his soul struggling from the darkness of worldly wickedness to the light of love" (Dostoevsky, *Brothers Karamazov,* 24–25).

35. Kenneth Burke to Ralph Ellison, 16 December 1945, Ralph Ellison Papers, box I:38, folder 8.

36. Rampersad, *Ralph Ellison,* 209.

37. Ralph Ellison to Richard Wright, 24 August 1946, Richard Wright Papers. See also Fabre, "From *Native Son* to *Invisible Man,*" 213.

38. Rampersad, *Ralph Ellison,* 204.

39. Ralph Ellison to Richard Wright, 24 August 1946, Richard Wright Papers.

40. Kenneth Burke to Ralph Ellison, 16 December 1945, Ralph Ellison Papers, box I:38, folder 8.

41. Rampersad, *Ralph Ellison,* 211.

42. L. Jackson, *Ralph Ellison,* 358; Rampersad, *Ralph Ellison,* 211.

43. Ralph Ellison to Stanley Edgar Hyman, 17 June 1947, Stanley Edgar Hyman Papers.

44. Rampersad, *Ralph Ellison,* 211.

45. Fanny Ellison to Shirley Jackson, 29 December [probably 1948], Shirley Jackson Papers; Fanny Ellison to Shirley Jackson, 4 April 1949, Shirley Jackson Papers; Jackson, *Ralph Ellison,* 362; Rampersad, *Ralph Ellison,* 233–34; Stanley Edgar Hyman to Ralph Ellison, 23 August 1948, Ralph Ellison Papers, box I:51, folder 14; Stanley Edgar Hyman to Ralph Ellison, 7 March 1949, Ralph Ellison Papers, box I:51, folder 14; Stanley Edgar Hyman to Ralph Ellison, n.d., Ralph Ellison Papers, box I:51, folder 15; Stanley Edgar Hyman to Ralph Ellison, 1 November 1949, Ralph Ellison Papers, box I:51, folder 14.

46. L. Jackson, *Ralph Ellison,* 414.

47. Murray and Callahan, *Trading Twelves,* 19. At this crucial point he was struggling with transitions; once he saw how simply Jackson was handling hers, he was heartened, and moved rather quickly through the remainder of his narrative.

48. Graham and Singh, *Conversations with Ralph Ellison,* 395.

49. Burke, "Ralph Ellison's Trueblooded *Bildungsroman,*" 350.

50. Genter, "Toward a Theory of Rhetoric," 195. For treatments of Ellison's use of Burkean themes and terms, see Adell, "Big E(llison)'s Texts and Intertexts," 386–87; Albrecht, "Saying Yes and Saying No," 55, 58–60; Crane, "Ralph Ellison's Constitutional

Faith," 115–16; O'Meally, "On Burke and the Vernacular," 256; O'Meally, "Rules of Magic," 255, 266–67; and Whitaker, "Spokesman for Invisibility," 394–95.

51. Ellison, *Invisible Man*, 3.

52. Ellison, *Collected Essays*, 349.

53. Ibid.

54. Ellison, *Invisible Man*, 3.

55. In what follows, I focus upon Ellison's Burkean borrowings in the novel. Obviously, this cannot tell the whole story; scholars have highlighted many influences: jazz, the vernacular, the tradition of the novel (specifically, Melville and James). Yet, I believe that reading Ellison's work against the backdrop of his relationship with Burke reveals something significant about his career—and, ultimately, as chapters 4 and 5 argue, something significant about the American racial divide.

56. Genter, "Toward a Theory of Rhetoric," 204.

57. Burke, *Attitudes toward History*, 211. The following discussion draws upon my examination of Ellison's personal library, housed in the Library of Congress. Although Ellison's collection also includes later editions of the text, at the time that he was writing the novel, Ellison was working in the first edition of *Attitudes*. For the convenience of contemporary scholars, though, throughout this chapter I have translated his notations into the current edition's pagination.

58. Ellison, *Invisible Man*, 4; hereafter cited parenthetically.

59. Burke, *Permanence and Change*, 49.

60. Burke, *Attitudes toward History*, 41.

61. For the other allusions to this Burkean conceit within the novel, see 273, 344, 508, 514, and 549.

62. In addition to dog-earing the page of *Attitudes* where this concept first appears, Ellison wrote the page number ("P.36") inside the front cover of the book—indicating that it was important that he be able to easily return to it in the future.

63. Burke, *Attitudes toward History*, 269.

64. Ibid., 210.

65. Burke, *Attitudes toward History*, 210.

66. Ibid., 210–11. Ellison's bracketing of these lines also included the next four lines on page 211.

67. Ibid., 269.

68. For a rich discussion of the role of technology and electricity in Ellison's thought—one suggestive of Ellison's indebtedness to Burke—see Wright, *Shadowing Ralph Ellison*, 131–59.

69. Burke, *Attitudes toward History*, 344.

70. Although this is admittedly speculative, I think there is textual evidence to support it—since Ellison's library clearly shows the connection between Burke and the conceptual framework of *Invisible Man*. Moreover, an acknowledgment, however oblique, of Burke's assistance makes sense—and "junk man" seems a fitting descriptor for someone whose eclecticism and idiosyncrasy are defining features.

71. Burke, *Attitudes toward History*, 43, 34.

72. Ibid., 5.

73. Ibid., 41.

74. Ibid., 43. Ellison's copy of *Attitudes* brackets Burke's detailed contrast between the heroic, the humorous, and the comic.

75. Ibid., 107.

76. Ellison, *Collected Essays,* 481.

77. For a different view on the relationship between Ellison and Burke on tragedy and comedy (focusing on the "tragicomedy" of the blues), see Eddy, *Rites of Identity,* 139–56. Though I find her discussion of this issue interesting, and occasionally compelling, our interpretive differences stem from a different understanding of the distinction Burke draws between tragedy, humor, and the comic. I believe that Ellison's "tragicomedy" deviates little, if at all, from Burkean comedy.

78. This is not to say that Burke's comic frame is restricted to the prologue and epilogue. Genter, for example, makes a compelling argument for the comic nature of the Golden Day episode ("Toward a Theory of Rhetoric," 206–8). However, I wish to focus attention upon the important opening and closing pages of the book; they are the most richly (and explicitly) Burkean portions of Ellison's novel.

79. Burke, *Attitudes toward History,* 171; original emphasis.

80. Ibid., 107, 171.

81. Ibid., 3.

82. For more on frames of acceptance, see ibid., 3–21.

83. Ibid., 21.

84. This passage echoes Burke's discussion of "yea-saying" (*Attitudes toward History,* 32–33).

85. Ibid., 28, 22, 256.

86. Ellison here alludes to Burke's famous statement: "In so far as an age is bent, a writer establishes equilibrium by leaning (leaning either as his age leans, or in the direction opposite to his age)" (Burke, *Counter-Statement,* vii). As Burke adds, the writer need not simply lean since "a writer will also desire to develop an equilibrium of his own, regardless of external resistances" (ibid.). I see, in Invisible's perspective, his achievement of such equilibrium.

87. The advice was "to overcome 'em with yeses, undermine 'em with grins, agree 'em to death and destruction, let 'em swoller [*sic*] you till they vomit or bust wide open" (*Invisible Man,* 16).

88. Original emphasis. This is an explicit reference to Burke's treatment of the dialectical convertibility of substance, such that two things sharing an ancestry ("a part of" each other) can be considered distinct—"apart from" each other (e.g., Burke, *Grammar of Motives,* 54, 78, 81, 107, 406, 415). In his copy of the first edition of the *Grammar,* Ellison highlighted the page where Burke links this dialectical logic to the scapegoat process (Burke, *Grammar of Motives,* 406).

89. The phrase "next phase" crops up repeatedly in Burke's correspondence and is a regular theme of his late writings. I thus think it likely that, here again, Ellison is imaginatively appropriating Burkean concepts.

90. Burke, *Attitudes toward History,* 213. Ellison marked this sentence and also made a marginal notation ("'Feedback'").

91. Ibid., 203.

92. Ibid. In his first edition of Burke's text, Ellison underlined the entire paragraph containing this quotation.

93. Ibid., 285. This quote is from a page heavily marked by Ellison. A combination of underlines and brackets emphasize Burke's discussion of symbolism, ritual renaming/rebirth, and the "three kinds of imagery" symbolizing "rituals of

change": fire, ice, and decay (ibid.). As a result, Ellison's marks cover almost the entire page.

94. Eddy, *Rites of Identity,* 18.

95. Burke, "Ralph Ellison's Trueblooded *Bildungsroman,*" 359.

96. Several authors (such as Eddy and Genter) link Norton to Ralph Waldo Emerson, though he might well also symbolize the philanthropist Julius Rosenwald, whose foundation helped support *Invisible Man.*

97. Ellison, *Invisible Man,* 37. Following the traumatic events of the day, when Invisible visits Norton in his room, he writes, "I could only look at him, a small silken-haired, white-suited St. Nicholas, seen through misty eyes" (ibid., 107).

98. Ibid., 40. During the Golden Day episode, the "vet" also refers to the attendant Supercargo as "a felled ox" during his conversation with Mr. Norton (ibid., 93).

99. Eddy, *Rites of Identity,* 18.

100. Ralph Ellison to Stanley Edgar Hyman, 16 August 1948, Stanley Edgar Hyman Papers. Ellison is referring to a preview of the first section of the *Rhetoric* ("The Range of Rhetoric"), published as "The Imagery of Killing" in *Hudson Review.*

101. Ralph Ellison to Stanley Edgar Hyman, 27 October 1949, Stanley Edgar Hyman Papers.

102. Stanley Edgar Hyman to Kenneth Burke, 9 November 1950, Kenneth Burke Papers; Kenneth Burke to Stanley Edgar Hyman, 12 November 1950, Kenneth Burke Papers; Stanley Edgar Hyman to Kenneth Burke, 15 November 1950, Kenneth Burke Papers; Stanley Edgar Hyman to Kenneth Burke, 28 November 1950, Kenneth Burke Papers.

103. Stanley Edgar Hyman to Kenneth Burke, 17 July 1951, Kenneth Burke Papers; Kenneth Burke to Stanley Edgar Hyman, 28 July 1951, Kenneth Burke Papers; Stanley Edgar Hyman to Kenneth Burke, 31 July 1951, Kenneth Burke Papers; Stanley Edgar Hyman to Kenneth Burke, 14 August 1951, Kenneth Burke Papers; Kenneth Burke to Stanley Edgar Hyman, 20 August 1951, Kenneth Burke Papers; Stanley Edgar Hyman to Kenneth Burke, 22 August 1951, Kenneth Burke Papers; Libbie Burke to Fanny Ellison, hand-dated "Wed," Ralph Ellison Papers, box I:38, folder 9.

104. Kenneth Burke to Stanley Edgar Hyman, 11 October 1951, Stanley Edgar Hyman Papers.

105. Stanley Edgar Hyman to Kenneth Burke, 18 October 1951, Kenneth Burke Papers.

106. Burke to Hyman, 20 October 1951, Hyman Papers.

107. Burke, *Rhetoric of Motives,* 219.

108. Fanny Ellison to Libbie Burke, 30 October, 1951, Ralph Ellison Papers, box I:38, folder 8.

109. L. Jackson, *Ralph Ellison,* 435–38, 440–41.

110. Burke and Davis, *Ralph Ellison,* 227.

111. Stanley Edgar Hyman to Kenneth Burke, 16 April 1952, Kenneth Burke Papers.

112. Stanley Edgar Hyman to Kenneth Burke, 22 April 1952, Kenneth Burke Papers.

113. Kenneth Burke to Ralph Ellison, 23 April 1952, Ralph Ellison Papers, box I:38, folder 8.

114. These terms play a central role in the "Traditional Principles of Rhetoric" in *A*

Rhetoric of Motives. By speaking "generically," he was not speaking "specifically"—in terms of the motives proper to group membership (i.e., racial identity).

115. Ralph Ellison to Stanley Edgar Hyman, 17 November 1952, Stanley Edgar Hyman Papers. Ellison is referring to Burke's work on the third volume of his *Motivorum* project, *A Symbolic of Motives*.

116. Stanley Edgar Hyman to Kenneth Burke, 26 November 1952, Kenneth Burke Papers.

117. L. Jackson, *Ralph Ellison*, 442–44.

118. Quoted in Jackson, *Ralph Ellison*, 444.

119. Ralph Ellison to Stanley Edgar Hyman, 12 January 1953, Stanley Edgar Hyman Papers.

120. Stanley Edgar Hyman and Shirley Jackson to Ralph Ellison, 24 January 1953, Ralph Ellison Papers, box I:51, folder 14.

121. Stanley Edgar Hyman to Kenneth Burke, 27 January 1953, Kenneth Burke Papers.

122. Kenneth Burke to Stanley Edgar Hyman, dated "January 1953," Stanley Edgar Hyman Papers. Despite this date, the letter is more likely from early to mid-February of that year. Burke's sardonic references are to T. S. Eliot (whose *The Waste Land* was vital to Ellison's development), Harvey Breit (the famed literary critic whose 1952 interview of Ellison appeared in the *New York Times*), and Irving Howe (the literary critic who was on the National Book Award selection committee, but later was the target of Ellison's "The World and the Jug").

123. Stanley Edgar Hyman to Kenneth Burke, 25 February 1953, Kenneth Burke Papers.

124. Kenneth Burke to Stanley Edgar Hyman, 3 March 1953, Stanley Edgar Hyman Papers.

125. Stanley Edgar Hyman to Kenneth Burke, 17 March 1953, Kenneth Burke Papers.

126. It is interesting that Burke described the novel as his "lessons," framing it as a rather unpleasant (if necessary) duty—as something more like a lecture than a work of art.

127. Kenneth Burke to Stanley Edgar Hyman, 2 June 1953, Stanley Edgar Hyman Papers.

128. Stanley Edgar Hyman to Kenneth Burke, 9 June 1953, Kenneth Burke Papers.

129. Fanny Ellison to Libbie Burke, 7 April 1954, Ralph Ellison Papers, box I:38, folder 8; Libbie Burke to Fanny Ellison, 29 April 1954, Ralph Ellison Papers, box I:38, folder 8; Fanny Ellison to Libbie Burke, 30 June 1954, Ralph Ellison Papers, box I:38, folder 8.

130. Ralph Ellison to Stanley Edgar Hyman, 1 July 1954, Stanley Edgar Hyman Papers. Ellison was invited to participate in the program by the seminar's president, and so he and Fanny spent several weeks touring Europe during the summer of 1954 (Rampersad, *Ralph Ellison*, 280, 300–308).

131. Ralph Ellison to Stanley Edgar Hyman, 22 June 1956, Stanley Edgar Hyman Papers. Ellison won a Prix de Rome in 1955, which awarded him a yearlong stay in Rome (see Rampersad, *Ralph Ellison*, 309). Ellison's letter refers to two figures with ties to Burke: Robert Penn Warren and Theodore Roethke. For more on Burke's relationship with Warren, see George and Selzer, *Kenneth Burke in the 1930s*, 41–45; for more

on Roethke, see Burke's essay "The Vegetal Radicalism of Theodore Roethke" (Burke, *Language as Symbolic Action*, 254–81).

132. Kenneth Burke to Stanley Edgar Hyman, 8 March 1955, Kenneth Burke Papers. Burke's efforts had begun at least two years previously. Burke's letter of nomination has not survived, but the reply from the Institute confirms Burke's support for Ellison (National Institute of Arts and Letters to Kenneth Burke, 21 April 1953, Kenneth Burke Papers).

133. Kenneth Burke to Stanley Edgar Hyman, 8 March 1955, Kenneth Burke Papers.

134. Stanley Edgar Hyman to Kenneth Burke, 22 March 1955, Kenneth Burke Papers.

135. Kenneth Burke to Stanley Edgar Hyman, 24 March 1955, Stanley Edgar Hyman Papers. There is no evidence to suggest that Hyman had already heard the news; it is more likely that he recognized Ellison from the mixed emotions conveyed in Burke's letter.

136. Kenneth Burke to George Knox, 16 July 1957, Kenneth Burke Papers. See also Knox, "Negro Novelist's Sensibility and the Outsider Theme."

137. Heilman, "Burke as Political Threat," 19. For Burke's candid statements on the controversy, see Jay, *Selected Correspondence of Kenneth Burke and Malcolm Cowley*, 310–16.

138. For more on the history of Burke's relationship to Communist and anti-Communist movements, see Burks, "Kenneth Burke"; Wander, "At the Ideological Front." For more on the "Red Panic" and the American Left, see Denning, *Cultural Front*, 463–72.

139. Burke, "Old Liberal Looks to the New Year, 1953," 238.

140. Burke, *Permanence and Change,* xlix. For more on these deletions, see Schiappa and Keehner, "'Lost' Passages of *Permanence and Change*."

141. Kenneth Burke to Stanley Edgar Hyman, dated January 1953, Stanley Edgar Hyman Papers.

142. Stanley Edgar Hyman to Kenneth Burke, 3 November 1964, Kenneth Burke Papers.

143. Kenneth Burke to Stanley Edgar Hyman, 6 November 1964, Kenneth Burke Papers.

144. Kenneth Burke to Ralph Ellison, 3 October 1964, Ralph Ellison Papers, box I:38, folder 8.

145. Ellison, *Collected Essays,* 60.

146. Kenneth Burke to Ralph Ellison, 3 October 1964, Ralph Ellison Papers, box I:38, folder 8.

147. Kenneth Burke to Ralph Ellison, 21 October 1965, Ralph Ellison Papers, box I:38, folder 8.

148. Kenneth Burke to Ralph Ellison, 1 November 1965, Ralph Ellison Papers, box I:38, folder 8.

149. Ibid.

150. Kenneth Burke to Stanley Edgar Hyman, 6 November 1965, Stanley Edgar Hyman Papers.

151. Kenneth Burke to Ralph Ellison, 12 November 1965, Ralph Ellison Papers, box I:38, folder 8; Richard Hughes to Kenneth Burke, 4 February 1966, Kenneth

Burke Papers; Kenneth Burke to Richard Hughes, 9 February 1966, Kenneth Burke Papers.

152. Kenneth Burke to Malcolm Cowley, 11 November 1965, Kenneth Burke Papers.

153. Hyman's persistence (and editorial efforts) produced two edited volumes of Burke's work during this time: *Terms for Order* and *Perspectives by Incongruity*. Though not best sellers, they helped renew scholarly interest in Burke's work.

154. The grant was awarded to cover "living, travel, and work costs during the completion of a Poetics and for work on a book of literary reminiscences" (Gerald Freund to Kenneth Burke, 2 June 1966, Kenneth Burke Papers). See also Gerald Freund to Kenneth Burke, 21 February 1966, Kenneth Burke Papers; Kenneth Burke to Gerald Freund, 2 March 1966, Kenneth Burke Papers; Gerald Freund to Kenneth Burke, 7 March 1966, Kenneth Burke Papers; Gerald Freund to Kenneth Burke, 2 June 1966, Kenneth Burke Papers; Kenneth Burke to Gerald Freund, 4 June 1966, Kenneth Burke Papers; Joseph Black to Kenneth Burke, 20 June 1966, Kenneth Burke Papers; and Kenneth Burke to Joseph Black, 11 August 1966, Kenneth Burke Papers.

155. Kenneth Burke to Stanley Edgar Hyman, 3 June 1966, Stanley Edgar Hyman Papers. See also Burke and Rueckert, *Letters from Kenneth Burke to William H. Rueckert, 1959–1987*, 86, 105.

156. Kenneth Burke to Ralph Ellison, 4 July 1966, Ralph Ellison Papers, box I:38, folder 8.

157. Kenneth Burke to Ralph Ellison, 19 October 1966, Ralph Ellison Papers, box I:38, folder 8.

158. Ralph and Fanny Ellison to Kenneth and Libbie Burke, 22 December 1966, Kenneth Burke Papers; Libbie Burke to Ralph and Fanny Ellison, 2 February 1967, Ralph Ellison Papers, box I:38, folder 8; Libbie Burke to Fanny Ellison, 13 March 1967, Ralph Ellison Papers, box I:38, folder 8; Kenneth Burke to Ralph Ellison, 13 March 1967, Ralph Ellison Papers, box I:38, folder 8; Libbie Burke to Fanny Ellison, 28 May 1967, Kenneth Burke Papers; Fanny Ellison to Kenneth Burke, 28 March 1969, Kenneth Burke Papers; Kenneth Burke to Fanny Ellison, 3 April 1969, Ralph Ellison Papers, box I:38, folder 8.

159. Fanny Ellison to Kenneth Burke, 5 June, 1969, Kenneth Burke Papers; Kenneth Burke to Fanny Ellison, 9 June 1969, Ralph Ellison Papers, box I:38, folder 8.

160. Burke, "Ralph Ellison's Trueblooded *Bildungsroman*," 354.

161. Kimberly Benston to Kenneth Burke, 28 February 1982, Kenneth Burke Papers.

162. Ralph Ellison to Kenneth Burke, 7 November 1982, Kenneth Burke Papers. Burke had mistakenly described Invisible's boss in the paint factory, Lucius Brockway, as a white man.

163. Kenneth Burke to Ralph Ellison, 20 May 1983, Kenneth Burke Papers.

164. Ralph Ellison to Kenneth Burke, 20 June 1983, Kenneth Burke Papers.

165. Kenneth Burke to Ralph Ellison, 16 August 1983, Ralph Ellison Papers, box I:38, folder 9.

166. Kenneth Burke to Ralph Ellison, 20 May 1983, Ralph Ellison Papers, box I:38, folder 9. The emphasis is Burke's.

167. Ralph Ellison to Kenneth Burke, 20 June 1983, Kenneth Burke Papers; original emphasis.

168. Burke, "Ralph Ellison's Trueblooded *Bildungsroman*," 349–50.

169. Kenneth Burke to Ralph Ellison, 26 December 1982, Ralph Ellison Papers, box I:38, folder 9.

4 / Was Kenneth Burke a Racist?

1. The last item preserved in the archives was a 1987 holiday card sent by Ralph and Fanny, inscribed: "We love you Kenneth. Keep well" (Ralph and Fanny Ellison to Kenneth Burke, 15 December 1987, Kenneth Burke Papers).

2. Ralph Ellison to Kenneth Burke, 20 June 1983, Kenneth Burke Papers; Ralph Ellison to Kenneth Burke, 7 November 1982, Kenneth Burke Papers.

3. Burke, *Rhetoric of Motives*, 208.

4. Ibid.

5. Graham and Singh, *Conversations with Ralph Ellison*, 321.

6. Eddy, *Rites of Identity*, 3; original emphasis.

7. Ibid.

8. Here I am passing over Eddy's brief account of Ellison's critique of Burke since it was included in the chapter 3 discussion of *Invisible Man* (see Eddy, *Rites of Identity*, 18). Certainly one should be cautioned not to reduce the depth and breadth of a friendship (or intellectual relationship) to social categories such as racial identity, but, as I argue in this chapter, it is also a mistake to allow broad statements to substitute for a more complex discussion of their differences in perspective and identity. Further, I believe that detailed attention to the issue of race in the Burke-Ellison relationship is necessary for the articulation of a more complete, Burkean-Ellisonian approach to race—the subject of chapter 5.

9. Pease, "Ralph Ellison and Kenneth Burke," 74.

10. It is for this reason that I would respectfully disagree with Eddy's choice to ignore this material in her examination of the Burke-Ellison connection. She writes, "I have not relied upon archival evidence of shared meals and social engagements, of mutual friends—Shirley Jackson and Stanley Hyman, of interactions at Bennington, in New York and New Jersey, but that evidence is also available to the curious who seek it out" (Eddy, *Rites of Identity*, 24). As I have tried to demonstrate in the first three chapters of this book, the "intellectual history" that she claims as her focus is not so easily disentangled from the personal history of this relationship; much is lost when one, like Eddy or Pease, restricts one's gaze to the published record.

11. Pease, "Ralph Ellison and Kenneth Burke," 73–74.

12. Ibid., 78.

13. Burke, *Rhetoric of Motives*, 193; hereafter cited parenthetically in this chapter.

14. Pease, "Ralph Ellison and Kenneth Burke," 88.

15. Yet, in the conclusion of his essay, Pease describes the appearance of a new phase in the relationship between these men. He reads Burke's late essay "Ralph Ellison's Trueblooded *Bildungsroman*" as a series of failed attempts to characterize the significance, structure, and plot of Ellison's novel from Burke's dramatistic perspective. These ultimately unsuccessful efforts, Pease contends, indicate Burke's inability to remaster Ellison's work, to again reduce it to the confines of his white-dominated system. The frustration he experienced led to a dawning realization of the "gaps" in his system—and thus eventually demonstrated to Burke the exclusionary acts upon

which it was built. Pease's argument partly rests on the assumption that Ellison broke with Burke following the publication of the *Rhetoric*, and only reconciled with him in the 1980s following the publication of Burke's so-called "retraction." Archival evidence casts doubt on this assumption since Ellison's collection of Burke's books grew through the 1950s, 1960s, and 1970s—and Ellison's later essays, like his early ones, continued to draw on Burke's ideas for their theoretical inspiration. The pieces collected in *Going to the Territory*, I would argue, are at least as indebted to Burke as are those in *Shadow and Act*. Certainly their relationship was more strained following the publication of *Invisible Man*, as detailed in chapter 3, but Ellison's library shows that, even by the mid-1960s, he was again deeply immersed in Burkean concepts.

16. Pease, "Ralph Ellison and Kenneth Burke," 74.

17. Over the eighteen months following Burke's 16 December 1945 letter to Ellison—the period that Burke spent planning and writing the earliest parts of the *Rhetoric*—the two met on several documented occasions (Kenneth Burke to Stanley Edgar Hyman, 20 April 1946, Stanley Edgar Hyman Papers; Ralph Ellison to Stanley Edgar Hyman, 20 June 1946, Stanley Edgar Hyman Papers; Kenneth Burke to Stanley Edgar Hyman, 21 July 1946, Stanley Edgar Hyman Papers; Kenneth Burke to Stanley Edgar Hyman 29 July 1946, Stanley Edgar Hyman Papers; Ralph Ellison to Kenneth Burke, 23 September 1946, Kenneth Burke Papers; Kenneth Burke to Ralph Ellison, 3 December 1946, Ralph Ellison Papers, box I:38, folder 8; Ralph Ellison to Kenneth Burke, 4 December 1946, Ralph Ellison Papers, box I:38, folder 8; Kenneth Burke to Stanley Edgar Hyman, 8 January 1947, Stanley Edgar Hyman Papers).

18. Ralph Ellison to Kenneth Burke, 25 August 1947, Kenneth Burke Papers. I return to the Ellisonian significance of this essay in chapter 5.

19. Kenneth Burke to Ralph Ellison, 14 January 1948, Ralph Ellison Papers, box I:38, folder 8.

20. See, for example, Kenneth Burke to Stanley Edgar Hyman, 13 January 1948, Stanley Edgar Hyman Papers; Kenneth Burke to Ralph Ellison, 14 January 1948, Ralph Ellison Papers, box I:38, folder 8; and Kenneth Burke to Stanley Edgar Hyman, 26 January 1948, Stanley Edgar Hyman Papers.

21. For this reason, Burke distinguishes between particular visions of dialectic (such as Plato's) and the dialectical order of terminology; for Burke, Plato's dialectic is an ultimate terminology, not a dialectical one. This is why Burke, when introducing the differences between the dialectical and ultimate orders of terminology, offers a qualification: "The 'ultimate' order of terms would thus differ essentially from the 'dialectical' (as we use the term *in this particular connection*)" (Burke, *Rhetoric of Motives*, 187; original emphasis). For more on this distinction between senses of "dialectic," and Plato's "ultimate" terminology, see Crable, "Distance as Ultimate Motive."

22. See also *Rhetoric of Motives*, 190, 191, 195.

23. Burke's discussions of Marxism (and Karl Mannheim's critique of it) suggest that it simply provides formal or rhetorical comfort through its resemblance to an ultimate order; it proclaims transcendence of polar opposition, in other words, while slyly adding one more dialectical voice to the parliamentary debate.

24. Ralph Ellison to Kenneth Burke, 23 November 1945, Kenneth Burke Papers. Burke bracketed this passage from Ellison's letter in pencil.

25. Ibid.

26. Kenneth Burke to Ralph Ellison 14 January 1948, Ralph Ellison Papers, box I:38, folder 8.

27. Stanley Edgar Hyman to Kenneth Burke, 10 October 1950, Kenneth Burke Papers.

28. Kenneth Burke to Ralph Ellison, 26 December 1982, Ralph Ellison Papers, box I:38, folder 9; original emphasis.

29. Burke, "Rhetorical Situation," 268.

30. Ibid., 269.

31. Burke, *Permanence and Change*, 14–15.

32. Kenneth Burke to Ralph Ellison, 16 December 1945, Ralph Ellison Papers, box I:38, folder 8.

33. Kenneth Burke to Ralph Ellison, 19 October 1966, Ralph Ellison Papers, box I:38, folder 8.

34. Kenneth Burke to Ralph Ellison, 13 March 1967, Ralph Ellison Papers, box I:38, folder 8.

35. Kenneth Burke to Malcolm Cowley, 14 March 1964, Kenneth Burke Papers.

36. Kenneth Burke to Ralph Ellison, 1 October 1971, Kenneth Burke Papers.

37. Kenneth Burke to Ralph Ellison, 9 March 1980, Ralph Ellison Papers, box I:38, folder 9.

38. Kenneth Burke to Ralph Ellison, 16 December 1945, Ralph Ellison Papers, box I:38, folder 8; original emphasis. Burke is here quoting a portion of Ellison's 23 November 1945 letter; as discussed in chapter 2, the quote is part of Ellison's description of blacks' desperation at the pervasiveness of racism in American social life—and whites' unwillingness to recognize it.

39. Kenneth Burke to Hugh Dalziel Duncan, 24 January 1963, Kenneth Burke Papers.

40. Ibid.

41. Ibid. Burke's reference to "the Faubus fuss" most likely refers to Arkansas Gov. Orval Faubus's infamous anti-integrationist action of 2 September 1957. Assuming that date is correct, there is no evidence in the correspondence to indicate that Ellison is the "Negro friend" in question. For more on Faubus and the civil rights struggle in Little Rock, see Anderson, *Little Rock*; and Reed, *Faubus*.

42. Burke similarly included a racially charged "Wadda Woild!" in his 1964 letter to Cowley—when describing the mix-up over the title of his speech to the Unitarians (Kenneth Burke to Malcolm Cowley, 14 March 1964, Kenneth Burke Papers). One could, of course, also read significance in Burke's stereotypically Yiddish phrasing of his frustration at the intractability of the "black-white" dialectical divide. As Jacobson points out in *Roots Too*, there is a significant link between the pressures of the civil rights movement and the reclamation or "rediscovery" of white ethnic identity in postwar America (e.g., 11–71).

43. The words are Jean Toomer's, quoted in Guterl, *Color of Race in America*, 6.

44. Burke's stories rely much more heavily upon the trope of the "Jew" (Burke, *Complete White Oxen*, 107, 119–20, 121, 123, 127, 199, 203–4), but there are some telling invocations of the stereotypical "Italian" (Burke, *Complete White Oxen*, 45, 127). In comparison, the "Irish" and "Chinese" play a much smaller role in these stories (Burke, *Complete White Oxen*, 103, 148, 204, 235, 276)—and there is a lone reference to "the Polish maid" (Burke, *Complete White Oxen*, 150). The "Negro" is conspicuously

absent from the book—except in Burke's apologia written for a later edition of the text (Burke, *Complete White Oxen*, xvii).

45. Jacobson, *Whiteness of a Different Color*, 10; original emphasis.

46. Ibid., 95–96.

47. Guterl, *Color of Race in America*, 6.

48. For example, witness Burke's reflection that "perhaps even the Jew-and-the-Irishman of the Broadway stage is an instance of repetitive form grown into conventional form" (Burke, *Counter-Statement*, 126). In his novel, Burke is even more explicit in his critique of such attitudes; as one character reflects: "Regardless of how humiliated I might feel, in my belittling of this race I took on dignity. In calling a man a Jew, with fury, I was assuaged—for here was a dishonour from which I was for ever saved" (Burke, *Towards a Better Life*, 165).

49. Burke, *Philosophy of Literary Form*, 310. According to George and Selzer, this essay ("Twelve Propositions") was written in 1938 (*Kenneth Burke in the 1930s*, 223).

50. For the comparison between the "southern races" and those of the North, see Burke, *Philosophy of Literary Form*, 347–48. It is significant, I would argue, that the essay including this comparison was written quite early in the 1930s (George and Selzer, *Kenneth Burke in the 1930s*, 211). It is a sign that, during the early part of the decade, Burke—like America as a whole—was caught between two quite different conceptions of race.

51. For his critique of Nordicism, see Burke, *Philosophy of Literary Form*, 231; for his analysis of Hitler, see Burke, "Rhetoric of Hitler's 'Battle,'" or chapter 1 of this book.

52. Burke, "Rhetoric of Hitler's 'Battle,'" 194, 202, 203.

53. Burke, *Philosophy of Literary Form*, 367–68. According to George and Selzer, Burke completed the essay in June 1933 (*Kenneth Burke in the 1930s*, 213).

54. Burke, *Permanence and Change*, 14–15.

55. Jacobson, *Whiteness of a Different Color*, 98.

56. Ralph Ellison to Kenneth Burke, 23 November 1945, Kenneth Burke Papers.

57. Indeed, at one point Burke even admits: "We had thought of calling [the ultimate order] mystical, but that designation too quickly makes readers take sides for or against us. So let us call it 'ultimate'" (186).

5 / From Turmoil to Peace

1. Ralph Ellison to Kenneth Burke, 23 November 1945, Kenneth Burke Papers.

2. Ellison, *Collected Essays*, 484; hereafter cited parenthetically. Unless otherwise noted, all citations from Ellison in this chapter are to this volume.

3. Ibid., 523.

4. Burke, *Rhetoric of Motives*, 189.

5. Although such imagery is less common in his essays, Ellison does occasionally venture into such territory, as in his description of "the deep dark bottom of the melting pot" as that realm "where the private is public and the public private, where black is white and white black, where the immoral becomes moral and the moral is anything that makes one feel good (or that one has the power to sustain)" (104).

6. We need look no further than the character of Bliss (later Sunraider), whose ambiguous intermixture of white and black identities complicates the apparent simplicity

of our racial categories. For more on Ellison's continued preoccupation with this theme, see Bradley, *Ralph Ellison in Progress*.

7. For the purposes of this chapter, I treat Ellison's works of nonfiction as a unified body of thought. For this reason, I jump between essays, without linking the concept or argument to its placement in the Ellisonian corpus. Though there are legitimate drawbacks to such an approach, and good reasons to choose otherwise, I wish simply to articulate the central arguments and insights of an Ellisonian rhetorical theory of race and identity—in order, at the end of the chapter, to emphasize the resonance between Ellison's nonfiction and Burke's ultimate order. Within the confines of this project, the biographical or chronological distinctions between the essays collected in *Shadow and Act* and *Going to the Territory* are less important than the interlocking nature of their assumptions and conclusions—which is why my citations refer to the *Collected Essays* throughout, rather than these individual texts.

8. According to Rampersad, this is "almost certainly" a reference to the black activist and artist Amiri Baraka, founder of the Black Arts movement and one of Ellison's critics (*Ralph Ellison*, 434).

9. I should note that the importance of blacks was due not simply to slavery since, as Ellison writes, even before the American Revolution "black people were already here causing all sorts of turbulence in the king's town—in religion, music, science, and so on" (453).

10. Although attention is occasionally drawn to this process (as when white artists like Benny Goodman, Elvis Presley, or Eminem garner fame by adopting black musical traditions), Ellison emphasizes that blacks have *always* played a leading role in American culture as a whole: "Without the presence of Negro American style, our jokes, tall tales, even our sports would be lacking in the sudden turns, shocks and swift changes of pace (all jazz-shaped) that serve to remind us that the world is ever unexplored, and that while a complete mastery of life is mere illusion, the real secret of the game is to make life swing" (582). See also 430–31, 510–11, 581, 587, 689.

11. Given Ellison's focus upon the interpenetration of whiteness and blackness, his emphasis is upon the black linguistic contribution to the American language. He does not, though, minimize the contributions made by other groups to our language, especially those whose presence predated the European. Reflecting his Oklahoma origins, Ellison muses: "The American language, this rich, marvelous, relatively unexplored organ, is the creation of many people, and it began with the Indians. As we walk through the streets of our cities their names sing in our heads; great poetry has been made of them, but we do not realize that they are Indian names" (762).

12. Cf. 430, 445.

13. For a complementary (and Burke-driven) account of Ellison's linking of the vernacular to the American tradition, see Wright, *Shadowing Ralph Ellison*, 52–77. See also Bigsby, "Improvising America"; Eddy, *Rites of Identity*, 99–119; and Magee, "Ralph Ellison."

14. This is also, Ellison argues, why the novel as an art form arose at the same time as the new American nation: "If the novel had not existed at the time the United States started becoming conscious of itself as a nation . . . it would have been necessary for Americans to invent it" (701; cf. 697–700).

15. At other points, Ellison refers to this as the "joke" at the heart of American life, the gap "that always lies between appearance and reality, between the

discontinuity of social tradition and that sense of the past which clings to the mind" (108; cf. 519).

16. Cf. 408, 453–54, 840, 851. Here Ellison draws explicitly upon the "Dialectic of Constitutions" from Burke's *Grammar of Motives* (323–401).

17. For a more legally driven analysis of this point—one that, significantly, emphasizes Burke's influence on Ellison—see Crane, "Ralph Ellison's Constitutional Faith."

18. Another trace of the Founders' incomplete break with Old World hierarchy was unearthed recently, when analysis revealed that Thomas Jefferson had originally included the word "subjects" in the text of the Declaration of Independence; he later blotted the word and replaced it with the more democratic term "citizens" (Associated Press, "Declaration of Dependence?" *CBS News*, 2 July 2010, www.cbsnews.com /stories/2010/07/02/national/main6641548.shtml).

19. Ellison also describes this as a situation where "the principles of equality and freedom were splintered into warring entities" (776).

20. I would point out the Burkean allusions—to the pentad and its key terms—within Ellison's argument.

21. This, Ellison might suggest, is why Barack Obama's inauguration was a ceremonial cleansing of national sins, through tears, laughter, and song—because his victory represented a milestone for the country. It also suggests a further motive for the consistent definition of Obama as black, and not as "nonwhite" or biracial, within public discourse; only by *being black* could he serve as a symbol of the nation's progress toward the realization of its principles.

22. This is not to deny that racial identity is performative—just that it has only *selectively* been acknowledged as such (e.g., Gross, *What Blood Won't Tell*). Though Ellison does not make this point, the same could be said of gender, ability, class, and sexuality.

23. Cf. 103–4, 777–78.

24. As Ellison puts it, "Negroes were seen as ignorant, cowardly, thieving, lying, hypocritical and superstitious in their religious beliefs and practices, morally loose, drunken, filthy of personal habit, sexually animalistic, rude, crude and disgusting in their public conduct, and aesthetically just plain unpleasant" (638).

25. According to Burke, this horrific process of victimage reflects the desire to avoid the anguish and complexity of social life. All social order, he writes, is premised upon an exclusionary act, the denial of other possible orders; it constitutes both a political and a moral order, a description of social life and a command. Since attempts to obey all dictates of a social order will fail, at least in part, the gap between command and response, order and disorder, requires symbolic rectification to allay the resulting guilt. This is a very brief, and somewhat superficial, explication of Burke's discussion of order, guilt, and redemption (see Burke, *Rhetoric of Religion*), but it captures the main lines of argument that Ellison adopted in his analysis of American culture. Although these themes appear in Ellison's early essays, they are more evident in later essays—those written after he digested Burke's 1961 text (e.g., Ellison, *Collected Essays*, 772–73).

26. Yet, as Ellison points out, this is a tricky kind of magic. The substitute of stereotype for complex images of humanity has impoverished our national discourse and literature, cheapened artist and audience, speaker and listener. According to Ellison,

it "conditions the reader to accept the less worthy values of society, and it serves to justify and absolve our sins of social irresponsibility" (95). Moreover, as Ellison frequently points out, the grounding of white identity upon black inferiority also produces a host of psychic deformations.

27. See, too, his meditations on the psychic impact of racism in "Harlem Is Nowhere" (320–27).

28. Indeed, the last third of Rampersad's biography focuses quite heavily upon Ellison's frosty relationship with the Black Power and Black Arts movements, and with other black activists and separatist groups (e.g., Rampersad, *Ralph Ellison*, 414–15, 452–53). Ellison's own reflections on this relationship can be found in his published interviews from that period (e.g., Graham and Singh, *Conversations with Ralph Ellison*, 326–32, 397–400).

29. Although Burke mentions this only in passing, this first order of terms takes its name from the philosophical position commonly known as "logical positivism." He does not make clear whether he is referring specifically to the Vienna Circle's doctrines or to derivatives of them; it appears he cares less about the particularities of the position than the basic attempt to reduce knowledge to empirical observation, and language to simple correspondence (see Burke, *Rhetoric of Motives*, 191–92).

30. Ibid., 183.

31. I use the phrase "logically prior" since, to use Burke's example, the nonsymbolic motions of the body are a prerequisite for any human symbol use. For Burke's complete statement on the relationship between the realms of the symbolic and nonsymbolic, see "(Nonsymbolic) Motion/(Symbolic) Action"; for a rereading of this relationship, one that focuses on the symbolic dimensions of the "natural" world, see Crable, "Symbolizing Motion."

32. Burke, *Rhetoric of Motives*, 183.

33. As a result, those using a positive vocabulary of race are not necessarily those who would self-identify as racist; one can appeal to "evident" physiological differences without also *explicitly* advocating the hierarchizing of those differences.

34. Burke, *Rhetoric of Motives*, 183.

35. For the history of efforts to correctly identify the number of human "natural kinds," see Bernasconi and Lott, *Idea of Race*; and Eze, *Race and the Enlightenment*. According to Bernasconi and Lott, Francois Bernier was the first to offer an explicitly racial taxonomy, which was first published in 1684.

36. Jacobson, *Whiteness of a Different Color*, 78–80.

37. Gossett, *Race*, 360–64.

38. U.S. Census Bureau, "Racial and Ethnic Classifications Used in Census 2000 and Beyond," www.census.gov/population/www/socdemo/race/racefactcb.html. The six major categories now recognized by the U.S. Government are: American Indian or Alaska Native; Asian; Black or African American; Native Hawaiian or Other Pacific Islander; White; and Other. For the 2010 Census, the categories were subdivided, creating a total of fifteen distinct racial identities (see Population Reference Bureau, "The 2010 Census Questionnaire: Seven Questions for Everyone," www.prb.org /Articles/2009/questionnaire.aspx). I return to the subject of the Census shortly.

39. By the 1930s and 1940s, taxonomies of race provided by those like Dillingham and Blumenbach were attacked for their unscientific roots. By 1950, even scientists who accepted the "three major divisions" of Caucasoid, Negroid, and Mongoloid

argued against taking such taxonomies too seriously: "These divisions were not the same in the past as they are at present, and there is every reason to believe that they will change in the future" (UNESCO, *Four Statements on the Race Question*, 31–32). As recently as 1997, the American Anthropological Association issued a statement contesting the government's official taxonomy of racial and/or ethnic groups, arguing that "these classifications must be transcended and replaced by more non-racist and accurate ways of representing the diversity of the U.S. population" (American Anthropological Association, "Response to OMB Directive 15: Race and Ethnic Standards for Federal Statistics and Administrative Reporting [Sept 1997]," www.aaanet.org/gvt/ombdraft.htm).

40. Burke, *Rhetoric of Motives*, 191.

41. Ibid.

42. Ibid., 186. This statement covers a good deal of ground—there are not, it appears, many subjects Burke would find suitable for treatment in positive terms. Scientific subjects are no exception: "A skeptic might offer reasons to believe that such science is less positive than its apologists take it to be. Particularly one might ask himself whether the terms for *relationships* among things are as positive as are the names for the things themselves" (*Rhetoric of Motives*, 184). However, as the first stage in a movement toward an ultimate vocabulary, the positive order forms a necessary part of Burke's argument—and thus my own.

43. Although these associations were developed in chapter 1, I would underscore the tenacity of this conception of race. The study of intelligence, for example, has been a favorite of those advancing racialist arguments—from the U.S. Army intelligence tests of World War I (Gossett, *Race*, 366–69) to the 1994 publication of *The Bell Curve* by Herrnstein and Murray.

44. See, for example, Barkan, *Retreat of Scientific Racism*, 76–88, 127–30; and Jacobson, *Whiteness of a Different Color*, 99–102.

45. The original typescript calls it "Statement by Experts on Race Problems," though it is typically referred to it as the UNESCO "Statement on Race" (see UNESCO Archives, "Statement on Race. Part I. 1949–1951," www.unesco.org/general/eng/infoserv/archives/files_online/32312A102_I.pdf). The document was "signed" by a group of prominent intellectuals from across the world: Ernest Beaglehold, Juan Comas, L. A. Costa Pinto, Franklin Frazier, Morris Ginsberg, Humayun Kabir, Claude Levi-Strauss, and Ashley Montagu. Although described as a group-authored statement, Montagu played a key role in developing and writing it—according to some, a too prominent role. Following extensive criticism of the original "Statement on Race," UNESCO released a revision two years later; two more followed, in 1964 and 1967. Together, they represent one of the most complete "official" statements of the twentieth century on matters of race.

46. UNESCO, *Four Statements on the Race Question*, 33.

47. Ibid., 31.

48. Jacobson, *Whiteness of a Different Color*, 98–113; Omi and Winant, *Racial Formation in the United States*, 14–23. Interestingly, Omi and Winant attribute the popularity of the "ethnicity paradigm" primarily to the work of Gunnar Myrdal, whose book *An American Dilemma* was the subject of a scathing review by Ellison (Ellison, *Collected Essays*, 328–40).

49. Though only one document, the Census represents a powerful context for the

examination of American racial discourse. We might assume that race has always been a part of Census tallies (Campbell Gibson and Kay Jung, "Historical Census Statistics on Population Totals by Race, 1790 to 1990, and by Hispanic Origin, 1970 to 1990, for the United States, Regions, Divisions, and States," U.S. Census Bureau, www.census .gov/population/www/documentation/twps0056/twps0056.html). However, mirroring the trends in racial discourse traced in chapter 1, "the term 'race' didn't appear on the census until 1900, and with the exception of 1950 it has been the sole descriptor (as opposed to 'color or race') for this census item only since 1990" (Jefferson Fish, "The Census and Race--Part II--Slavery [1790-1860]," *Psychology Today*, 13 July 2010, www.psychologytoday.com/blog/looking-in-the-cultural-mirror/201007/the-census -and-race-part-ii-slavery-1790-1860). Since the Census form is constructed using the standards approved by the Office of Management and Budget for the classification of the U.S. population, it reflects the "official" view of race in the United States. I would thus agree, at least in part, with Nobles's contention that "censuses help form racial discourse, which in turn affects the public policies that either vitiate or protect the rights, privileges, and experiences commonly associated with citizenship" (*Shades of Citizenship*, 1). The last part of this quote underscores the profound consequences of this national tally for communities and individuals. As Omi and Winant remark, the Census affects "such matters as access to employment, housing, or other publicly or privately valued goods; social program design and the disbursement of local, state, and federal funds; [and] the organization of elections" (*Racial Formation in the United States*, 3). The Census is both the embodiment of a governmental racial vocabulary and a site where racial assumptions translate into material consequences for those tallied.

50. Even on this revised form, there was no "box" labeled "biracial" or "multiracial"; the 2000 Census was merely the first to allow respondents to claim more than one race (cf. U.S. Census Bureau, "Race Data," www.census.gov/population/www /socdemo/race/racefactcb.html). In the months leading up to the 2010 Census—following the election of Obama—attention returned to the practical issues surrounding the "counting" of biracial and multiracial individuals (Haya El Nasser, "Multiracial No Longer Boxed in by the Census," *USA Today*, 15 March 2010, www.usatoday.com /news/nation/census/2010-03-02-census-multi-race_N.htm).

51. For an example of the difference in the attention paid to these stories from the 2000 Census, see, for example, Eric Schmitt, "For 7 Million People in Census, One Race Category Isn't Enough," *New York Times*, 13 March 2001.

52. The 2000 Census was not the first time that the "origins" question had been used with regard to Latino/as. A version of the item was first used on the 1970 Census and was revised prior to the 1980 Census. As Nobles explains: "The Census Bureau added the 'Hispanic Origins' question to the 1980 census under pressure from the Hispanic Advisory Committee and in the absence of a satisfactory alternative method. Previously the bureau had not assigned persons of 'Spanish heritage' and/or with 'Spanish surnames' to a separate group. They were generally categorized as 'white,' except when they were, in the words of census manuals, 'definitely Negro or Indian'" (*Shades of Citizenship*, 82). For more on this issue, see Rodriguez, *Changing Races*.

53. The 2000 Census was not the first time that Latino/as had "complicated" the results in this fashion—it was just the first time that the government had complained publicly about it. On the previous two censuses, it appears that the government

accepted the responses of Latino/as who identified as members of an "Other" race; by contrast, "in 1970, such responses in the Other race category were reclassified and tabulated as White" (Gibson and Jung, "Historical Census Statistics on Population Totals by Race, 1790 to 1990, and by Hispanic Origin, 1970 to 1990, for the United States, Regions, Divisions, and States," U. S. Census Bureau, www.census.gov/population /www/documentation/twps0056/twps0056.html).

54. Thomas Ginsberg, "Latino Replies Complicate Census' 1st Multiracial Tally," *Philadelphia Inquirer*, 13 March 2001.

55. The government's position further implies that individuals can (somehow) misidentify their own race. For over a decade, the American Anthropological Association has argued that the ambiguous mix of self- and other-reports of race represents a key flaw in Census procedures since "research has shown substantial differences of racial/ethnic identification by these two methods" (American Anthropological Association, "Response to OMB Directive 15: Race and Ethnic Standards for Federal Statistics and Administrative Reporting [Sept 1997]," www.aaanet.org/gvt/ombdraft.htm).

56. U.S. Census Bureau, "Explore the Form," http://2010.census.gov/2010census/ how/interactive-form.php.

57. For the past fifty years, no other group has been accorded this same duality of identity by the Census—even though ethnic identity has become as salient to white Americans as to any other segment of the population (Jacobson, *Roots Too*).

58. Population Reference Bureau, "The 2010 Census Questionnaire: Seven Questions for Everyone," www.prb.org/Articles/2009/questionnaire.aspx. As Fish points out, Asians, too, occupy an interesting place within the Census's categories: "Asian or Pacific Islander was a race with sub-categories in 1990; but in 2000 and 2010 it became 11 races. (One might also ask why Guamanian and Samoan are considered separate races, but Other Pacific Islander merges numerous possibilities—such as Tahitian—into a single race. Is U.S. citizenship the distinguishing feature of a race—Tahitians are French—and if so, how can race be a biological category?)" (Jefferson Fish, "The Census and Race—Part V—[1990–2010]," *Psychology Today*, 3 August 2010, www.psychologytoday.com/blog/looking-in-the-cultural-mirror/201008 /the-census-and-race-part-v-1990-2010).

59. Burke, *Rhetoric of Motives*, 186.

60. Although this term is widely recognized, and has even been called a "dominant view," it is not universally embraced by critical race scholars (Machery and Foucher, "Social Construction and the Concept of Race," 1208). For the purposes of this chapter, I use the term to group all those who seek to expose the dialectical nature of racial discourse, regardless of whether they would self-identify as constructionists.

61. Burke, *Rhetoric of Motives*, 184.

62. For examples of science-driven constructionist arguments, see Graves, *Race Myth*; and Sweet, *Legal History of the Color Line*.

63. Hirschfeld, *Race in the Making*; Van Ausdale and Feagin, *The First R*.

64. Cosmides, Tooby, and Kurzban, "Perceptions of Race," 176.

65. This link between perception and assumption explains why, as Jacobson points out, "The American eye sees a certain person as black, for instance, whom Haitian or Brazilian eyes might see as white" (*Whiteness of a Different Color*, 10).

66. In a sense, these results are not new; as early as 1941, Ashley Montagu predicted

that genetic research would disprove the reality of race (see, for example, Montagu, "Concept of Race in the Human Species in the Light of Genetics").

67. Sweet, *Legal History of the Color Line*, 46–47. Though his is a helpful book, I would still mention that Sweet, at times, fails to fully interrogate the terminology upon which his analysis relies. That is, within his text, "African" and "European" often are used without a great deal of critical reflexivity.

68. American Anthropological Association, "Statement on 'Race' (May 17, 1998)," www.aaanet.org/stmts/racepp.htm. See also Cosmides, Tooby, and Kurzban, "Perceptions of Race"; Graves, *Emperor's New Clothes*; J. Marks, *Human Biodiversity*; and Sweet, *Legal History of the Color Line*.

69. For example, the genetic trait related to sickle cell anemia, often used as evidence for the naturalness of race, instead disputes it, since it "is found among populations in tropical ecological niches in Africa as well as in certain environments in southern Europe and western Asia" (Harrison, "Introduction," 7). The trait is indeed common to some (though not all) Africans and African Americans, but also to some populations, such as Greeks, Italians, and Arabs, that Americans would not categorize as black. To cite another example: "Sorting human populations by the O allele of the ABO blood group gives a characteristically counterintuitive result, with Icelanders clustering with Japanese, Ethiopians clustered with Swedes, and so forth" (Cosmides, Tooby, and Kurzban, "Perceptions of Race," 173). Moreover, it is not simply that genetically based categorizations violate our racial distinctions, but that there is *no single scheme of categorization* suggested by these genetic markers. In fact, "the patterns of genetic and phenotypic variation are sufficiently rich that by choosing alternative criteria, the human mind could be trained to cluster humans into a large number of alternative, mutually contradictory groupings" (ibid.).

70. Templeton, "Human Races," 647. As Graves indicates, some scientists still adhere to a biological theory of race, but this position does not represent the dominant view of physical anthropology or population genetics (*Race Myth*, 2–3).

71. See Baker, *From Savage to Negro*; Baum, *Rise and Fall of the Caucasian Race*; Feagin, *White Racial Frame*; Gross, *What Blood Won't Tell*; Jacobson, *Whiteness of a Different Color*; Omi and Winant, *Racial Formation in the United States*; Smedley, *Race in North America*; and Sweet, *Legal History of the Color Line*.

72. Burke, *Rhetoric of Motives*, 184; original emphasis.

73. Ibid., 185; original emphasis.

74. Baker, *From Savage to Negro*, 1.

75. Omi and Winant, *Racial Formation in the United States*, 55; original emphasis.

76. Although Burke does not explicitly make this argument in the *Rhetoric*, I believe that his second order incorporates the contextual view of language popularized in the 1930s by Richards, Ogden, and Malinowski—the view of language that opposed the positivists' correspondence view. This is also why, I would argue, Burke's later essay "What Are the Signs of What?"—focused upon language as "entitlement"—leans heavily upon Malinowski (Burke, *Language as Symbolic Action*, 359–79).

77. Burke, *Rhetoric of Motives*, 184.

78. Just as constructionist scholars incorporate bodies into their definitions of race, Burke does not deny the relevance of the nonsymbolic realm to the dialectical order. He argues that the nature of this relationship is altered by the dialectical order's transcendence of the positive; the relationship is one of entitlement, not representation. In

other words, dialectical terms do not deny the positive, nonsymbolic realm—much as constructionists do not deny the material elements included under the title of race—they simply transcend the simple relationship of correspondence between word and world.

79. Smedley, *Race in North America*, 6.

80. Gross, *What Blood Won't Tell*, 8.

81. Feagin, *White Racial Frame*, ix; original emphasis.

82. Burke, *Rhetoric of Motives*, 187.

83. This is, admittedly, a bit of an extrapolation. Burke does not explicitly indicate that the dialectical order displays conflict on multiple levels—both *within* dialectical titles and *between* them. However, I would argue that, without this slight clarification, it is difficult to make sense of this second order. To be sure, in his discussion of this order Burke emphasizes the conflict between distinctly individual titles (e.g., capitalism vs. socialism), but he also identifies the possibility of a vocabulary that itself encompasses conflicting titles. For example, in his discussion of Plato's four types of government, he suggests that a dialectical vocabulary would "leave the four kinds [of government] merely confronting one another in their diversity . . . in the sense of the parliamentary jangle" (Burke, *Rhetoric of Motives*, 188–89). This section of text, as illustrated by this quote, implies that *a dialectical vocabulary itself can constitute a parliamentary arrangement* of the subtitles that fall beneath its head.

84. Gross, *What Blood Won't Tell*, 9.

85. See, for example, Feagin, *White Racial Frame*; Guterl, *Color of Race in America*; Marable, *Beyond Black and White*; Martin, *White African American Body*; and Webster, *Racialization of America*.

86. See, for example, Ancheta, *Race, Rights, and the Asian American Experience*; O'Brien, *Racial Middle*; Saunt, *Black, White, and Indian*; Walker, *Black, White, and Jewish*; and Wu, *Yellow*.

87. Burke, *Rhetoric of Motives*, 184.

88. Ibid., 187.

89. These unpublished notes are drawn from a folder labeled "Myth," archived within the Kenneth Burke Papers.

90. Burke, *Rhetoric of Motives*, 198.

91. Ibid.

92. See, for example, Matt Nuenke, "What Does It Mean to Say, 'Race Is a Social Construction?'" Majorityrights.com, http://majorityrights.com/index.php/weblog/comments/what_does_it_mean_to_say_race_is_a_social_construction/). This entry, and the comments appended to it, are typical of this kind of reaction to the constructionist argument.

93. Klein and Takahata, *Where Do We Come From?* 384. To be fair to this position, there is disagreement among anthropologists as to whether physical anthropology has entirely abandoned the concept of race (e.g., Cartmill and Brown, "Surveying the Race Concept"; and Lieberman, Kirk, and Littlefield, "Perishing Paradigm"). Similar debates are reflected in news coverage of forensic anthropology (e.g., Willow Lawson, "Anthropologists Disagree about Race and Bones," ABC News.com, October 6, 2009, http://abcnews.go.com/Technology/story?id=119897&page=1). The American Anthropological Association emphatically states that the constructionist position represents "the contemporary thinking and scholarly positions of a majority

of anthropologists," but it is clear that dissenters do exist (American Anthropological Association, "Statement on 'Race' [May 17, 1998]," www.aaanet.org/stmts/racepp.htm).

94. This line of argument is quite common in conservative blogs and commentaries; a particularly systematic example of this can be found at the website for the organization Adversity.net (www.adversity.net), self-described as "A Civil Rights Organization for Color Blind Justice." However, this position is also common within American public discourse, often appearing as an argument against "reverse discrimination." Inadvertently highlighting the Burkean dimensions of this point, Burstein finds that critics of "reverse discrimination" have essentially formed a social movement, one founded upon—a dialectical—opposition to the groups supporting civil rights (see Burstein, "'Reverse Discrimination' Cases in the Federal Court").

95. Burke, *Rhetoric of Motives*, 187; original emphasis.

96. Ibid., 201.

97. Burke, "Ideology and Myth," 307. I draw upon this essay to help explain the ultimate order because Burke explicitly identifies it as the foundation for the *Rhetoric*'s third section, "Order" (e.g., Kenneth Burke to Stanley Edgar Hyman, 26 January 1948, Stanley Edgar Hyman Papers). For Ellison's reflections on Burke's essay, see Ralph Ellison to Kenneth Burke, 25 August 1947, Kenneth Burke Papers.

98. Burke, "Ideology and Myth," 307.

99. Ibid.; original emphasis.

100. The only danger in this shift to the "beyond" of the ultimate order, Burke writes, is if the mythic image is interpreted literally—if it is taken to represent a real or accurate account of origins. Such an account would act as though it were positive, conflating a logical "first" with a temporal "first." Burke contends that myths are no less symbolic acts than are ideologies; indeed, he writes that "insofar as [myths] are taken literally, they do function as ideologies" (*Rhetoric of Motives*, 201). However, if we resist the abstraction of the mythic image from the movement through the first two orders, Burke argues, we will not mistake it for a reflection of reality—collapsing logical and temporal priority (e.g., Burke, *Rhetoric of Motives*, 201–3). Said another way, by retaining our myth's connection to the hierarchical movement through the three orders, we will recognize the narrative order of myth as an imagistic portrayal of a logical order—and not as an accurate, objective account of origins (cf. Burke, *Grammar of Motives*, 430–40). Just as Platonic transcendence cannot be separated from its embodiment in a dialogue, a mythic image cannot be separated from the process that produced it, the systematic transcendence of both positive sensation and dialectical ideas; a mythic image is not a metaphysical statement of essence, but a process of ordering opposing voices through a summarizing, imagistic statement of origins. In this way, Burke suggests that the disciplined movement through the three orders must be continually reenacted to account for the addition of new voices or perspectives to the dialectical realm. For a more detailed treatment of this portion of Burke's argument in the *Rhetoric*, see Crable, "Distance as Ultimate Motive."

101. Burke, "Ideology and Myth," 310. In other words, Burke's mythic image should not be confused with empirical imagery, since it does not indicate a tangible portion of the experienced world. It is of the ultimate, and not positive, order of terms.

102. Ibid., 308.

103. Burke, *Rhetoric of Motives*, 188.

104. Ibid., 187.

105. From the left, Ellison's dialectical vocabulary invites a particular kind of counter-statement. One might counter that his account ignores the importance of political economy in the Founding Fathers' acceptance of racial hierarchy. Their decision, in short, was motivated by a need to consolidate their economic position within the new nation; race, then, is rooted in class warfare. From the right, Ellison's position invites a different sort of counter-statement: his account ignores the reality of evident racial differences that the colonists, rightly or not, used to differentiate slaves from citizens. Race, its defenders would claim, is rooted in nature, despite our desire to claim otherwise. Without moving to an ultimate terminology, I believe, Ellison is drawn into heated, endless debate with opposing dialectical positions such as these.

106. Burke, "Ideology and Myth," 310. Burke's "ideal myth" involves, quite literally, questions of peace and war—a very pressing issue when he wrote this essay, in the aftermath of World War II. However, when read alongside Ellison's work, it appears no less relevant to the theorizing of race in America.

107. See Dalton, *Racial Healing*; Shearer, *Enter the River*; Unterschuetz and Unterschuetz, *Longing*; and Yancey, *Beyond Racial Gridlock*. The language of "healing" is also widely used in the popular press to portray the possibilities for racial peace.

108. Burke, "Ideology and Myth," 312; original emphasis.

109. Burke, *Rhetoric of Motives*, 140. Unfortunately, among Burkean scholars this myth is given much less attention than the version of the myth that it supersedes; the latter fits much more readily with our common assumptions about the reality of the divisions separating individuals from one another. For a more detailed critique of this position and the typical reading of Burke's *Rhetoric*, see Crable, "Distance as Ultimate Motive."

110. Burke, *Rhetoric of Religion*, 256.

111. Also lurking within this myth is the origin of our racial categories, since the "'fall' into terms" makes possible the relentless division of humanity into "natural kinds," culminating in our American "racial divide." In the wake of our symbolically generated rebellion, the "loving" primary presymbolic unity is replaced with an antagonism of partiality, a discordant babble of terms, of parts whose only reconciliation can be through transcendence. Burke's myth draws not upon the familiar terms of the political or sociological, but it is no less a statement of the motives generating our "racial divide."

112. Burke, *Rhetoric of Motives*, 192.

113. Burke, *Language as Symbolic Action*, 5.

114. Burke, *Permanence and Change*, 272.

115. Here I refer the reader to Mark Smith, *How Race Is Made*. Although the data collected in this text are powerful, I would suggest that Smith's overrationalistic framework has less explanatory power than the Burkean-Ellisonian vocabulary sketched here. To put it simply, it was not southerners' irrationality that led them to claim that they could smell blacks; it was instead the "terministic screen" of racial discourse that directed their perceptual attention in patterned ways. They saw, smelled, tasted, heard, and felt what they had first learned to speak.

116. Given the "'mystery' of courtship" produced "when 'different kinds of beings' communicate with each other," it is little wonder that our American "racial divide" has spawned a host of social devices to manage the social embarrassment between

blacks and whites (Burke, *Rhetoric of Motives*, 208). In addition to a long-standing tradition of racialized "pastoral" literature, rumor has been a consistent product of the "mystery" of race relations, as some fascinating scholarship has demonstrated (see, for example, Fine and Turner, *Whispers on the Color Line*; and Odum, *Race and Rumors of Race*).

    117. Burke, "Ideology and Myth," 312; original emphasis.

    118. Burke, *Rhetoric of Motives*, 195.

BIBLIOGRAPHY

Aaron, Daniel. *Writers on the Left: Episodes in American Literary Communism.* New York: Harcourt, Brace and World, 1961.

Aaron, Daniel, Malcolm Cowley, Kenneth Burke, Granville Hicks, and William Phillips. "Thirty Years Later: Memories of the First American Writers' Congress." *American Scholar* 35, no. 3 (1966): 495–516.

Abu-Lughod, Janet L. *Race, Space, and Riots in Chicago, New York, and Los Angeles.* New York: Oxford University Press, 2007.

Adell, Sandra. "The Big E(llison)'s Texts and Intertexts: Eliot, Burke, and the Underground Man." *CLA Journal* 37 (1994): 377–401.

Albrecht, James M. "Saying Yes and Saying No: Individualist Ethics in Ellison, Burke, and Emerson." *PMLA* 114, no. 1 (1999): 46–63.

Allen, Frederick Lewis. *Only Yesterday: An Informal History of the 1920s.* New York: Wiley, 1997.

———. *Since Yesterday: The Nineteen-Thirties in America: September 3, 1929–September 3, 1939.* New York: Harper and Brothers, 1940.

Ancheta, Angelo N. *Race, Rights, and the Asian American Experience.* 2nd ed. New Brunswick, N.J.: Rutgers University Press, 2006.

Anderson, Karen. *Little Rock: Race and Resistance at Central High School.* Princeton: Princeton University Press, 2009.

Arnesen, Eric. *Black Protest and the Great Migration: A Brief History with Documents.* New York: Bedford/St. Martin's, 2002.

Astor, Gerald. *The Right to Fight: A History of African Americans in the Military.* Cambridge: Da Capo Press, 1998.

Bak, Hans. *Malcolm Cowley: The Formative Years.* Athens: University of Georgia Press, 1993.

Baker, Lee D. *From Savage to Negro: Anthropology and the Construction of Race, 1896–1954.* Berkeley and Los Angeles: University of California Press, 1998.

Baker, Lewis. "Biography in Progress: Little Kenny Has His Fits." *Pre/Text* 6 (1985): 379–80.

Barkan, Elazar. *The Retreat of Scientific Racism: Changing Concepts of Race in Britain and the United States between the World Wars.* Cambridge: Cambridge University Press, 1992.

Barrett, William, Kenneth Burke, Malcolm Cowley, Robert Gorham Davis, and Hiram Haydn. "American Scholar Forum: The New Criticism." *American Scholar* 20 (Winter 1950): 86–104; *American Scholar* 20 (Spring 1951): 218–31.

Baum, Bruce. *The Rise and Fall of the Caucasian Race: A Political History of Racial Identity.* New York: New York University Press, 2008.

Bayor, Ronald H., ed. *Race and Ethnicity in America: A Concise History.* New York: Columbia University Press, 2003.

Benston, Kimberly W., ed. *Speaking for You: The Vision of Ralph Ellison.* Washington, D.C.: Howard University Press, 1990.

Bernasconi, Robert, and Tommy L. Lott, eds. *The Idea of Race.* Indianapolis: Hacket, 2000.

Biesecker, Barbara A. *Addressing Postmodernity: Kenneth Burke, Rhetoric, and a Theory of Social Change.* Tuscaloosa: University of Alabama Press, 1997.

Bigsby, C. W. E. "Improvising America: Ralph Ellison and the Paradox of Form." In *Speaking for You: The Vision of Ralph Ellison*, edited by Kimberly W. Benston, 173–86. Washington, D.C.: Howard University Press, 1990.

Blankenship, Jane. "Kenneth Burke on Ecology." In *Extensions of the Burkeian System*, edited by James Chesebro, 251–68. Tuscaloosa: University of Alabama Press, 1993.

Bobbitt, David A. *The Rhetoric of Redemption: Kenneth Burke's Redemption Drama and Martin Luther King, Jr.'s I Have a Dream Speech.* Lanham: Rowman and Littlefield, 2007.

Bodnar, John, Roger Simon, and Michael P. Weber. *Lives of Their Own: Blacks, Italians, and Poles in Pittsburgh, 1900–1960.* Urbana: University of Illinois Press, 1982.

Bradley, Adam. *Ralph Ellison in Progress: From "Invisible Man" to "Three Days before the Shooting . . . "* New Haven: Yale University Press, 2010.

Brock, Bernard L., ed. *Kenneth Burke and the 21st Century.* Albany: State University of New York Press, 1999.

Brophy, Alfred L. *Reconstructing the Dreamland: The Tulsa Riot of 1921: Race, Reparations, and Reconciliation.* New York: Oxford University Press, 2002.

Burke, Bob, and Denyvetta Davis. *Ralph Ellison: A Biography.* Oklahoma City: Oklahoma Heritage Association, 2003.

Burke, Kenneth. *Attitudes toward History.* 3rd ed. Berkeley and Los Angeles: University of California Press, 1984.

———. "Auscultation, Creation, and Revision." In *Extensions of the Burkeian System*, edited by James Chesebro, 42–172. Tuscaloosa: University of Alabama Press, 1993.

———. "Comments." *Western Speech* 32 (1968): 181–82.

———. *The Complete White Oxen*. Berkeley and Los Angeles: University of California Press, 1968.

———. *Counter-Statement*. Berkeley and Los Angeles: University of California Press, 1968.

———. "The Five Master Terms, Their Place in a 'Dramatistic' Grammar of Motives." *View* 3, no. 2 (1943): 50–52.

———. *A Grammar of Motives*. Berkeley and Los Angeles: University of California Press, 1969.

———. "Ideology and Myth." In *On Symbols and Society*, edited by Joseph R. Gusfield, 303–15. Chicago: University of Chicago Press, 1989.

———. *Language as Symbolic Action*. Berkeley and Los Angeles: University of California Press, 1966.

———. "(Nonsymbolic) Motion/(Symbolic) Action." *Critical Inquiry* 4, no. 4 (1978): 809–38.

———. "An Old Liberal Looks to the New Year, 1953." *Communication Studies* 42, no. 3 (1991): 238–39.

———. *Permanence and Change: An Anatomy of Purpose*. 3rd ed. Berkeley and Los Angeles: University of California Press, 1984.

———. *The Philosophy of Literary Form: Studies in Symbolic Action*. 3rd ed. Berkeley and Los Angeles: University of California Press, 1973.

———. "Ralph Ellison's Trueblooded *Bildungsroman*." In *Speaking for You: The Vision of Ralph Ellison*, edited by Kimberly W. Benston, 349–59. Washington, D.C.: Howard University Press, 1990.

———. "The Rhetoric of Hitler's 'Battle.'" In *The Philosophy of Literary Form: Studies in Symbolic Action*, 3rd ed., 191–220. Berkeley and Los Angeles: University of California Press, 1973.

———. *A Rhetoric of Motives*. Berkeley and Los Angeles: University of California Press, 1969.

———. *The Rhetoric of Religion*. Berkeley and Los Angeles: University of California Press, 1970.

———. "The Rhetorical Situation." In *Communication: Ethical and Moral Issues*, edited by Lee Thayer, 263–75. New York: Gordon and Breach, 1973.

———. "The Tactics of Motivation." *Chimera* 1 (Spring 1943): 21–33; *Chimera* 2 (Summer 1943): 37–53.

———. *Towards a Better Life*. New York: Harcourt, Brace, 1932.

———. *The White Oxen, and Other Stories*. New York: A. & C. Boni, 1924.

Burke, Kenneth, and Malcolm Cowley. "Kenneth Burke and Malcolm Cowley: A Conversation." *Pre/Text* 6 (1985): 181–200.

Burke, Kenneth, and William H. Rueckert. *Letters from Kenneth Burke to William H. Rueckert, 1959–1987*. West Lafayette, Ind.: Parlor Press, 2003.

Burke, Michael. "Visitors." *Journal of New Jersey Poets* 42 (Spring/Summer 2005).

Burks, Don M. "Kenneth Burke: The Agro-Bohemian 'Marxoid.'" *Communication Studies* 42, no. 3 (1991): 219–33.

Burstein, Paul. "Reverse Discrimination Cases in the Federal Courts: Legal Mobilization by a Countermovement." *Sociological Quarterly* 32, no. 4 (1991): 511–28.

Bygrave, Stephen. *Kenneth Burke: Rhetoric and Ideology.* London: Routledge, 1993.

Carlson, A. Cheree. "'You Know It When You See It': The Rhetorical Hierarchy of Race and Gender in *Rhinelander v. Rhinelander.*" *Quarterly Journal of Speech* 85, no. 2 (1996): 111–28.

Carter, Dan T. *Scottsboro: A Tragedy of the American South.* Baton Rouge: Louisiana State University Press, 1979.

Cartmill, Matt, and Kaye Brown. "Surveying the Race Concept: A Reply to Lieberman, Kirk, and Littlefield." *American Anthropologist* 105, no. 1 (2003): 114–15.

Chafe, William Henry, Raymond Gavins, and Robert Rodgers Korstad. *Remembering Jim Crow: African Americans Tell about Life in the Segregated South.* New York: New Press, 2001.

Cosmides, Leda, John Tooby, and Robert Kurzban. "Perceptions of Race." *Trends in Cognitive Sciences* 7, no. 4 (2003): 173–79.

Cowley, Malcolm. *The Dream of the Golden Mountains: Remembering the 1930s.* New York: Viking Press, 1980.

———. *Exile's Return.* New York: Penguin, 1994.

———. *A Second Flowering: Works and Days of the Lost Generation.* New York: Viking Press, 1973.

Crable, Bryan. "Distance as Ultimate Motive: A Dialectical Interpretation of *A Rhetoric of Motives.*" *Rhetoric Society Quarterly* 39, no. 3 (2009): 213–39.

———. "Ideology as 'Metabiology': Rereading Burke's *Permanence and Change.*" *Quarterly Journal of Speech* 84, no. 3 (1998): 303–19.

———. "Race and *A Rhetoric of Motives*: Kenneth Burke's Dialogue with Ralph Ellison." *Rhetoric Society Quarterly* 33, no. 3 (2003): 5–25.

———. "Symbolizing Motion: Burke's Rhetoric and Dialectic of the Body." *Rhetoric Review* 22, no. 2 (2003): 121–37.

Crane, Gregg. "Ralph Ellison's Constitutional Faith." In *The Cambridge Companion to Ralph Ellison*, edited by Ross Posnock, 104–20. New York: Cambridge University Press, 2005.

Crusius, Timothy W. *Kenneth Burke and the Conversation after Philosophy.* Carbondale: Southern Illinois University Press, 1999.

———. "Kenneth Burke's 'Auscultation': A 'De-Struction' of Marxist Dialectic and Rhetoric." *Rhetorica* 6, no. 4 (1988): 355–79.

Curtis, Thomas Quinn. *The Smart Set: George Jean Nathan & H. L. Mencken.* New York: Applause, 1998.

Dalton, Harlon L. *Racial Healing: Confronting the Fear between Blacks and Whites.* New York: Anchor, 1996.

Daniels, Roger. *Coming to America: A History of Immigration and Ethnicity in American Life.* New York: HarperCollins, 2002.

Denning, Michael. *The Cultural Front.* London: Verso, 1997.

Deutsch, Leonard J. "Ellison's Early Fiction." *Negro American Literature Forum* 7 (1973): 53–59.

Dostoevsky, Fyodor. *The Brothers Karamazov.* Translated by Constance Garnett. Revised by Ralph E. Matlaw. New York: Norton, 1981.

Du Bois, W. E. Burghardt. *The Souls of Black Folk: Essays and Sketches.* New York: Fawcett World Library, 1961.

Eddy, Beth. *The Rites of Identity: The Religious Naturalism and Cultural Criticism of Kenneth Burke and Ralph Ellison.* Princeton: Princeton University Press, 2003.

Ellison, Ralph. *The Collected Essays of Ralph Ellison.* Edited by John F. Callahan. New York: Modern Library, 1995.

———. *Flying Home and Other Stories.* Edited by John F. Callahan. New York: Random House, 1996.

———. *Going to the Territory.* New York: Random House, 1986.

———. *Invisible Man.* New York: Random House, 1995.

———. *Juneteenth: A Novel.* New York: Random House, 1999.

———. *Shadow and Act.* New York: Vintage, 1995.

———. *Three Days before the Shooting . . .* Edited by John F. Callahan and Adam Bradley. New York: Modern Library, 2010.

Ellison, Ralph, Ishmael Reed, Quincy Troupe, and Steve Cannon. "The Essential Ellison." *Y'Bird Magazine* 1 (1977): 126–59.

Ellsworth, Scott. *Death in a Promised Land: The Tulsa Race Riot of 1921.* Baton Rouge: Louisiana State University Press, 1982.

Epstein, Abraham. *The Negro Migrant in Pittsburgh.* Pittsburgh: S. N., 1918.

Eze, Emmanuel Chukwudi, ed. *Race and the Enlightenment: A Reader.* Malden, Mass.: Blackwell, 1997.

Fabre, Michel. "From *Native Son* to *Invisible Man*: Some Notes on Ralph Ellison's Evolution in the 1950s." In *Speaking for You: The Vision of Ralph Ellison,* edited by Kimberly W. Benston, 199–216. Washington, D.C.: Howard University Press, 1990.

———. *The Unfinished Quest of Richard Wright.* 2nd ed. Champaign: University of Illinois Press, 1993.

Faires, Nora. "Immigrants and Industry: Peopling the 'Iron City.'" In *City at the Point: Essays on the Social History of Pittsburgh,* edited by Samuel P. Hays, 5–32. Pittsburgh: University of Pittsburgh Press, 1989.

Feagin, Joe R. *The White Racial Frame: Centuries of Racial Framing and Counter-Framing*. New York: Routledge, 2009.

Felgar, Robert. *Richard Wright*. Boston: Twayne, 1980.

Fine, Gary Alan, and Patricia A. Turner. *Whispers on the Color Line: Rumor and Race in America*. Berkeley and Los Angeles: University of California Press, 2001.

Foley, Barbara. "Ralph Ellison as Proletarian Journalist." *Science and Society* 62, no. 4 (1998): 537–56.

Folsom, Franklin. *Days of Anger, Days of Hope: A Memoir of the League of American Writers 1937–1942*. Boulder: University Press of Colorado, 1994.

Forrest, Leon. "Luminosity from the Lower Frequencies." In *Speaking for You: The Vision of Ralph Ellison*, edited by Kimberly W. Benston, 308–21. Washington, D.C.: Howard University Press, 1990.

Frank, Armin Paul. *Kenneth Burke*. New York: Twayne, 1969.

Gayle, Addison. *Richard Wright: Ordeal of a Native Son*. Garden City, N.Y.: Anchor/Doubleday, 1980.

Genter, Robert. "Toward a Theory of Rhetoric: Ralph Ellison, Kenneth Burke, and the Problem of Modernism." *Twentieth Century Literature* 48, no. 2 (2002): 191–214.

George, Ann, and Jack Selzer. *Kenneth Burke in the 1930s*. Columbia: University of South Carolina Press, 2007.

Gibson, Richard. "A No to Nothing." *Kenyon Review* 13, no. 2 (1951): 252–55.

Ginzburg, Ralph. *100 Years of Lynchings*. Baltimore: Black Classic Press, 1962.

Glasco, Laurence. "Double Burden: The Black Experience in Pittsburgh." In *City at the Point: Essays on the Social History of Pittsburgh*, edited by Samuel P. Hays, 69–110. Pittsburgh: University of Pittsburgh Press, 1989.

———. *The WPA History of the Negro in Pittsburgh*. Pittsburgh: University of Pittsburgh Press, 2004.

Gossett, Thomas F. *Race: The History of an Idea in America*. New York: Oxford University Press, 1997.

Gottlieb, Peter. *Making Their Own Way: Southern Blacks' Migration to Pittsburgh, 1916–1930*. Champaign: University of Illinois Press, 1987.

———. "Migration and Jobs: The New Black Workers in Pittsburgh, 1916–1930." In *African Americans in Pennsylvania: Shifting Historical Perspectives*. Edited by Joe William Trotter Jr. and Eric Ledell Smith, 272–86. University Park: Pennsylvania State University, 1997.

Graham, Maryemma, and Amritjit Singh, eds. *Conversations with Ralph Ellison*. Jackson: University Press of Mississippi, 1995.

Graves, Joseph L., Jr. *The Emperor's New Clothes: Biological Theories of Race at the Millennium*. New Brunswick, N.J.: Rutgers University Press, 2003.

———. *The Race Myth: Why We Pretend Race Exists in America*. New York: Dutton, 2004.

Griffiths, F. T. "Ralph Ellison, Richard Wright, and the Case of Angelo Herndon." *African American Review* 35, no. 4 (2001): 615–36.

Gross, Ariela J. *What Blood Won't Tell: A History of Race on Trial in America.* Cambridge: Harvard University Press, 2008.

Guterl, Matthew Pratt. *The Color of Race in America, 1900–1940.* Cambridge: Harvard University Press, 2001.

Harrison, Faye V. "Introduction: Expanding the Discourse on 'Race.'" *American Anthropologist* 100, no. 3 (1999): 609–31.

Hawhee, Debra. "Burke on Drugs." *Rhetoric Society Quarterly* 34, no. 1 (2004): 5–28.

———. *Moving Bodies: Kenneth Burke at the Edges of Language.* Columbia: University of South Carolina Press, 2009.

Heilman, Robert B. "Burke as Political Threat: A Chronicle of the 1950s." *Horns of Plenty: Malcolm Cowley and His Generation* 2, no. 1 (1989): 19–26.

Herrnstein, Richard J., and Charles A. Murray. *The Bell Curve: Intelligence and Class Structure in American Life.* New York: Free Press, 1994.

Hirsch, James S. *Riot and Remembrance: America's Worst Race Riot and its Legacy.* New York: Houghton Mifflin, 2002.

Hirschfeld, Lawrence A. *Race in the Making: Cognition, Culture, and the Child's Construction of Human Kinds.* Cambridge: MIT Press, 1996.

Hoffman, Frederick John, Charles Albert Allen, and Carolyn F. Ulrich. *The Little Magazine: A History and a Bibliography.* Princeton: Princeton University Press, 1946.

Huggins, Nathan Irvin. *Harlem Renaissance.* Oxford: Oxford University Press, 1971.

Hyman, Stanley Edgar. *The Armed Vision: A Study in the Methods of Modern Literary Criticism.* New York: Vintage, 1955.

Jack, Jordynn. "'The Piety of Degradation': Kenneth Burke, the Bureau of Social Hygiene, and *Permanence and Change.*" *Quarterly Journal of Speech* 90, no. 4 (2004): 446–68.

Jackson, John P., Jr. *Science for Segregation: Race, Law, and the Case against Brown v. Board of Education.* New York: New York University Press, 2005.

Jackson, Lawrence Patrick. "The Birth of the Critic: The Literary Friendship of Ralph Ellison and Richard Wright." *American Literature* 72, no. 2 (2000): 321–55.

———. *Ralph Ellison: Emergence of Genius.* New York: Wiley, 2002.

———. "Ralph Ellison's Invented Life: A Meeting with the Ancestors." In *The Cambridge Companion to Ralph Ellison*, edited by Ross Posnock, 11–34. Cambridge: Cambridge University Press, 2005.

Jacobson, Matthew Frye. *Barbarian Virtues: The United States Encounters Foreign Peoples at Home and Abroad.* New York: Hill and Wang, 2000.

———. *Roots Too: White Ethnic Revival in Post–Civil Rights America.* Cambridge: Harvard University Press, 2006.

———. *Whiteness of a Different Color: European Immigrants and the Alchemy of Race.* Cambridge: Harvard University Press, 1999.

Jay, Paul, ed. *The Selected Correspondence of Kenneth Burke and Malcolm Cowley, 1915–1981.* New York: Viking Press, 1988.

Johnson, Franklin. *The Development of State Legislation Concerning the Free Negro.* New York: Arbor Press, 1919.

Joost, Nicholas. *Scofield Thayer and "The Dial": An Illustrated History.* Carbondale: Southern Illinois University Press.

Josephson, Matthew. *Life among the Surrealists: A Memoir.* New York: Holt, Rinehart and Winston, 1962.

Klein, Jan, and Naoyuki Takahata, *Where Do We Come From?: The Molecular Evidence for Human Descent.* New York: Springer, 2002.

Klumpp, James F. "Burkean Social Hierarchy and the Ironic Investment of Martin Luther King." In *Kenneth Burke and the Twenty-first Century,* edited by Bernard L. Brock, 207–41. Albany: State University of New York Press, 1999.

Knox, George. "The Negro Novelist's Sensibility and the Outsider Theme." *Western Humanities Review* 11, no. 2 (1957).

Lantz, Kenneth. *The Dostoevsky Encyclopedia.* Westport, Ct.: Greenwood Press, 2004.

Lemann, Nicholas. *The Promised Land: The Great Black Migration and How It Changed America.* New York: Vintage, 1992.

Lentricchia, Frank. *Criticism and Social Change.* Chicago: University of Chicago Press, 1983.

Lewis, David Levering. *When Harlem Was in Vogue.* New York: Penguin, 1997.

Lieberman, Leonard, Rodney C. Kirk, and Alice Littlefield. "Perishing Paradigm: Race—1931–99." *American Anthropologist* 105, no. 1 (2003): 110–13.

Locke, Alain, ed. *The New Negro: Voices of the Harlem Renaissance.* New York: Simon and Schuster, 1992.

Lubove, Roy. *Pittsburgh.* Princeton: Markus Wiener, 1976.

———. *Twentieth-Century Pittsburgh: Government, Business, and Environmental Change.* Pittsburgh: University of Pittsburgh Press, 1995.

Lynch, John A. "Race and Radical Renamings: Using Cluster Agon Method to Assess the Radical Potential 'European American' as a Substitute for 'White.'" *KB Journal* 2, no. 2 (2006). www.kbjournal.org/lynch.

Machery, Edouard, and Luc Foucher. "Social Construction and the Concept of Race." *Philosophy of Science* 72 (2005): 1208–19.

Magee, Michael. "Ralph Ellison: Pragmatism, Jazz and the American Vernacular." *Transactions of the Charles S. Peirce Society* 39, no. 2 (2003): 227–58.

Marable, Manning. *Beyond Black and White: Transforming African-American Politics.* New York: Verso, 1995.

Marks, Carole. "The Social and Economic Life of Southern Blacks during the Migration." In *Black Exodus: The Great Migration from the American South,* edited by Alfredteen Harrison, 36–50. Jackson: University Press of Mississippi, 1991.

Marks, Jonathan. *Human Biodiversity: Genes, Race, and History.* Piscataway, N.J.: Aldine Transaction, 1995.

Martin, Charles D. *The White African American Body: A Cultural and Literary Exploration.* New Brunswick, N.J.: Rutgers University Press, 2002.

McGreevy, John T. *Parish Boundaries: The Catholic Encounter with Race in the Twentieth-Century Urban North.* Chicago: University of Chicago Press, 1998.

Montagu, Ashley. "The Concept of Race in the Human Species in the Light of Genetics." In *The Idea of Race,* edited by Robert Bernasconi and Tommy L. Lott, 100–107. Indianapolis: Hackett, 2000.

Munson, Gorham B. *The Awakening Twenties.* Baton Rouge: Louisiana State University Press, 1985.

Murray, Albert, and John F. Callahan, eds. *Trading Twelves: The Selected Letters of Ralph Ellison and Albert Murray.* New York: Modern Library, 2000.

Murray, Hugh T. "The NAACP versus the Communist Party." In *The Negro in Depression and War: Prelude to Revolution, 1930–1945,* edited by Bernard Sternsher, 267–81. Chicago: Quadrangle, 1976.

Naison, Mark. *Communists in Harlem during the Depression.* Urbana: University of Illinois Press, 1983.

Nobles, Melissa. *Shades of Citizenship: Race and the Census in Modern Politics.* Stanford: Stanford University Press, 2000.

O'Brien, Eileen. *The Racial Middle: Latinos and Asian Americans Living Beyond the Racial Divide.* New York: New York University Press, 2008.

Odum, Howard W. *Race and Rumors of Race: The American South in the Early Forties.* Baltimore: Johns Hopkins University Press, 1997.

Oestreicher, Richard. "Working-Class Formation, Development, and Consciousness in Pittsburgh." In *City at the Point: Essays on the Social History of Pittsburgh,* edited by Samuel P. Hays, 111–50. Pittsburgh: University of Pittsburgh Press, 1989.

O'Meally, Robert. "On Burke and the Vernacular: Ralph Ellison's Boomerang of History." In *History and Memory in African-American Culture,* edited by Genevieve Fabre and O'Meally, 244–60. New York: Oxford University Press, 1994.

———. "The Rules of Magic: Hemingway as Ellison's 'Ancestor.'" In *Speaking for You: The Vision of Ralph Ellison,* edited by Kimberly W. Benston, 245–71. Washington, D.C.: Howard University Press, 1990.

Omi, Michael, and Howard Winant. *Racial Formation in the United States: From the 1960s to the 1990s.* 2nd ed. New York: Routledge, 1994.

Oppenheimer, Judy. *Private Demons: The Life of Shirley Jackson.* New York: Putnam, 1988.

Packard, Jerrold M. *American Nightmare: The History of Jim Crow.* New York: St. Martin's Press, 2002.

Paris, Bernard J. *Dostoevsky's Greatest Characters.* New York: Palgrave Macmillan, 2008.

Parker, Donald, and Warren Herendeen. "KB and MC: An Interview." *Visionary Company* 2, no. 3 (1987): 87–98.

Pauley, Garth. "Criticism in Context: Kenneth Burke's 'The Rhetoric of Hitler's "Battle."'" *KB Journal* 6, no. 1 (2009). www.kbjournal.org/garth_pauley.

Pease, Donald. "Ralph Ellison and Kenneth Burke: The Nonsymbolizable (Trans)Action." *boundary 2* 30, no. 2 (2003): 65–96.

Rampersad, Arnold. *1902–1941: I, Too, Sing America.* Vol. 1 of *The Life and Times of Langston Hughes.* Oxford: Oxford University Press, 2002.

———. *Ralph Ellison: A Biography.* New York: Vintage, 2008.

Reed, Roy. *Faubus: The Life and Times of an American Prodigal.* Fayetteville: University of Arkansas Press, 1997.

Rodriguez, Clara E. *Changing Race: Latinos, the Census and the History of Ethnicity.* New York: New York University Press, 2000.

Roediger, David R. *How Race Survived U.S. History: From Settlement and Slavery to the Obama Phenomenon.* London: Verso, 2008.

Roorda, Randall. "KB in Green: Ecology, Critical Theory, and Kenneth Burke." *ISLE: Interdisciplinary Studies in Literature and Environment* 4, no. 2 (1997): 39–52.

Rountree, J. Clarke, III. "Richard Kostelanetz Interviews Kenneth Burke." *Iowa Review* 17, no. 3 (1987): 1–14.

Rowley, Hazel. *Richard Wright: The Life and Times.* New York: Holt, 2001.

Rueckert, William H. *Kenneth Burke and the Drama of Human Relations.* 2nd ed. Berkeley and Los Angeles: University of California Press, 1982.

Saunt, Claudio. *Black, White, and Indian: Race and the Unmaking of an American Family.* New York: Oxford University Press, 2006.

Scales, James R., and Danney Goble. *Oklahoma Politics: A History.* Norman: University of Oklahoma Press, 1982.

Schiappa, Edward, and Mary F. Keehner. "The 'Lost' Passages of Kenneth Burke's *Permanence and Change.*" *Communication Studies* 42, no. 3 (1991): 191–98.

Schweik, Susan M. *The Ugly Laws: Disability in Public.* New York: New York University Press, 2009.

Scruggs, Charles. *Sweet Home: Invisible Cities in the Afro-American Novel.* Baltimore: Johns Hopkins University Press, 1993.

———. "Jean Toomer and Kenneth Burke and the Persistence of the Past." *American Literary History* 13, no. 1 (2001): 41–66.

Sealander, Judith. *Private Wealth and Public Life: Foundation Philanthropy and the Reshaping of American Social Policy from the Progressive Era to the New Deal.* Baltimore: Johns Hopkins University Press, 1997.

Seaton, James. "Review: Ellison the Essayist." *Hudson Review* 49, no. 3 (1996): 497–502.

Seigel, Marika A. "'One Little Fellow Named Ecology': Ecological Rhetoric in Kenneth Burke's *Attitudes toward History.*" *Rhetoric Review* 23, no. 4 (2004): 388–404.

Selzer, Jack. *Kenneth Burke in Greenwich Village: Conversing with the Moderns, 1915–1931*. Madison: University of Wisconsin Press, 1996.

Selzer, Jack, and Robert Wess, eds. *Kenneth Burke and His Circles*. West Lafayette, Ind.: Parlor Press, 2008.

Shearer, Jody Miller. *Enter the River: Healing Steps from White Privilege toward Racial Reconciliation*. Scottdale, Pa.: Herald Press, 1994.

Simons, Herbert W. "Introduction: Kenneth Burke and the Human Sciences." In *The Legacy of Kenneth Burke*, edited by Herbert W. Simons and Trevor Melia. Madison: University of Wisconsin Press, 1989.

Sitkoff, Harvard. *The Depression Decade*. Vol. 1 of *A New Deal for Blacks: The Emergence of Civil Rights as a National Issue*. New York: Oxford University Press, 1978.

Smedley, Audrey. *Race in North America: Origin and Evolution of a Worldview*. Boulder: Westview Press, 2007.

Smith, Mark M. *How Race Is Made: Slavery, Segregation, and the Senses*. Chapel Hill: University of North Carolina Press, 2006.

Smith, Shawn Michelle. *Photography on the Color Line: W. E. B. DuBois, Race, and Visual Culture*. Durham, N.C.: Duke University Press, 2004.

Sweet, Frank W. *Legal History of the Color Line: The Rise and Triumph of the One-Drop Rule*. Palm Coast, Fla.: Backintyme, 2005.

Templeton, Alan R. "Human Races: A Genetic and Evolutionary Perspective." *American Anthropologist* 100, no. 3 (1999): 632–50.

Terborg-Penn, Rosalyn. "African-American Women's Networks in the Anti-Lynching Crusade." In *Gender, Class, Race, and Reform in the Progressive Era, Part 3*, edited by Noralee Frankel and Nancy S. Dye. Lexington: University Press of Kentucky, 1994.

Toomer, Jean. *Cane*. New York: Boni and Liveright, 1993.

United Nations Educational, Scientific and Cultural Organization. *Four Statements on the Race Question*. Paris: UNESCO, 1969.

Unterschuetz, Phyllis A., and Eugene F. Unterschuetz. *Longing: Stories of Racial Healing*. Wilmette, Ill.: Bahai Publishing, 2010.

Van Ausdale, Debra, and Joe R. Feagin. *The First R: How Children Learn Race and Racism*. Lanham, Md.: Rowman and Littlefield, 2001.

Voogd, Jan. *Race Riots and Resistance: The Red Summer of 1919*. New York: Peter Lang, 2008.

Walker, Rebecca. *Black, White, and Jewish: Autobiography of a Shifting Self*. New York: Riverhead, 2001.

Wander, Philip C. "At the Ideological Front." *Communication Studies* 42, no. 3 (1991): 199–218.

Warren, Austin. "Kenneth Burke: His Mind and Art." *Sewanee Review* 41 (1933): 227–36.

Weber, Michael P. "Community-Building and Occupational Mobility in Pittsburgh, 1880–1960." In *City at the Point: Essays on the Social History of Pitts-*

burgh, edited by Samuel P. Hays, 361–84. Pittsburgh: University of Pittsburgh Press, 1989.

Webster, Yehudi O. *The Racialization of America*. New York: St. Martin's Press, 1992.

Weiser, Elizabeth M. "Burke and War: Rhetoricizing the Theory of Dramatism." *Rhetoric Review* 26, no. 3 (2007): 286–302.

Wess, Robert. "Ecocriticism and Kenneth Burke: An Introduction." *KB Journal* 2, no. 2 (2006). www.kbjournal.org/wess2.

———. *Kenneth Burke: Rhetoric, Subjectivity, Postmodernism*. Cambridge: Cambridge University Press, 1996.

Whitaker, Thomas R. "Spokesman for Invisibility." In *Speaking for You: The Vision of Ralph Ellison*, edited by Kimberly W. Benston, 386–403. Washington, D.C.: Howard University Press, 1990.

Williamson, Joel. *The Crucible of Race: Black-White Relations in the American South since Emancipation*. New York: Oxford University Press, 1984.

Wolin, Ross. *The Rhetorical Imagination of Kenneth Burke*. Columbia: University of South Carolina Press, 2001.

Woodcock, John. "An Interview with Kenneth Burke." *Sewanee Review* 55, no. 4 (1977): 704–18.

Woods, Arthur. *Dangerous Drugs: The World Fight against Illicit Traffic in Narcotics*. New Haven: Yale University Press, 1931.

Woodward, C. Vann. *The Strange Career of Jim Crow*. New York: Oxford University Press, 1974.

Wright, John S. *Shadowing Ralph Ellison*. Jackson: University of Mississippi Press, 2006.

Wright, Richard. *American Hunger*. New York: Harper and Row, 1977.

———. *Native Son*. New York: HarperPerennial, 1998.

Wu, Frank H. *Yellow: Race in America beyond Black and White*. New York: Basic, 2002.

Yagoda, Ben. "Kenneth Burke: The Greatest Literary Critic since Coleridge?" *Horizon* 23 (1980): 66–69.

Yancey, George A. *Beyond Racial Gridlock: Embracing Mutual Responsibility*. Downers Grove, Ill.: InterVarsity Press, 2006.

Zangrando, Robert L. *The NAACP Crusade against Lynching, 1909–1950*. Philadelphia: Temple University Press, 1980.

Index

acceptance, frame of, 56, 93–96. *See also* comic frame; rejection, frame of
allegiance, problem of, 65–66, 71, 75, 121, 123–24
American Revolution, 142–47, 166, 168–69, 214n9. *See also* democracy; vernacular
"Anglo-Saxon" race, 14–16, 24–25, 132, 179n31, 183n103. *See also* racial pluralism
anti-Semitism, 14–15, 43–44, 171, 179n31; and Kenneth Burke, 14, 43, 133, 179n31, 186n140, 212n44, 213n48; and racial binarism, 44, 132–33, 192n246
anxiety: and symbolicity, 170–74, 215n25; and white identity, 147–49
Armstrong, Louis, 91, 94. *See also* "see around the corner"

Batterham, Lily, 27, 185n131
Benston, Kimberly, 109–10
Birth of a Nation, 22. *See also* Klan, Ku Klux
black Americans: influence of, 141–43, 149, 214n9, 214n10; symbolic role of, 146–49, 215n21. *See also* cultural pluralism
Black Boy, 55, 62, 68–69, 75–76, 117, 124, 196n61; critical reaction to, 55, 57; Ralph Ellison's review of, 55–58
blues, music of, 51, 58, 75, 94

Blumenbach, Johann, 25, 152, 183n105, 216n39
Bureau of Social Hygiene, 26, 28, 184n111, 186n137
Burke, Libbie (Batterham), 28, 60, 73, 100, 103, 109, 112, 185n131, 197n88
Burke, James, 12, 15–18, 179n31, 180n48, 185n125
Burke, Kenneth: aestheticism of, 28–29, 48–49, 193n10; Andover residence of, 27, 67, 71–73, 77, 85, 99, 103, 105, 107–8, 176n16, 185n126, 194n34, 201n1; and Bennington College, 54, 200n142; college career of, 26; and Colonel Arthur Woods, 28, 184n111, 186n132, 186n137; conception of rhetoric, 1, 47, 68, 124, 127, 192n7; "counter-statement" of, 1, 18–19, 48, 63, 181n65, 205n86; and the *Dial*, 28, 185n127, 185n130; early writings of, 26–28; experience of class difference, 16–18, 180n43; and the First American Writers' Congress, 39, 190n209; and Greenwich Village, 26–27; idiosyncrasy of, 1–2, 204n70; introduction to Ralph Ellison, 45, 50, 52; jealousy of Ralph Ellison, 102–8, 111; marriage of, 27, 185n131; and McCarthyism, 105–6, 193n13; near-death experience of, 17, 180n50; as quintessentially American,